The Undiscovered Country

PETER LANG
New York • Washington, D.C./Baltimore • Bern
Frankfurt am Main • Berlin • Brussels • Vienna • Oxford

The Undiscovered Country

The Later Plays of Tennessee Williams

EDITED BY
Philip C. Kolin

PETER LANG
New York • Washington, D.C./Baltimore • Bern
Frankfurt am Main • Berlin • Brussels • Vienna • Oxford

Library of Congress Cataloging-in-Publication Data

The undiscovered country: the later plays of Tennessee Williams /
[edited by] Philip C. Kolin.
p. cm.
Includes bibliographical references.
1. Williams, Tennessee, 1911–1983—Criticism and interpretation.
2. Drama—Technique. I. Kolin, Philip C.
PS3545.I5365 Z848   812'.54—dc21   2002004438
ISBN 0-8204-5130-4

Die Deutsche Bibliothek-CIP-Einheitsaufnahme

The undiscovered country: the later plays of Tennessee Williams /
ed. by: Philip C. Kolin.
–New York; Washington, D.C./Baltimore; Bern;
Frankfurt am Main; Berlin; Brussels; Vienna; Oxford: Lang.
ISBN 0-8204-5130-4

Cover photo: *Tennessee as* Doc *in* Small Craft Warnings; courtesy of World Wide
Photo, Richard Freeman Leavitt Collection, University of Tennessee

Cover design by Dutton & Sherman Design

The paper in this book meets the guidelines for permanence and durability
of the Committee on Production Guidelines for Book Longevity
of the Council of Library Resources.

© 2002 Peter Lang Publishing, Inc., New York

Printed in the United States of America

For Maureen,
with love

CONTENTS

ACKNOWLEDGMENTS

An editor of a collection of original essays happily incurs debts, and I am honored to record mine here. First off, I thank the contributors whose work for *The Undiscovered Country: The Later Plays of Tennessee Williams* made this volume possible. Their essays reflect the quality of critical work that the later canon deserves and which it repays. I see the essays in this volume kindling a new and far more just investigation of Williams's work written, revised, staged, and revised during the last three decades of his life. Our collective thanks also go to the many theatre companies and libraries that assisted us in our research and in obtaining photographs. To Richard Freeman Leavitt go my special thanks for the cover photo of this collection.

Second, I am grateful to the University of Southern Mississippi for its continued enthusiastic support of my research. In particular, I thank President Shelby Thames; Dean of the College of Liberal Arts Glenn T. Harper; and Chair of the Department of English Michael N. Salda. I am also grateful to my research assistant J. Marcus Weekley for his invaluable computer help.

Third, I joyfully acknowledge the encouragement and sage advice of Phyllis Korper, my editor at Peter Lang, and the efficiency of my production editor Lisa Dillon.

Last of all, I thank God Almighty for my immediate family who bless my life with their love—my wife Maureen, my children Kristin Julie, Eric Howard, Theresa, and Evan Philip; and my extended family whose prayers keep me afloat—Margie and Al Parish; Sister Carmelita Stinn; Father Tommy Conway; and Abbot Cletus Meagher, o.s.b. God bless them all!

Philip C. Kolin
May 2002

Philip C. Kolin

INTRODUCTION

Over twenty years after his death, Tennessee Williams's post-*Night of the Iguana* (1961) canon still remains largely undiscovered country, elusively difficult to edit, classify, and interpret. Williams's later plays evoke uneasiness and even embarrassment from the critical establishment. As Annette Saddik documents in her *Politics of Reputation*, the reception of these plays has been by and away negative: "By the 1970s, the reviewers had essentially given up on Williams, altogether expecting him to fail" (29). Williams's plays fared no better in the theatre. They folded after only a few performances, with only one play (*Small Craft Warnings*) having an extended, though not praiseworthy, run. Even more perniciously, Williams's later canon has been superciliously ostracized by a majority of critics who continue to explore the 1945–1961 canon while they extol his recently rediscovered apprentice plays of the late 1930s.

Given the scope and complexity of Williams's later canon, such critical opprobrium and/or myopia is lamentable. The plays that Williams wrote from *Night of the Iguana* until his death at the Elyses Hotel in 1983, a 21-year period, far outnumber those he created between the premieres of *The Glass Menagerie* in 1944 and *Iguana*, a 17-year period. As Ruby Cohn accurately observes, too, the exact number of these later plays is uncertain (232). A trunkload of them may still be unearthed. Also discomforting, many of the later plays we know about are unavailable in print. *Kirche, Kutchen, und Kinder, THIS IS (An Entertainment)*, and *A House Not Meant to Stand* are currently available only in manuscript, access to which is guarded by the Williams estate.

The later Williams canon merits much more attention and appreciation. Yet it has been hard to disentangle these plays from the antagonistic biographical criticism that has voraciously fed upon them. Almost all of these later works are shrouded in a biographical pallor, even in the most current assessment of two key plays (*Vieux Carré* and *Something Cloudy, Something Clear*) by Bruce J. Mann. Critics have manipulated Williams's biography as both filter and flagellum, reading these later plays through his personal and often decadent life, venomously attacking the script as if it were nothing more (or less) than a performance of his *Memoirs*. Booze, drugs, the failed dreams of an artist—these, according to many critics, were the stuff out of which Williams's scripts were made. "Williams himself, rather than his works, was becoming the main attraction" (Saddik 27). This critical penchant occurred, to be sure, before *Night of the Iguana,* but the habit only worsened over time. C.W.E. Bigsby, otherwise one of the more astute readers of American drama, declared that the plays Williams wrote in the 1960s exhibited "a kind of narcissism which reflected his paranoia and self concern. His talent fed off itself" (63). Bigsby's opinion—commonly held in the academy and paraded in the press by reviewers for the major New York dailies—persisted in similar dismissal of Williams's work of the 1970s. As Bigsby again stressed, "His plays had always borne directly out of his life, but the years the degree of refraction lessened until he began to write more and more about himself as a blighted gay poet or debilitated artist for whom writing was a way of denying his mortality" (65).

Readings such as Bigsby's have, unfortunately, become gospel. According to Marc Robinson, "Tennessee Williams spent a lifetime trying to escape cliches, but cliches cling to him" (29). This predicament was especially true for Williams in the case of his later plays; they have become supercharged electromagnetic fields attracting responses like Bigsby's, though not always so eloquently expressed. All too predictably, the characters in Williams's later plays have been analyzed as his psychic look-alikes, however dissimilar their physical appearances. The one-eyed Fräulein in *The Gnädiges Fräulein,* for example, was, according to Harold Clurman, a picture of Williams fallen upon hard times, battling off the critics who wanted to mutilate him just as the cocaloony birds do the soubrette. Like her, the argument goes, Williams was a "social derelict." Surely she is and yet she is so much more. Every predatory gay character—Quentin in *Small Craft Warnings* or Mark in *Chalky White Substance*—was the aging Williams in dramatic drag.

The plots of Williams's later work have also been assailed, branded as fragmentary, a "rambling discourse with little or no movement toward climax," as Arthur Ganz asserted (120). *Out Cry, Small Craft,* or *Bar of a Tokyo Hotel,* for example, have been held to the same tired standards of realism that Williams revolted from in the 1930s with *Stairs to the Roof* or in the 1940s with *Glass Menagerie*. Rather than empowering Williams as a highly innovative and effective dramatist in line with Artaud, Beckett, or Pinter, he was diminished as "uncreatively derivative." Where Williams was praised in the early plays for his genius at selecting haunting symbolism, the critics have pummeled him in the later plays for imitating himself. What V.S. Naipaul said of Dickens has too often been said of Williams: he "died from self parody" (qtd. in Levine). In the critics' eyes, for instance, Chicken in *Kingdom of Earth* is an imitation Stanley Kowalski and not a very good one at that, and the rooming house in *Vieux Carré* nostalgically billets too many well-known, well-worn Williams boarders/denizens.

Labels, however, have concealed Williams's accomplishments in his later plays. The diversity and breadth of this part of the Williams canon defies easy, homogenized rubrics. Not even the convoluted classification system of Polonius — "pastoral, comical, historical pastoral, tragical-historical, tragical-comical-historical-pastoral" — can do justice to the highly experimental plays of Williams's last three decades. "I am writing differently now," he told Donald Spoto (366), but few readers have understood or appreciated the difference(s). Typical of the critical misunderstanding and dis-ease with Williams's later plays is Martin Denton's view of *Small Craft Warnings* (1972): "It falters into the weird blend of experiment and mean-spirit grotesqueness that characterizes so much of Williams's later work." Coming closest, perhaps, to establishing a critical rubric containing Williams's later work, Ruby Cohn divides them into "sociopolitical plays," plays of "poetic regionalism," plays on "aged or dying" characters, "lyric plays," and those that are "Gothic and/or grotesque." While pedagogically challenging, Cohn's categories still collapse or coalesce. The "spare and monochromatic" (236) *Out Cry* or *In the Bar of a Tokyo Hotel* might qualify as Gothic, poetically regional, and, depending on how one views theatre as weapon, platforms for change, sociopolitical forays into actors'/artists' inquiry into selves, interrogations of audience/other, or even attacks on the institutionality of theatre itself.

This collection of fifteen original essays by many leading Williams scholars attempts to reappraise and recuperate Williams's later work. Moving to new territory, the essays here do not disclaim biography, but they do not substitute it for confronting Williams's scripts as highly experimental and carefully crafted for a theatre of mind and body. The fifteen essays in *Undiscovered Country* situate and study the later plays, not disparagingly as dim shadows of the earlier ones but as creative, original works that testify to the evolution of Williams's art over a period of three decades. No other volume of essays on Tennessee Williams — not even Robert F. Gross's recent *Casebook* (which looks at only six of the post-*Iguana* plays) — offers readers so much on the later canon. While in no way striving for a comprehensive appraisal of the later Williams canon the fifteen essays here do address a fairly large share of that body of work, offering new (and in many ways provocative) readings of *The Gnädiges Fräulein, In the Bar of a Tokyo Hotel, Small Craft Warnings, A Lovely Sunday for Crueve Coeur, Clothes for a Summer Hotel, Out Cry, Two Character Play, Vieux Carré, Red Devil Battery Sign, Something Cloudy, Something Clear,* and *A House Not Meant to Stand.* Significantly, *Undiscovered Country* begins with a group of essays — by Allean Hale, Annette Saddik, and Una Chaudhuri — that provide new and in some senses radical, responses to one of the least understood and most denigrated of Williams's plays — *The Gnädiges Fräulein.* And two other essays — by George Crandell and Norma Jenckes — pack challenging readings of Williams's much overlooked *Clothes for a Summer Hotel.*

Taken as a group, then, the essays in *Undiscovered Country* seek to advance our understanding of a substantial, expansive body of Williams's work and to advance these plays as triumphs of the American theatre in the 1960s, 1970s, and 1980s. Readers, *en avant!*

Works Cited

Bigsby, C. W. E. *Modern American Drama, 1945–2000*. Cambridge: Cambridge UP, 2000.
Clurman, Harold. "Theatre." *Nation* 14 (Mar. 1966): 3009.
Cohn, Ruby. "Tennessee Williams: The Last Two Decades." Ed. Matthew C. Roudané. *The Cambridge Companion to Tennessee Williams*. Cambridge: Cambridge UP, 1997. 232–43.
Denton, Martin. "*Small Craft Warnings*." nytheatre.reviews.com
Gross, Robert F., ed. *Tennessee Williams: A Casebook*. New York: Routledge, 2002.
Gunz, Arthur. *Realms of the Self*. New York: New York UP, 1980.
Levine, Samantha. "The Notorious Naipaul Wins a Nobel." *US News & World Report* 22 Oct. 2001: 8.
Mann, Bruce. "Memories and Muses: *Vieux Carré* and *Something Cloudy, Something Clear*." *Tennessee Williams: A Casebook* Ed. Robert F. Gross. New York: Routledge, 2002. 139–52.
Robinson, Marc. *The Other American Drama*. Cambridge: Cambridge UP, 1994.
Saddik, Annette. *The Politics of Reputation: The Critical Reception of Tennessee Williams' Later Plays*. Madison, NJ: Associated University Presses, 1999.
Spoto, Donald, *The Kindness of Strangers: The Life of Tennessee Williams*. New York: Ballantine Books, 1985.

Annette J. Saddik

"THE INEXPRESSIBLE REGRET OF ALL HER REGRETS": TENNESSEE WILLIAMS'S LATER PLAYS AS ARTAUDIAN THEATER OF CRUELTY

In my opinion art is a kind of anarchy, and the theater is a provence of art. . . . It runs counter to the sort of orderliness on which organized society apparently must be based. It is a benevolent anarchy: it must be that and if it is true art, it is. It is benevolent in the sense of constructing something which is missing, and what it constructs may be merely criticism of things as they exist.

—*Tennessee Williams*, "Something Wild," 1945

In the true theater a play disturbs the senses' repose, frees the repressed unconscious, incites a kind of virtual revolt (which moreover can have its full effect only if it remains virtual), and imposes on the assembled collectivity an attitude that is both difficult and heroic.

—*Antonin Artaud*, The Theater and Its Double, 1958

(originally appeared in French in 1938)

In *The Theater and Its Double,* Antonin Artaud proposes a "theater of cruelty" that does not involve "the cruelty we can exercise upon each other by hacking at each other's bodies, carving up our personal anatomies . . . but the much more terrible and necessary cruelty which things can exercise against us. We are not free. And the sky can fall on our heads. And the **theater** has been created to teach us that first of all" (79). While Artaud's cryptic description of his theater of cruelty has been applied to authors such as Jean Genet and August Strindberg (in the later experimental plays), the work of Tennessee Williams, most commonly associated with long, poetic speeches, does not immediately seem to correspond with Artaud's vision of changing the primary role of speech, "of reducing its position, of considering it as something else than a means of conducting human characters to their external ends" (72). Yet from his earliest beginnings, Williams's vision of a "new, plastic theatre which must take the place of the exhausted theatre of realistic conventions" in his production notes to *The Glass Menagerie* echoed Artaud's insistence on a theater which is "not psychological but plastic and physical" (71),[1] highlighting the inadequacy of language to represent human experience.

It is with his later plays, however, that Williams finally began to achieve his vision of this Artaudian "plastic" theater which expresses a "metaphysical fear" (Artaud 44) beyond language, one that exists to explore what cannot be expressed in words. Clearly, the eruption of violence in Williams's work is a manifestation of the fear and frustration of being trapped in language, and so the physicality of the theater makes it the perfect medium through which to explore the chaos signified by that violence. It is precisely this chaos beyond rational constructs—the primal scream—with which Artaud's theater of cruelty concerns itself. Artaud is not directly interested in violence per se but rather in the impulse behind the violent act, the primitive instincts and desires in their purest states *before* they become repressed by culture and emerge in what he sees as distorted, sublimated forms. Honoring, capturing, and presenting these impulses in ritualistic spectacle are key to the theater of cruelty, and there are clearly elements of this philosophy in *The Two-Character Play/Out Cry* (1967), which Williams revised throughout the 1970s, as well as many, if not most, of his later one-acts, such as *The Mutilated* (1966), *The Frosted Glass Coffin* (1970), and *Lifeboat Drill* (1981). While it would be difficult to say that any one play corresponds exactly to Artaud's vision of a theater of cruelty, Williams's late plays *The Gnädiges Fräulein* (1966), *Kingdom of Earth* (also known as *The Seven Descents of Myrtle*) (1968, 1975),[2] *Now the Cats with Jewelled Claws* (1981), and *This is the Peaceable Kingdom* (1981), succeed in liberating the spectator from a reliance on plot and its linguistic constructs, creating through sound, gesture, and spectacle the cruelty of the real which remains linguistically "untranslatable" (Artaud 71). One key element that links Artaud's work with Williams's later anti-realistic plays is precisely a revelation of the metaphysical cruelty that lies beyond logical representation, marginalizing language and instead taking advantage of the physicality of the theater.

While Williams's later work was largely characterized as unsuccessful when it was first presented, recent scholarship argues that a nostalgia for the "poetic realism" which had established his early reputation prevented critics and audiences from fully understanding the later anti-realistic projects.[3] In *The Gnädiges Fräulein, Kingdom of Earth, Now the Cats with Jewelled Claws,* and *This is the Peaceable Kingdom,* Williams was ready to move completely beyond psychological characterization and conventional moral ideology, beyond theater as mimetic representation, and therefore his style became more concurrent with a focus on the eclectic and immediate "happenings" of the 1960s-1980s, which emphasized the physical presence of the sexualized body and the illusive energy of the spirit and was very much influenced by Artaud. Representation in these "events," therefore, becomes symbolic and ritualistic—representation without a mimetic referent— outside immediate repetition. All these plays share an element of the "grotesque," a term used frequently in discussions of Williams's later plays[4] and one that is consistent with Artaud's technique of exaggeration. His one-act play *The Gnädiges Fräulein* (loosely translated as "Gracious Miss" or "An Honorable Woman"), for example, is a work that relies heavily on the aural, the visual, and the physical, articulating the world of the outcast through ritualistic spectacle. While the familiar Williams theme of survival—of going forward in the midst of personal and social adversity, echoed by the famous "En Avant" with which he signed his letters—is certainly present in this play, the mode of representation is very different from that of his earlier works. The characters are presented as two-dimensional rather than as human beings with complex psychological histories, and the form *Gnädiges Fräulein* takes is certainly more physical and much less reverent than the psychological realism of works such as *A Streetcar Named Desire* or *The Glass Menagerie,*[5] functioning more as a metalinguistic expression that laughs sadly at the inevitability of cruelty, rife with irony and using parody as its backdrop. In this sense, *Gnädiges* comes across more like Williams's *Camino Real* or Beckett's *Waiting For Godot* than any of Williams's earlier work. The 1960s gave Williams a freedom and a style to explore what had been taboo and unaccepted in America during the 1940s and '50s, and he was able to finally realize his opinion of art as a "kind of anarchy" that he discussed in 1945.

This "benevolent anarchy" Williams claimed as the role of theater was very much in line with Artaud's sense of a "virtual revolt" that lay at the core of dramatic representation. For both, artistic rebellion was effective precisely *because* it was *not* reality but a true image laden with symbolic status that begged to be read as spectacle, not a mere random event. Representation and, therefore, mimetic repetition have no place in the theater of cruelty, as the theater exists to create something new and explore a terror beyond rational expression. Jacques Derrida usefully untangles Artaud's explanation of the primitive and pre-logical nature of the theater of cruelty as not a representation but "life itself, in the extent to which life is unrepresentable. Life is the nonrepresentable origin of representation" (42).[6] For Artaud, "cruelty" is manifested in the theater's disruption of all the audience's prior conceptions, and it is that disruption which leads to social awakening, forcing us to experience in the theater what civilization doesn't allow. Theater then becomes the transformative and the real. Like Artaud, Williams was no longer interested in the exploration of psychological problems of individuals commonly associated with realism, nor was he completely committed to the politically charged emphasis on social transformation through the motivations of intellect that other critics of realism such as Bertolt Brecht emphasized. Instead, Williams's

Artaudian plays are concerned with aspects of theater connected to the *unconscious* mind, favoring intuition, feeling, and experience over reason and the cataclysmic celebration of these sensory functions through ritualistic presentation.

Artaud's theoretical imaginings can probably be seen in practice most clearly in the plays of writers such as Genet, who, although he had read little of Artaud's work, shared his goals for the theater. Artaud, like Genet, was very interested in pre-logical consciousness and primitive existence, which they both felt could primarily be reached through ritual in the theater, where all activities (all actions) are separated from their functions, thereby becoming symbolic. Both writers sought to invert the conventional moral code of good and evil, and, therefore, what was deemed "good" in traditional society (culture, repression, self-control, obedience to the law) became universally evil, and what was considered "evil" (nature, sexuality, violence, power) was encouraged as good. While I have found no evidence that Williams was directly familiar with Artaud's work, it is possible that he encountered his theories during his studies at the New School in New York City during the 1940s, and he was certainly familiar with Genet's work. In fact, in an essay which appeared in *New York Magazine* in 1960, Williams cited Camus, Genet, Brecht, Beckett, Anouilh, Ionesco, Duerrenmatt, and Albee as his "fellow defendants" in writing honestly about life (Day and Woods 114–115). His late plays *Kirche, Küche und Kinder: An Outrage for the Stage* (unpublished, 1979) and *THIS IS (An Entertainment)* (unpublished, 1976) contain moments of remarkable similarity to Artaud's and Genet's work. A scene in *Kirche, Küche und Kinder,* for example, where a Minister throws a paper bag over the character Hotsy's head and "plops a huge Bible under [her] derriere and mounts her [as] members of THE PRESS" burst in is reminiscent of the same dismissal of good taste in Count Cenci's violent pursuit of his daughter as he seeks to rape her in Artaud's *The Cenci*. In *THIS IS,* the role-playing of the Count and Countess that opens the play is strikingly similar to that of Genet's *The Maids,* and the invasion of the hotel by the revolution outside, with the Countess's lover, General Eros, leading the way echoes the ending of Genet's *The Balcony*.[7]

Like Nietzsche, Artaud and Genet want characters to be judged outside of good and evil, and Artaud's theater of cruelty forces the spectator to confront the harsh facts of a cruel world and his or her own isolation.[8] These writers explore the contradictions and hypocrisies of bourgeois society and often champion the "primitive" impulses of the socially marginalized. Williams's well-known focus on the world of outcasts or social outlaws, beginning as early as his 1937 play titled *Fugitive Kind* (not to be confused with *The Fugitive Kind,* the title of the film version of *Orpheus Descending*), was typically expressed in a much more romanticized manner in the pre-1960 work than one would normally associate with Artaud or Genet. While he often valorized the overtly sexual outcast as charismatic and spiritually alive, there is clearly a split in his sympathies, stemming from what he has often claimed as the "combination of Puritan and Cavalier strains in [his] blood" (Day and Woods 58). The paragons of an animalistic desire in his plays—Val Xavier, Stanley Kowalski, Chance Wayne, Sebastian Venable, for example—are morally problematized

Patti Chambers as Polly, Nancy Castle as Molly in *The Gnädiges Fräulein*. Courtesy of Theater Ten Thousand at The Ohio Theatre (October 1999).

and are often punished for their transgressions.[9] In the later plays I cite above, however, this moral split virtually disappears as he committed to a more starkly anti-realistic, physical, and morally inverted theater characteristic of Artaud and Genet.

The Gnädiges Fräulein obviously resists realistic coherency from the beginning, yet although the title of the double bill which included both *Gnädiges* and *The Mutilated—Slapstick Tragedy*—indicates a strong reliance on the physical, "slapstick" is hardly a sufficient description of the action. This is a play which is certainly meant to be seen, as Arnold Barkus's excellent 1999 production at New York's Ohio Theatre made overwhelmingly clear. The play opens with Polly, the Society Editor of the *Cocaloony Gazette,* introducing the scene to the audience among the swooshing of the cocaloony birds above. We then encounter Molly, the caretaker of a boardinghouse for drifters, mopping up blood. Hungry for publicity, she offers Polly material for an intense story of human interest and proceeds to tell the tale of her most tragic boarder, the Gnädiges Fräulein, who, we find out, once performed before European royalty as part of a famous artistic trio, the other two being a trained seal and the trained seal's trainer, a beautiful "Viennese dandy" who was the object of her unrequited love. One day, in order to gain his attention, the Fräulein suddenly leapt into the air and intercepted the fish that was thrown to the seal by catching it in her own jaws. This absurd novelty was popular for some time, until one day the seal rebelled and attacked her in defense of its territory. Molly tells us that after this failed career in show business, the Gnädiges Fräulein just drifted until she finally wound up lodging in Molly's "big dormitory." When it became clear that the Fräulein was not earning her keep, the business-minded Molly, aware of the Fräulein's acrobatic past, sent her off to the fish docks to compete with the cocaloony birds for fish just as she had competed with the seal for attention. The cocaloonies, however, like the seal, did not welcome the competition and would increasingly terrorize the Fräulein, chasing her from the docks. By the end of the play, the cocaloonies have gauged out both her eyes and ripped out most of her hair; her skirt and legs are streaked with blood, but still she takes her fish bucket and runs to the docks to compete for fish as the scene closes. This is the degraded condition to which the once great Fräulein is reduced, but her survival in the face of life's cruelties makes her "an honorable woman" for Williams.

Language as a means of direct expression is not at all primary in *Gnädiges Fräulein,* and even the long speeches are impressionistic rather than narratively coherent, interrupted by lapses of "lost concentration" with Molly and Polly "star[ing] blankly for a couple of moments" (219). Words are not important in terms of rational signification, so it becomes easy, even inevitable, for Molly and Polly to forget what they were saying in the middle of a sentence. Narrative is also frequently interrupted by gesture, as Polly's long opening speech is punctuated with loud "swooshes" of the cocaloony birds countered by her cries of "OOPS!" amidst bits of gossip. Throughout the speech the term "southernmost" is used more as a rhythmic mantra than a crucial signifier, even though it does locate the action in the Florida Keys. The specific setting, however—"Cocaloony Key"—is the fantastic arena where birds called cocaloonies dominate and dictate the cruelty of a "survival of the fittest" social order, where human and beast are on equal terms and the metaphysical cruelties imposed on us both by others and by the ways of the world are highlighted. The pathetic pretenses of a civilized world, such as gossip columns, "social position" (250), or Polly's proclamation that "a lady never steps out of her house, unless her house is on fire, without a pair of gloves on" (219) become meaningless. When Polly suggests that she could interview the Gnädiges Fräulein and "ask her opinions," Molly's reply is that "She's long past having opinions" (229). Since "opinion" relies on cultural context and social exchange, the primary physical predatory world that the Gnädiges Fräulein now occupies entertains no such illusions.

Although Linda Dorff sees the cocaloony birds as "unlike the predatory black birds of *Suddenly Last Summer,*" having "degenerated to a two-dimensional cartoon image of 'natural' life grotesquely and comically disfigured by the presence of civilization and its everpresent garbage" (17–18), the picture of the cruel cycle of the black birds devouring the sea turtles in the Encantadas still comes to mind, even as Williams has turned from sentimental horror to liberating mockery. The fact that he has moved from using the birds as a metaphor for the off-stage, never-seen devouring of Sebastian to a more literal, on-stage mutilation of the outrageous Fräulein does certainly make the image in *Gnädiges Fräulein* much more cartoonish, but unlike the characteristic response to violence in cartoons, the audience doesn't typically laugh as the Fräulein's eyes are ripped out of their sockets and her hair is torn out. When I saw the play, this was an undeniably sad and tragic image, even as (or maybe more so because of it) Molly and Polly dismissed her condition somewhat comically. We can laugh all we want, but this is still a world where Artaudian nature and culture clash, and the cruel superiority of nature unquestionably wins out.

For Artaud, "culture" was synonymous with repression and artificiality and imposed unhealthy boundaries which "have never been coincident with life, which in fact has been devised to tyrannize over life" (7). He considers it "right that from time to time cataclysms occur which compel us to return to nature, i.e., to rediscover life" (10). Nature is liberating, primitive, and perhaps cruel, but inevitable and healthy. It is the repression of our "natural" impulses (in the most basic, primitive, instinctual sense) through culture and the refusal to give the dark forces any respect or acknowledgment through even the ritual of theater that Artaud believes is at the root of a sick and destructive culture. In 1933, as the winds of World War II were stirring, Artaud prophetically articulated the *real* violence which he felt must result from culture's repression and denial of our inevitable natures and culture's refusal to pay homage to these forces through the celebration of *ritualistic* violence (88). He called for a theater whose "object is not to resolve social or psychological conflicts, to serve as battlefield for moral passions, but to express objectively certain secret truths" (70). The "secret truths" of human domination, cruelty, and survival are brought to light absurdly yet poignantly in *The Gnädiges Fräulein* without ever directly articulating them.

The clash of nature and culture plays itself out everywhere in this play—in the natural world of the cocaloonies versus the "society" with which Molly and Polly are so concerned, the seal (albeit a "trained" seal), which represents nature in contrast to the high society of the Viennese Dandy—and the Fräulein is always caught in between, trying to retain her social dignity while her physical senses deteriorate, and she is reduced to competing in nature for basic survival. She can no longer see—both her eyes having been gouged out—and she reads clips of her scrapbook from memory (246). Her hearing is going, so Molly and Polly must use a megaphone to address her, and her vocabulary is essentially limited to reciting from memory on command. The Fräulein's pronunciation, too, is deteriorating, and this was made especially clear in the Barkus production, where the Fräulein repeatedly mispronounced vowels—"Mah I cohm out?" for example, instead of "May I come out?" as written in the text. The Fräulein's use of language—reading it, hearing it, speaking it—has broken down and is replaced primarily by gesture and onomatopoeia. She can still sing, but even her singing is interrupted by those moments of "lost concentration" (233).

In "The Shudder of Catharsis," Elin Diamond writes that Artaud sought "an immediate and physical language" (Artaud's words), which

> would penetrate its spectators, "act . . . upon [them] like a spiritual therapeutics."
> Artaudian cruelty is a theater of "total spectacle" intended to destroy barriers
> between "analytic theater and plastic world, mind and body"—a theater composed

of and addressed to the "entire organism." . . . For Artaud, the bubonic plagues of Europe provided the best metaphors for physical, psychical and cultural transgressions. (165)

Artaud felt that "the theater is a formidable call to the forces that impel the mind by example to the source of its conflicts," and that

> If the essential theater is like the plague, it is not because it is contagious, but because like the plague it is the revelation, the bringing forth, the exteriorization of a depth of latent cruelty by means of which all the perverse possibilities of the mind, whether of an individual or a people, are localized. . . . We can now say that all true freedom is dark, and infallibly identified with sexual freedom, which is also dark, although we do not know precisely why. (Artaud 30)

Sexuality is represented in *The Gnädiges Fräulein* primarily through the "erotic fantasy" of Indian Joe, who is emblematic of the culture of mimetic representation—described as "blond" and dressed like a "Hollywood Indian." The cruel competition over access to Indian Joe's sexuality is one example of the struggle for domination in the natural world in this play. Not only is there competition between Polly and the Gnädiges Fräulein (who confuses him with the memory of her love, Toivo, the Viennese Dandy, who similarly didn't pay her any attention) for the attentions of Indian Joe, but his sexuality is linked to a macho sense of competition and domination with both the Fräulein and the Giant Cocaloony, coupled with a breakdown of rational language in a vocabulary limited essentially to "Ugh" and "Pow." He squares off several times with the Giant Cocaloony, matches described in the text as a "standoff" (240) in pantomime, to the Cocaloony's eventual retreat (240). Later, when the Giant Cocaloony appears once again, screeching "AWK. AWK,"[10] Joe merely has to utter "Ugh" and shake his tomahawk at the window to ensure retreat. In *Postmodernist Culture,* Steven Connor writes that

> In the influential work of Antonin Artaud the theatre is seen as a colonized or dispossessed cultural form, dominated as it is by written language. Artaud argues that the theatre should abandon its fealty to the authority of Text and learn to speak its own intrinsically theatrical language of light, colour, movement, gesture, and space. This is not to say that language should be banished from the theatre . . . but language is to be made physical too, communicating as pure sound and sensation rather than through abstract correspondence. (143–144)

At the close of scene ii, Joe runs out onto the porch drumming his bare chest and proclaiming the most articulate sentence he utters throughout the play: "I feel like a bull!" to which Polly can only reply lasciviously several times: "MOOOO! MOOOO!" (250). This primal utterance of animal sound is what closes the scene. By the end of the play, Molly snatches the fish that the Fräulein has caught and lovingly prepared for Indian Joe, leaving him shouting at her, "NO FISH IN

John Howard as "Indian Joe" in *The Gnädiges Fräulein*. Courtesy of Theater Ten Thousand at The Ohio Theatre (October 1999). Photo by Arnold Barkus.

SKILLET!" as he pushes aside both Molly and Polly and sits down at the table to eat the fish that Molly had snatched. Polly is left offering him the wine, as the Gnädiges Fräulein responds to the whistle which calls her back to the docks with a desperate blind dash.

The guttural utterances beyond rational language—communication as "pure sound and sensation rather than through abstract correspondence"—primacy of sexual dominance, and the heartless competition in the last scene articulate through action the cruelty of a world in which language cannot begin to address the natural forces which drive us. *The Gnädiges Fräulein* presents a dialogue which is constantly interrupted by gesture and sound and, therefore, does not (re)-present any logically coherent referent, thereby resisting repetition. Artaud puts forth the notion that "the stage is a concrete physical place which asks to be filled, and to be given its own concrete language to speak . . . and that this concrete physical language to which I refer is truly theatrical only to the degree that the thoughts it expresses are beyond the reach of the spoken language" (37). He calls for an "aspect of pure theatrical language which does without words, a language of signs, gestures and attitudes having an ideographic value as they exist in certain unperverted pantomimes," which he describes as "direct Pantomime where gestures— instead of representing words or sentences . . . represent ideas, attitudes of mind, aspects of nature, all in an effective, concrete manner, i.e., by constantly evoking objects or natural details" (39–40).

Artaud's "unperverted pantomime" is clearly manifested in Williams's "Giant Cocaloony bird," who terrorizes the Gnädiges Fräulein along with Molly and Polly, and in Barkus's production the physical significance of this "character" was made overwhelmingly clear through Sam Chan's presentation. Similarly, the Gnädiges Fräulein's penetrating scream, which Molly describes as "the inexpressible regret of all her regrets" (248) and Polly calls the "Saddest soliloquy on the stage since Hamlet's" is expressed "regretfully" through three instances of "AH-HHHHHHHHHHHHHH!" and is one of the most powerful and poignant moments I have ever seen on the stage. Surely this moment articulates Artaud's emphasis on the difficulty of communicating in mere words "the feeling of a particular sound or the degree and quality of a physical pain" (46), and a movement toward a more organic and hieroglyphic "language in space, language of sounds, cries, lights, onomatopoeia" (90). Diamond discusses a similar moment in Helene Weigel's performance in the well-known scene in Bertolt Brecht's *Mother Courage,* in which Mother Courage is forced to identify the corpse of her son. She writes that

> In Brecht's text, Mother Courage refuses, twice, to identify the corpse. In performance, when the questioners left, Helene Weigel completed the moment by turning her head with mouth extended fully and mimed, silently, the cathartic scream her character could not utter. (162)

Diamond goes on to quote George Steiner, who witnessed this "silent scream" at the first Berliner Ensemble production in 1949 and compared it to the screaming horse in Picasso's *Guernica:*

> The sound that came out was raw and terrible beyond any description that I could give of it. But in fact there was no sound. Nothing. The sound was total silence. It was silence which screamed and screamed through the whole theatre so that the audience lowered its head as before a gust of wind. (162)

Although their social goals for the theater were certainly very different, the written text was not at all primary for Artaud and Brecht, and Artaud repeatedly stated the importance of particular productions, which demonstrate "what can be determined only on the stage" (Artaud 46)—as in Weigel's "silence which screamed" in a moment "beyond . . . description." In Williams's later one-act play, *The Frosted Glass Coffin,* a similar outcry that defies language occurs at the very end. The final moment of the play focuses on the physically and mentally deteriorated Mr. Kelsey, who has slowly come to realize that his wife is dead, as he "closes his cataract-blinded eyes and opens his jaws like a fish out of water. After a few moments, a sound comes from his mouth which takes the full measure of his grief" (214).[11]

This intense reliance on gesture is also evident throughout the Fräulein's "recitations" of old songs, attempts at repetition which never fully succeed. Like Myrtle in *Kingdom of Earth,* the Fräulein has fallen from show business but is trapped into performing failed and absurd representations of herself. During one of her musical numbers, she interrupts herself and initiates a non-sequitur gesture of opening and closing her mouth like a goldfish, which Molly explains as "demonstrating." When Polly asks exactly what the Fräulein is demonstrating, Molly replies "Either a goldfish in a goldfish bowl or a society reporter in a soundproof telephone booth" (233)—representations of both animal and human trapped by cultural artificiality. This scene strongly echoes modern and postmodern ideas of alienation, and, among other things, is representing on a physical level Val Xavier's sad realization in *Orpheus Descending* that "Nobody ever gets to know *no body!* We're all of us sentenced to solitary confinement inside our own skins, for life!" (II.i.271). This ability to express alienation in rational language breaks down in *The Gnädiges Fräulein,* as the Fräulein is reduced to the absurd gesture of signification which is beyond rationality and signifies nothing that can be absolutely located or determined. Similarly, the pantomime scene between Harry and Tom in Susan Glaspell's *The Verge* (1921), in which Harry attempts to communicate to Tom through the glass door of the greenhouse that he wants him to go fetch salt for the breakfast eggs, prompts Claire to comment that "It was all so queer. He locked out of his side of the door. You locked in on yours. Looking right at each other and—" (233–34). Claire's interpretation of the moment recalls the incommunicability of the human condition, where we are all trapped, be it inside our own skins, goldfish bowls, telephone booths, or greenhouses, trying desperately to connect through word or gesture, but the signifying universe fails us.

Artaud's emphasis on gesture over language in the theater as well as Williams's similar emphasis in *Gnädiges Fräulein* do not offer us an escape from the futility of trying to make connections, but they do powerfully highlight the illusion of rational language that this connection ("communication," "expression") can occur unproblematically. Artaud sees a "rupture between things and words, between things and the ideas and signs that are their representations" (7) at the root of social and metaphysical confusion, and, like Williams, who aimed to present the cruelties of the human condition through his tragicomic "slapstick tragedy," seeks a theater which will address that rupture or gap.

Although I focus on the Artaudian aspect of cruelty in this play, Dorff reads *Gnädiges*, along with the later works *THIS IS (An Entertainment), Kirche, Küche und Kinder: An Outrage for the Stage, A Lovely Sunday for Creve Coeur* (1975–1979), and a fragment entitled *The Everlasting Ticket* (1981) in a more comic vein, labeling them the "outrageous plays," works which appropriate "metadrama and the aesthetics of the cartoon to parody the state of contemporary theater" (13). She argues that the outrageous qualities of these plays have often led critics to view them as uncontrolled excesses on Williams's part, ignoring the violent critique underneath. Dorff's focus on the Bahktinian aspects of the "grotesquely comic" nature of the play is undeniably present and is not at all incompatible with a more Artaudian reading. The operation of the grotesque on the everyday world, transforming it into a "terrifying" one "alien to man," which Dorff cites from Bahktin (16) is akin to the goals of Artaud's theater of cruelty, a theater which aimed to present life in an exaggerated, unfamiliar form in order to shock and liberate. The significance of *Gnädiges Fräulein* lies precisely in its multifaceted nature, in the contradictory layering of style that marks it as a postmodern work. Both the tragic and the comic aspects of this play stress its anti-mimetic and exaggerated foundation, but while Dorff's essay unravels its "comic grotesque" side, an Artaudian reading can certainly incorporate this aspect of the play and yet go further in exploring what this interpretation cannot—the inexpressible tragedy and underlying metaphysical cruelty of a cosmic pain beyond language, the primal screams that defy rational comprehension and embrace the pre-logical utterances of unadulterated nature.

Williams's full-length play *Kingdom of Earth* opens with the threat of the overwhelming powers of nature—an impending flood in the "muted warning of the river" and the "whining wind" (I.i.126). The central characters Myrtle, Lot, and Chicken all serve as symbolic figures rather than representations of complex human beings, and the "plot" is limited in any traditional sense. Myrtle and Lot, now married, return to Lot's childhood home, where his half-brother Chicken lives and hopes to take possession if he can withstand the flood which threatens to destroy the house along with those who occupy it. We eventually learn that Myrtle—a "rather fleshy" young woman—has been a professional performer, the last surviving member of "The Four Hot Shots from Mobile," the other women all having come to rather cruel and violent ends. She continues, however, to perform parodies of herself in gaudy outfits that emphasize her sexuality and vitality. Lot, by contrast, is a frail young man who is obsessed with the memory of his dead mother, "Miss Lottie," and is affectionately dominated by Myrtle. Myrtle's domination over Lot, however, is not the driving force of this play. The overtly sexual Chicken, who is aptly named and described as being "like a crouched animal" (I.i.127), "seems a suitable antagonist to a flooding river" (I.i.125) and, apparently, to Myrtle as well.

The struggle for domination, however, is not so much represented in this play by the simple struggle between Myrtle and Chicken, but rather between what Lot and Chicken symbolize, emissaries of culture and nature, death and life, respectively—

with Myrtle as the virgin/whore who shifts back and forth between them. Like the Gnädiges Fräulein, Myrtle is caught in the struggle between nature and culture, a symbol of the battle within us all. She comes on the scene first as a maternal figure, protecting Lot as her husband/child and insisting that she finds his inability to perform sexually and his "refined" appearance attractive, "superior to a man." She claims that his impotence touched "the deepest chord in [her] nature, which is the maternal chord" (I.i.135). Chicken, the perfect contrast to his "invalid" (I.i.140) brother, appears to upset Myrtle at first, as she objects strongly to his sexual innuendoes and "filthy talk" and insists that "we should all talk and act like gentlemen an'—ladies" (I.i.147). She refers to Chicken as "that man, that animal" (I.ii.155), unsure whether he is human or beast, but certainly not part of the civilized world of "gentlemen," and approaches the kitchen downstairs to him "as if approaching a jungle" (I.ii.161). With each descent down the stairs to Chicken, however, she descends deeper into his world, the "lower" order antithetical to society. By scene iv of Act I, they are singing and drinking together in what appears to be true comradery, until eventually Myrtle, who knows "lots of church songs but—can't think of any" in the presence of Chicken (I.iv.175), is forgetting the repressions of cultured society. Just as the Fräulein's singing was interrupted by moments of "lost concentration," Myrtle's rational coherency breaks down and degenerates into physical "instink" [*sic*], a term she uses repeatedly. Like Artaud, she comes to the conclusion that life is made out of "Evil," and Chicken replies that "life just plain don't care for the weak" (II.ii.199).

Myrtle's duality is further complicated by her reaction to Chicken's mixed racial heritage—the union of his white father and black mother marginalizes him and forces him into the position of social outcast. Lot makes it clear that although he and Chicken share the same father, they had *"Very* diff'rent mothers!" (I.i.138). Lot's and Chicken's father seemed to be a part of nature as he "wouldn't let Mother build a dining room into the house," presumably having no use for the social functions of a dining room. He died "howling like a wild beast" but still a winner, as even though "Mother was free to transform this place or tear it down to the ground, life was cruel to Mother. It gave her no time to carry out her plans" (I.i.129) and defeat the wild forces of the natural world which overtook her home. Chicken, with his "savage" (I.i.129), "wolfish grin" (II.i.184), is the product of parents who both lie outside of culture—an animalistic father and a mother who is already dismissed as bestial by virtue of her race.

Yet Myrtle at first denies being "disgusted" by Chicken, claiming to be "pleased an' relieved" that he wanted to kiss her (II.ii.201). Her sexuality, like her "uncontrollable" voice, which Lot attempts to curtail at various points, is characterized as chaotic and beyond repression. She describes herself as "a warm-natured woman" whose doctor prescribed her some pills to "keep down the heat of [her] nature," but alas, they had no effect (II.ii.201). The "terrific attraction" (II.iii.203) between the hysterical Myrtle and the constantly masturbating Chicken culminates in the crude scene of fellatio suggested between scenes ii and iii of Act II, with Myrtle crying as Chicken, like Lot before him, calls her a whore. After the consummation, however, Myrtle is indeed disgusted by her relations with Chicken as she moves her chair back from the table "like a monster was on it" (II.iii.205), and Williams's stage notes explain that she "has the typical Southern lower-class dread and awe of negroes" (II.iii.204). She returns to virgin mode as she asks Chicken not to talk crudely to her. But her "cultured" (i.e., learned) revulsion of Chicken's race, which again signifies his bestial, "natural" sexuality, is discarded as she opts for a life of physicality, priding herself on "noticin' an' appreciatin' a man's appearance. Physical," seeking salvation in Chicken's sexuality and brutal strength as he "look[s] like a man who could hold back the flood of a river!" (II.iii.208). Like Indian Joe who speaks primarily in grunts, Chicken's physical sexuality is beyond language, and this is what appeals to Myrtle. Together, they will meet the forces of nature head on, celebrate the cataclysm, and survive, drinking warm chicken blood to keep them alive.

Lot, on the other hand, is the picture of sterile civilization, taking pains to transform himself into the perfect mimetic representation. He carefully bleaches his hair so that it appears natural and is very proud of his artistic ability, learned, of course, from his mother. He spends the play dressing up first in his mother's white silk wrapper and posing with her ivory cigarette holder, then progressing to full drag in gauzy white dress, blond wig, and wide picture hat trimmed with faded flowers in an attempt to recapture her image. Yet, like Chicken, there is something menacing in his performance, as by Act II his "'Mona Lisa' smile is more sardonic and the violet shadows about his eyes are deeper" (II.i.177). This entire play, in fact, is laden with a menacing tone similar to Artaud's plays, particularly, *The Cenci*. At the end, Lot's crossdressing transforms him into both a mimetic image and a sinister parody of his dead mother, Miss Lottie. Obsessed with the past and refusing to move forward, Lot, like his Biblical namesake's wife, looks back and becomes frozen in representation, an object of art transformed in his own death "by the sexless passion of the transvestite" (II.iii.212). Chicken, by contrast, embraces survival in the present and aligns himself with the earth, the land, waiting with his home to take on the chaos of the flood, "a natural act of God" (II.ii.200). Here, God is not the spirit cultivated by organized religion and glorified in the "church songs" Myrtle can no longer remember but a force of nature and chaos. Chicken chooses reality over representation, life over art, nature over culture, and a life with Myrtle, who, although "no match" for the picture of a centerfold on the wall, is real, not a two-dimensional image frozen in time. The struggle between the "spiritual gates" and the "lustful body" (II.iii.210) is resolved, and the body dominates and incorporates the spirit as the forces of nature become the way to salvation. The mind (the rational, the logical) is pushed aside, and the spirit/body split that Artaud insists must be destroyed in order to celebrate natural life collapses. *Kingdom of Earth* echoes the familiar Lawrencian split that often appears in Williams's work—sexuality is equated with nature and the life force in a struggle with the cultured repression that seeks to destroy it. In a note to his one-act play about D. H. Lawrence's last days, *I Rise in Flame, Cried the Phoenix* (1951), Williams wrote that

Lawrence felt the mystery and power of sex, as the primal life urge, and was the life-long adversary of those who wanted to keep the subject locked away in the cellars of prudery. Much of his work is chaotic and distorted by tangent obsessions, . . . but all in all his work is probably the greatest modern monument to the dark roots of creation. (56)

This observation strongly echoes Artaud's similar descriptions of the primal life urge discussed above as well as the dark roots of creation associated with sexuality. The celebration and presentation of these urges are what lie at the core of both Artaud's theories and *Kingdom of Earth*. The last words of the play *"Up! Quick!"* carry a sexual connotation of triumph which serves to completely drown out the civilized impotence symbolized by Lot.

Like *The Gnädiges Fräulein* and *Kingdom of Earth*, Williams's 1981 one-act, *Now the Cats with Jewelled Claws*, an odd play which critics have not quite known how to address, becomes much more accessible when viewed through a nonlinear Artaudian lens of spectacle and inverted moral logic. At the rise of the curtain a cinema marquee appears, and the attraction offered is titled *Defiance of Decency*, setting the stage for an Artaudian debacle. Violence, wailing, singing, dancing, disjointed language, vulgar sexual gestures/remarks, chanting, and Brechtian placards come together in a spectacle of the senses in this play. The first third of scene ii is sung in the style of a Gregorian chant, and the music as well as the style of singing change for the remainder of the scene. In the first performance of *The Cenci* in 1935, Artaud's gruesome drama based on Stendhal's and Shelley's fictional adaptations of historical events, Artaud himself played Count Cenci, and his ritual chanting of the text was an attempt to get beyond the rational signification of language and reach what he saw as the mythic space between and beyond it. Although his approach did not succeed with the audience and led the play to financial failure, it does aid in highlighting the play's importance as spectacle, as presenting an immediate reality beyond logic and psychological understanding.

Now the Cats with Jewelled Claws takes place in a luncheon restaurant, centered first around two women, Madge and Bea, using the commotion of the "after-Christmas sales" as, eventually, a metaphor for social relations. Like the language of another late Williams one-act, *In the Bar of a Tokyo Hotel*, the language of *Now the Cats* is truncated and fragmented, with incomplete sentences/thoughts cut off with a period, then completed by another character. The following lines from scene i are typical of this sort of symbiosis in the play:

> BEA [sitting down and placing the rabbit beside her]. Oh, yes, the rabbit was wrapped, but the wrapping was torn off in a riot of shoppers at Guffle's. The after-Christmas sales have created.
> MADGE. An atmosphere of hysteria in the department store.(299)

Not only are attempts at rational, linear communication broken down in this example, but thematically these lines set the stage for the atmosphere of "hysteria" and "riot" that is always just below the surface of this play. Like the riots of *Now the Cats with Jewelled Claws,* the looting in *Peaceable Kingdom* (355) is emblematic of Artaud's description of the spectacle of human reaction to the plague, since "once the plague is established in a city, the regular forms collapse," and the "dregs of the population, apparently immunized by their frenzied greed, enter the open houses and pillage riches they know will serve no purpose or profit." For Artaud, this is the moment "the theater is born. The theater, i.e., an immediate gratuitousness invoking acts without use or profit" (24). The chaotic frenzy of rioting and looting evident in the plague scene is Artaud's perfect metaphor for theater. Like the plague, Artaud saw theater of cruelty as the great leveler—destroying the veneers of civilization and forcing us to confront a more primitive state, undermining the rational discourse of the audience.

References to unleashed sexuality and the threat of death, violence, fear, and anarchy are scattered everywhere in this play. When The Waitress first appears, she is pregnant and has a black eye. Later, Madge "wails, histrionically" (305) in the style of the Gnädiges Fräulein's "soliloquy" of the pain beyond language discussed above. In the middle of scene i, The Manager performs "a furious dance, around the ladies' table, Dionysian and vulgar," which he interprets linguistically to mean that "The porno show is directly across the street" (312). Madge suggests that "a massacre" could occur as a result of the different preferences in TV channels at her hotel, and the "panic to buy," which has been stimulated by "recession," has caused the streets to be "stampeded with panic-purchasers" (314). "Perverse" sexuality is introduced with the entrance of the First Young Man and Second Young Man amid their discussions of love, death, and sexual/social degeneration, as the First Young Man exclaims: "Did I ever tell you that I'm a social alien? Anarchist?" (317).

In this play as well as (less blatantly) in *This is the Peaceable Kingdom,* Williams also combined Brechtian with Artaudian anti-realistic elements, as different as the two are ideologically, in an effort to marginalize language on several levels. Brechtian placards are used to identify key points in the performance, first with the title "Trivialities" (306) followed shortly by Bea and Madge's dance to which the Manager sings (308), another Brechtian trademark to break up realistic illusion, found frequently in plays such as *The Threepenny Opera* and *The Good Person of Setzuan.* This particular song emphasizes a chaotic excess of sensual frenzy as the "banalities" (309) of life are discussed shortly afterwards. Once again in true Brechtian fashion, lines suddenly are sung a cappella, breaking up any rational coherency of plot, in a discussion of sexual "kink" and hustling (320). The next placard is worn by a "hunched man" labeled "Mr. Black," an obvious symbol of death whom several characters deny they see. More interpretive dance and singing duets carry us into the second scene, which begins with dialogue sung in the style of Gregorian chant that changes after a shattering crash is heard out on the street. After the violence of the car accident and the removal of the body, the chaotic ending is performed, like Artaud's plague scene, outside of language:

> Outside the great window they form a tight circle, milling about in confusion, shoving each other with their huge purchases—their hats are knocked awry and they

begin to exchange kicks and punches. Then there is a sound like the roar of an ogre in the sky. They disperse, screaming, running. The street is dark and silent. (328–29)

The Waitress then proclaims that she will not be back at work ever again, since she was attacked on the subway and there's no other way for her to get to work, as taxi fare is too high. The Manager leads a lyric on the subject of spectacle, its audience "The Cats with Jewelled Claws," full of ineffectual disdain:

> And now the cats with jewelled claws
> glide down the wall of night
> softly to crouch with bated breath
> and glare at all below,
> their malice on each upturned face
> descending cool as snow . . . (329)

Clearly there is a social message in this play concerning the civilized city in a state of anarchy, violence, and chaos and the muted spectatorship of the privileged who sit and watch the pain of the dispossessed without action or comment beyond "malice." This play could be seen as both Artaudian and Brechtian in form and content. The refusal to privilege rational linguistic constructs, interrupting mimetic illusionism with song, dance, and slogans, are devices common to both theorists, and the emphasis on the chaos of our unleashed natures, typified by Artaud's plague scene, is paired with an (albeit vague) social commentary on violence, fear, and the inaction of those in power. Spectacle interrupts any attempt at rational coherency, and, once again, it is the "basest" forms of our natures that are revealed and presented as inevitable in true Artaudian fashion. What makes this play different from *Gnädiges Fräulein,* however, as well as from *Kingdom of Earth,* is the refusal to celebrate this chaotic nature fully in an embrace of moral reversal and a dismissal of culture, curbing it instead with a Brechtian message of social contempt. It could be argued that the Brechtian moment occurs most strongly in the ambiguity of the ending, as the Manager leads the Young Man out toward the revolving door, offering to introduce him to "his future," which remains unknown and presumably malleable, the state of the world not final but left for the audience to determine.

A similar plea for social action is evident in the one-act play *This is the Peaceable Kingdom (or, Good Luck God),* as Man becomes God—culture's only hope—by the end of this play. Yet this play is much more pessimistic in its vision of the role of culture—and while nature is not entirely celebrated over culture here, it is certainly exhibited as the ugly, primary force that drives us and reveals itself more fully the closer we get to death. Williams picks a very specific and realistic location for his setting—"a nursing home in one of the drearier sections of Queens during the 'nursing home strike' in New York City in the spring of 1978"—marking its social context from the beginning. The patients are "staring grimly out at us as the curtain rises," and for the first half minute "no word is spoken" during a "pantomimic performance that should provoke the two tragic elements of pity and terror" (333). While the element of tragedy here is strong, as in *The Gnädiges Fräulein,* there are moments of bizarre humor, which Williams describes as "gallows humor" (333). This is a place where "decent existence is ended and indecent existence begins" (335), the natural drowning out cultural restraints.

Like *Now the Cats with Jewelled Claws,* "Hysteria is the condition of this place, this city, the world!" (353) and the action of the play is marked by riots and the explosion of grotesque gestures that mark desires outside linguistic expression. The inmates are starving, and cultural niceties are mocked in a scene where a gloved matron offers charitable food contributions. A lengthy history of the "Colonial Dames of America" is presented, however, before any food is given out, and the cultural cachet becomes meaningless in a world where basic needs are not met. The inmates riot wildly, taking food by force. One inmate, Lucretia, ends scene i by "banging her head against the wall . . .[with] despairing outcries" (358), the frustrated expression of human pain beyond language presented in this spectacle of human suffering. Moreover, the self-consciousness of the spectacle throughout the play is made evident by the journalists and photographers who chronicle and display all the events on television, the ultimate cultural manipulator of the real. The violence of human nature is repackaged and re-presented to society in a more palatable, distanced form.

Of all Williams's plays discussed here, the physical degeneration, tragi-comic elements, and loneliness along with a "Strange Voice" which periodically announces that "This is the Peaceable Kingdom" and sets the mood, make it the most Beckettian in content and form and certainly in line with Artaud's theories. In the play Saul's observation that humans are ultimately defined by desire and lack—"Nothing but an open mouth left at the end" (350)—can easily be associated with both Beckett's *Not I* as well as Sebastian's ultimate fate in *Suddenly Last Summer,* recalled here in the "greedy sounds, mouth open" made by Bernice. Mrs. Shapiro similarly "smacks her mouth repeatedly open and shut for more food" (350), with the grotesque gesture of "her head lolling this way and that" (351). This intense reliance on gesture signifies one of the most notable elements of this play, the undisguised fear and suspicion of language on many levels. Not only is the language unreliable and inadequate, often giving way to pantomime, but the constant awareness of the danger of language in warnings to "be careful what you say" (342), with a rather realistic social context of the fear of anti-semitic language, runs throughout. Ultimately, however, the social and religious struggles created by culture become irrelevant— we are all equal in the end as we fall to the chaotic powers of nature. The inmate Ralston names himself God and is eventually confirmed by Lucretia, but unlike *Now the Cats with Jewelled Claws,* hope seems extinguished as God the savior becomes "just an old man in a nursin' home in a wheelchair" (361).

What distinguishes Williams's later work discussed above from his earlier forms is primarily the anti-realistic marginalization of language and an emphasis on the physicality of the theater influenced by both Artaud and Brecht, while the more specific ideological elements of the presentation of ritualistic spectacle, a moral reversal in the primacy of nature over culture, and a revelation of inevitable metaphysical cruelty that occur throughout these plays mark them as much more specifically Artaudian in their goals. Therefore, I would argue that while *Kingdom of Earth* is highly successful in fulfilling Artaud's philosophical vision, the "total spectacle" that Artaud articulated, one that would liberate the spectator from mimetic representation, is most effectively present in Williams's plays that rely strongly on gesture, dance, song, color, and light. In that sense, the one-acts *The Gnädiges Fräulein, Now the Cats with Jewelled Claws,* and *This is the Peaceable Kingdom* even more powerfully achieve the chaotic liberation from the rational that Artaud sought, a return to the "popular, primal theatre sensed and experienced directly by the mind, without language's distortions and the pitfalls in speech and words (Artaud 82–83).

Notes

1. One of the only references I have found linking Artaud with Williams occurs in C.W.E. Bigsby's *Modern American Drama: 1945–1990,* where he points out that Mary Caroline Richards's translation of Artaud uses the same term—a "plastic" theatre—that Williams used for the new theatre he desired to create.
2. Unless otherwise noted, I refer to Williams's 1975 version of the play printed in *The Theatre of Tennessee Williams,* vol. 5.
3. See, for example, my book on Williams's later career, *The Politics of Reputation: The Critical Reception of Tennessee Williams' Later Plays.*
4. Linda Dorff, in her article for *The Tennessee Williams Annual Review,* categorizes *The Gnädiges Fräulein* as one of the "outrageous works," where "Williams plays on the comic grotesque" (24). In the same issue of *TWAR,* Michael R. Schiavi's article on *Kingdom of Earth* cites critics' reactions to Williams's later works as "grotesque" (104).
5. In his article, "The Two *Glass Menageries:* Reading Edition and Acting Edition," Geoffrey Borney reads *Menagerie* as ironic, citing the playful distance that the Brechtian titles and images create, but as it was first performed with the titles omitted, the play typically has been read as psychological, sentimental realism.
6. For a more complex discussion of theater of cruelty as non-representative, see Jacques Derrida, "The Theater of Cruelty and the Closure of Representation."
7. The description of scenes from *Kirche, Küche und Kinder* and *THIS IS (An Entertainment)* come from Linda Dorff's article in *The Tennessee Williams Annual Review.*
8. For a more comprehensive discussion of Artaud and Genet in relation to the Nietzschean reversal of cultural values, see Christopher Innes, *Avant-Garde Theatre 1892–1992.*
9. For a discussion of the atonement and punishment of the sexually transgressive Sebastian Venable, see my article "The (Un)Represented Fragmentation of the Body in Tennessee Williams' 'Desire and the Black Masseur' and *Suddenly Last Summer.*"
10. In *The Mutilated,* a character that comes on stage briefly, the "Bird-Girl" (a woman, presumably "Rampart Street Rose," with chicken feathers glued to her) is paraded around as "the world's greatest freak attraction" (85), and also screeches "AWK AWK AWK!" This "freak," whom Celeste sees as being treated cruelly, can be seen as a cross between the Fräulein and the Giant Cocaloony in *Gnädiges.*

11. For more on *The Frosted Glass Coffin,* see Philip C. Kolin's piece in *Explicator,* one of the only commentaries I have found on this much-neglected play.

Works Cited

Artaud, Antonin. *The Theater and Its Double,* trans. Mary Caroline Richards. New York: Grove Press, 1958.

Bigsby, C.W.E. *Modern American Drama: 1945–1990.* Cambridge: Cambridge University Press, 1992.

Borney, Geoffrey. "The Two *Glass Menageries:* Reading Edition and Acting Edition." *Modern Drama: Selected Plays from 1879 to the Present.* Ed. Walter Levy. Upper Saddle River, NJ: Prentice-Hall, 1999. 928–40.

Connor, Steven. *Postmodernist Culture: An Introduction to Theories of the Contemporary.* Oxford: Blackwell Publishers, 1997.

Day, Christine, and Bob Woods. *Where I Live: Selected Essays by Tennessee Williams.* New York: New Directions, 1978.

Derrida, Jacques. "The Theater of Cruelty and the Closure of Representation." *Mimesis, Masochism, and Mime.* Ed. Timothy Murray. Ann Arbor: University of Michigan Press, 1997. 40–62.

Diamond, Elin. "The Shudder of Catharsis in Twentieth-Century Performance." *Performativity and Performance.* Ed. Andrew Parker and Eve Kosofsky Sedgwick. New York: Routledge, 1995. 152–72.

Dorff, Linda. "Theatricalist Cartoons: Tennessee Williams's Late, 'Outrageous' Plays." *Tennessee Williams Annual Review* 2(1999): 13–33.

Glaspell, Susan. *The Verge. Modern Drama: Selected Plays from 1879 to the Present.* Ed. Walter Levy. Upper Saddle River, NJ: Prentice-Hall, 1999. 227–53.

Innes, Christopher. *Avant-Garde Theatre (1892–1992).* London: Routledge, 1993.

Kolin, Philip C. "'a play about terrible birds': Tennessee Williams's *The Gnadiges Fraulein* and Alfred Hitchcock's *The Birds.*" *Journal of the South Atlantic Modern Language Association* 66.1 (2001): 1–22.

———. "Williams's *The Frosted Glass Coffin.*" *The Explicator* 59.1 (2000): 44–46.

Saddik, Annette. *The Politics of Reputation: The Critical Reception of Tennessee Williams' Later Plays.* London: Associated University Presses, 1999.

———. "The (Un)Represented Fragmentation of the Body in Tennessee Williams' 'Desire and the Black Masseur' and *Suddenly Last Summer.*" *Modern Drama* 41 (1998): 347–54.

Schiavi, Michael R. "Effeminacy in the *Kingdom:* Tennessee Williams and Stunted Spectatorship." *Tennessee Williams Annual Review* 2 (1999): 99–113.

Williams, Tennessee. *The Theatre of Tennessee Williams.* 8 vols. New York: New Directions, 1971–92. All quotations from Williams's plays are taken from this source.

Michael Paller

THE DAY ON WHICH A WOMAN DIES:
THE MILK TRAIN DOESN'T STOP HERE ANYMORE AND NŌ THEATRE

Since its first production at the Spoleto Festival in 1962, *The Milk Train Doesn't Stop Here Anymore* has been regarded as a Tennessee Williams low-point, an embarrassing failure of which the less said the better. The play was fortunate to open on Broadway during a newspaper strike in January 1963, when reviews were hard to come by, and it eked out a run of two months (although Howard Taubman's supportive but very mixed review appeared in the Western Edition of *The New York Times*). In an unusual move and an indication of how hard Williams had worked revising the script and wanted it to succeed, it re-opened a year later with a new cast, director, and designers. This time there was an abundance of reviews—and the play closed after five performances. The notices were at best mixed, at worst, devastating. Williams must have been especially hurt by the opinion of his first important New York mentor, John Gassner: ". . . the fiasco . . . cannot but serve as a reminder that silk purses cannot be made out of sow's ears no matter how fine the stitching" (76). Walter Kerr, another long-time champion, heard the sound of self-parody, a jangling tune that many critics would claim to hear in most Williams plays to come (*Thirty* 222). Academic critics have not been much kinder, complaining that the play is little more than a series of long, disconnected speeches, the characters more symbolic than real. As late as 1977, Gerald Weales would write, ". . . there is no conflict, no real abrasion . . . *Milk Train* suggests *Camino Real* in its imaginative ponderousness, its determination to make its point, but, for all its obviousness, there is more fun in the earlier work" (66).

For all its "obviousness," however, what has escaped virtually every critic since 1963 (and most theatre-makers, as well) is that Williams did not suddenly become inept or tone deaf to the sound of his inner music. The truth was that Williams had written a kind of play that critical ears had not been trained to hear: a drama based on something other than Aristotelean notions of conflict. *Milk Train* has little meaningful conflict because Williams had replaced it with something else. It is a play in which two-dimensional characters exchange long, often narrative speeches, the subjects of which are the memories of a life almost done and the need to welcome death. *Milk Train* occurs on the border between living and dying, in which a pilgrim meets a character whose unfulfilled, restless spirit needs release from the world of materialistic illusion. In short, Williams was writing his version of a Nō play. More than that, in *Milk Train*, Williams opened the way to a new personal dramaturgy, with which he would sweep away most of his past statements and values, explore new territories, and arrive at new conclusions about the value of living—and dying.

Even those few critics who have tried hard to like the play insist on admiring it on Western terms. Their intentions may be good, but in the end they only condescend to the play and contribute to the general misunderstanding. Some, as we will see, have tried to redeem a "bland" Chris Flanders by viewing him as a St. Christopher figure or even as Christ himself. Chris is, indeed, a religious figure, but again, his origin is Eastern: the bodhisattva, a Zen Buddhist figure who, forsaking Buddhahood, devotes his life to others. Indeed, everything in *Milk Train*'s symbolism, structure, and characters that struck critics as inept in western terms is, in Nō theatre, beautiful and appropriate.

Not that Williams hadn't planted many clues about his new method along the way. For audiences of the first Broadway production, Williams provided a hint of his intentions in a program note, asking them to view Sissy not as a human being but as a "universal condition of human beings: The apparently incomprehensible but surely somehow significant adventure of being alive that we all must pass through for a time" (Taubman). Before the revised version opened for a tryout at the Barter Theater in Abingdon, Virginia, in September 1963, Williams told *The New York Times* that a trip to Japan in 1961 had left him "deeply impressed" with Eastern philosophy. With ironic understatement, he described *Milk Train* as "vaguely Oriental with Occidental variations" ("'Milk Train'"). The published version of the text is preceded by an epigram Williams borrowed from Yeats (another playwright influenced by Nō), in which the poet yearns for his heart to be set free from his dying body and released into eternity.

Among critics, only Allean Hale has taken Williams's interest in Japanese dramaturgy seriously, and her work, especially on *In the Bar of a Tokyo Hotel*, is crucial to any real understanding of several of Williams's later plays ("Tennessee's" 211–12). No one to date has examined *Milk Train* in any depth to discover the roots of its apparent strangeness. Those few critics who have acknowledged any Eastern influence in the play at all have limited themselves to its most obvious and least important manifestation, the two Kabuki stage assistants, which they easily dismiss as "bogus" (Weales 66) and "camp Kabuki nonsense" which, one says, Williams had fallen victim to "after spending more time in Japan than was good for him" (Coveney). Occasionally, a critic will make a general statement, such as one by Falk, which manages to minimize the play's Japanese influence and inflate the importance of its

Christian symbolism: "The playwright seems to combine the Oriental idea of resignation, of accepting death, with the myth of Christ wrestling with the problem
of good and evil, and finally, in behalf of mankind, carrying his burden of sins"
(127). Indeed, Falk's assessment of *Milk Train* comes in a chapter entitled, "The
Deteriorating Artist." Far from deteriorating, Williams was setting out on a new
course. This chapter will show that, for *The Milk Train Doesn't Stop Here Anymore*,
the direction of that course was due east; its destination, the Nō theatre.

Why would Williams attempt something as alien to American audiences in 1963 as a
Nō play? Hale has documented the galvanizing effect of Williams's introduction to
Yukio Mishima in 1957 and how it inspired him to revitalize his work with explorations into the theatre of the East. Williams read Mishima's *Five Modern Nō Plays*
and visited him in Japan in 1959, where he saw a great deal of Nō and Kabuki theatre. On the trip home, he began writing what he referred to as "an occidental Noh
play" called *The Day on Which a Man Died,* which would become the template for
In the Bar of a Tokyo Hotel. He was working on four other plays on that voyage; one
of them was *The Milk Train Doesn't Stop Here Anymore.* As Hale has demonstrated,
Eastern influences would also find their way into another work begun on that fertile journey, *The Night of the Iguana* ("Secret" 366–367). *Milk Train,* however, represents a more thorough-going attempt to integrate significant amounts of Nō philosophy and dramaturgy with his own unmistakable brand of Western theatre.

    Williams might not have been so attracted to Japanese forms had his life and
work not reached a crisis point. Most significantly, Williams's fourteen-year relationship with Frank Merlo was disintegrating; by the time *Milk Train* debuted at
Spoleto in 1962, they had separated and Merlo was dying of lung cancer. When the
revised version of *Milk Train* opened on Broadway in January 1964, Merlo was
dead, after a long and dreadful struggle. Williams's use of alcohol, which had risen
precipitously ever since he started work on *Cat on a Hot Tin Roof* in 1954, continued to spiral, and he had begun adding large amounts of barbiturates to his regi-
men as well.

    His professional life had also reached a crossroads. In 1962, as he was working
on *Milk Train,* he told Lewis Funke and John E. Booth in *Theatre Arts* magazine
that he sensed that his kind of writing was going out of style (qtd. in Devlin 99).
More important, he sensed it had become insufficient to express the new depths of
suffering and loss he was experiencing. Some kind of change in form and content
was called for, but what?

    He would find the answer primarily by way of his acquaintance, through Mis-
hima, with Nō. Williams's affinity for the Japanese writer went deep. Although he
was only thirty-two, Mishima had already published thirty-five novels as well as a
number of plays and was one of Japan's most visible cultural figures (Hale "Secret" 364). Both writers were devoted to their work above everything else, which
led, on the one hand, to prodigious output but, on the other, to largely unsatisfactory relationships with other people. Both came from families that claimed dis-
tantly aristocratic pasts, and both had childhoods that were almost mirror images

of each other's: violent fathers, over-protective mothers, early illnesses that isolated them from other children. And, of course, both were gay men who, despite
their respective cultures' oppressive attitudes, recreated their loves and desires in
their work (Hale "Secret" 364). Nonetheless, Williams's attraction to Eastern
dramaturgy at this particular time can be better understood by the relevance of
Nō's philosophy to the circumstances of his life than by the reasons for his friendship with Mishima.

To see just how thematically different the Nō-infused *Milk Train* would be from
Williams's previous work—and why it would be so thoroughly and even angrily
misunderstood—it would be useful to briefly examine his earlier principal thematic pattern. At the beginning of the decade, the outline of a "typical" Williams
play was well established in the public's mind, along with the set of values that it
championed. In that "typical" play, a character who embodies a life force arrives in
a community where he or she meets stiff resistance from the local population. The
newcomer finds a companion whose spiritual aspirations and physical desires have
been crushed by the community's simple, unconscious Puritanism or by their
more organized and determined oppression of vitality. A struggle ensues between
interloper and community, often, a battle to the death, with healthy doses of melodramatic violence and sex marking the stations along the way. In this conflict, the
right to individual expression, the satisfaction of sexual desire, and the determination to cling to spiritual and physical life are all highly valued; should the character
embodying these elements perish in the conflict, a tragedy has occurred. Struggle
and endurance are valued in and of themselves; they comprise, as Williams had
long ago written, ". . . the sort of life for which the human organism is created."
(Williams *Menagerie* 131)
   The pattern varies in its details and strategies from play to play, and some plays
are different animals altogether. But by 1963, audiences had seen that struggle
between physical or spiritual vitality and death played out between Val and Myra
Torrance and the men of Two-River County in *Battle of Angels* and between Alma
and her divided self in *Summer and Smoke;* Alvaro Mangiacavallo reawakens Sara-
fina Della Rosa in *The Rose Tattoo;* Maggie longs to impart her survivor's spirit to
her spiritually paralyzed husband Brick in *Cat on a Hot Tin Roof,* and a resurrected
Val Xavier does the same for Lady Torrance in *Orpheus Descending*. In the latter
play, Williams's revision of *Battle of Angels,* Carol Cutrere, another embodiment of
the life force as expressed in sensual terms, exhorts Val to heed the ghosts in Cy-
press Hill Cemetary, who chatter to any who will listen, "Live, live, live, live, live!"
(252). The pattern is varied to a greater extent in *Camino Real,* in which a collection
of literary but impotent Romantics array themselves against the armed forces of
the state; it is visible in *Suddenly Last Summer,* in which Sebastian Venable, in his
quest for life on the very edge of sensuality, sacrifices himself to his terrible god,
while his cousin Catharine will likely be lobotomized for telling the true story of
his death. The pattern is perhaps at its richest and most complex in *A Streetcar
Named Desire,* in which Stanley Kowalski is both Lawrencian life force and the

representative of community oppression. Even *The Glass Menagerie,* so often mislabeled a gentle memory play, is populated by characters who engage in a desperate struggle for survival in a hostile world.

In its many variations, this pattern—the life-enhancing outsider who champions individual expression and sexual fulfillment and represents the merit of struggle and endurance battling a repressive community for psychic or physical survival—contained all the themes, values, and dramatic action audiences expected of Tennessee Williams. No wonder audiences and critics would be baffled by *Milk Train,* which not only contains none of the familiar Williams tropes but undermines and repudiates every single one of them.

Williams based his Nō play on the 1953 short story, "Man Bring This Up Road." It was not published until 1959, when it appeared in *Mademoiselle.* Williams may have had the magazine galley with him as he and Merlo sailed home from Japan that year, and found the story to be a suitable framework for the play in which he would strike out for new thematic and formal territory. The central character's name, Mrs. Flora Goforth, may have suggested to him the action that a Nō play's principal figure must accomplish.

"Man Bring This Up Road" is a stark, simple story about the meeting of a washed-up poet and maker of mobiles named Jimmy Dobyne and the wealthy Mrs. Flora Goforth at her estate on a cliff north of Amalfi. He arrives hungry and exhausted, desperate for rest. Any chance of his recuperating at the villa is dashed, however, when he rejects Mrs. Goforth's amorous advances, and he is sent packing down the road almost as soon as he came up.

Williams transformed this material with ideas he had gleaned from the Japanese theatre. His initial sources would be Mishima's *Five Modern Nō Plays,* including its excellent Introduction by the translator Donald Keene and the classic English work on Nō by Arthur Waley, *The Nō Plays of Japan.* He may have consulted other books, and, of course, he learned a great deal from the performances he saw in Japan, but the bulk of what he needed he derived from these sources.

In his Introduction to Mishima's plays, Keene provides an outline for Nō, the form of which has changed little since the seventeenth century. The play

> was likely to begin with a priest on a journey to some holy spot. There he meets a person of the vicinity whose strangely poetic words belie his humble appearance. The priest questions the unknown reaper or fishergirl, who gradually reveals the story of his former glory, and leads us to understand that some unsatisfied attachment to the world has kept his spirit behind. At the end of the play, a hope of salvation, of deliverance from the attachment, is offered, and the ghost fades away. (*Five Modern Nō Plays* x–xi)

The humble reaper or fisherwoman (this figure is called the *shite*) has another identity. After shedding an outer costume, the *shite*'s true nature is revealed in a climactic dance: a demon, perhaps, or a warrior or a beautiful woman.

Williams was steered to Waley's *The Nō Plays of Japan* by Keene's bibliographical note, in which he mentions that four of the five original plays on which Mishima based his modern versions were available in English, in Waley's famous volume. The book first appeared in America in 1922; it was reissued in 1957. Internal evidence in *Milk Train* strongly suggests that it was to Waley that Williams turned next. In addition to the brief play texts, Williams found a detailed history and description of Nō theatre and, crucially, a "Note on Buddhism." From the former, Williams learned that a Nō play is without active, meaningful conflict per se, that the story is told retrospectively, through narration, as the now-humble character tells the pilgrim of his or her earthly life, and that the play's significant colors are "memory, longing or regret" (53). "The Note on Buddhism" informed Williams that at the heart of Nō were tenets of Zen Buddhism: the belief that the soul's being will be absorbed into Nirvana, or Buddha, the understanding that the physical world is mere illusion, and that the only escape from material existence, or the "Wheel of Life and Death," is Enlightenment (58). The Note also contains information on the Bodhisattvas, "intermediaries between Buddha and man . . . beings who, though fit to receive Buddhahood, have of their own free will renounced it, that they may better alleviate the miseries of mankind." According to Waley, the most well known of the Bodhisattvas was Kwannon, who might take either a woman or a man's form but in Japan was generally considered to be a woman (57).

Here was the new philosophical underpinning for which Williams had been searching. Once, he had valued struggle and championed sexual desire, equating it with salvation. Now, unable to get through the day without increasing amounts of alcohol and drugs, guilt-ridden over selfish behavior which had contributed to the separation from Merlo and terrified at the prospect of Merlo's impending death, Williams was lured by the message of Zen—rejection of personal ego and all earthly conflict and craving—and its serene representation in Nō.

According to Hale, Williams was especially interested in Mishima's "woman play," *The Lady Aoi,* a story of possession, in which the soul of a jealous mistress invades the wife of her lover ("Secret" 366). The original version of this play, *Aoi Nō Uye,* appears in Waley and contains a character who does not appear in Mishima's adaptation. She is the Witch of Teruhi, a diviner, who, by plucking a bow-string calls forth the angry spirit of Rokujō, who is assaulting the ailing body of the Princess Aoi. Williams would borrow part of her name, if not her mystical powers, for *Milk Train.*

Now, prepared by his reading and by seeing several performances both in Japan and in New York (Hale "Secret" 368), Williams could transform "Man Bring This Up Road" into his own version of a Nō play, *The Milk Train Doesn't Stop Here Anymore* in the following steps: Jimmy Dobyne, now named Christopher Flanders, carries in his heavy white sack a mobile called "The Earth Is a Wheel in a Great Big Gambling Casino," and his practice of calling on dying millionairesses earns him the nickname "The Angel of Death." He has come calling because the formerly robust Mrs. Goforth of "Man Bring This Up Road" has acquired a fatal illness. Steeped in denial, Flora (now nicknamed "Sissy") is nonetheless racing against the clock to finish dictating her memoirs to her secretary, Blackie, and meditating on the meaning of life and death. A friend, unnamed in the story, who lives on a neighboring island and fills Sissy in on Chris's background and frightening sobriquet, is now called the Marchesa Constance Ridgeway-Condotti, with the additional, unexplained honorific, the Witch of Capri, Williams's playful tribute to the diviner of *The Lady Aoi*. In scene iii, her face lit by the eerie blue flame of a copper brazier, Williams's Witch performs "a stylized recitation" in which she tells Sissy the story of Chris's first mystical—and fatal—visitation to a wealthy old woman (51).

Sissy Goforth's immense wealth, barely mentioned in the story, is conspicuous in the play, telling us from the beginning just how wedded to the material world she, as a *shite*, is. "Blackie," she tells her young secretary, "this estate contains things appraised by Lloyd's at over two million pounds sterling, besides my jewels and summer furs, and that's why it has to be guarded against trespassers, uninvited intruders" (16). Indeed, her estate of three villas is more like a fortress, perched atop a rocky mountain overlooking the Divina Costiera of Italy and guarded by armed watchmen and attack dogs. This hold is perched "Above the oldest sea in the Western world" (7), somewhere between earth and sky, between the material world and the realm of the spirit.

The play is bracketed by the appearance of those two "invisible" Stage Assistants. During a Prologue, they raise Sissy's heraldic banner, the device on which is the image of a griffin, "mythical monster, half lion, and half eagle. And completely human" (7). This Prologue is as Brechtian as it is Asian, for the Assistants tell us that the play occurs over "the course of the two final days of Mrs. Goforth's existence." In other words, like a Brecht play, *Milk Train* will contain little in the way of conventional suspense: there is no question that the principal character will die. The vital question will be, *how well does she die?* The play will end with the Stage Assistants lowering the banner—life is over – but with a muted bugle playing Reveille rather than Taps. Reveille, the call that signals the beginning of another day, suggests that Sissy is moving on to the next stage of life.

Like her griffin, Sissy is something of a monster herself, a devouring, egomaniacal demon, deeply afraid of death. Her first line, as she awakens to another day of pain, is ego personified: "Ahhhhhhhh, Meeeeeeeeee . . . " (8). As she becomes conscious, she utters a line which would not be out of place in a Beckett play, a cry of physical pain and existential angst: "Another day, Oh, Christ, Oh, Mother of Christ!" (8). The ill, pain-wracked Sissy needs to die. Still, although faced with the prospect of unbearable pain from the abscess in her lung, she cannot confront the mystery of what will come after. Like the Lady Aoi in Mishima's play, Sissy sleeps only under sedation, always accompanied by nightmares.

In one of the play's first Nō analogues, Williams literalizes Sissy's monstrous ego by demonstrating how it has devoured the villa. She has wired every building for sound, her voice penetrating wood, plaster, and stone in order to summon Blackie and launch into dictation at any moment. Sissy's ego demands immediate satisfaction and pervades every inch of her mountain kingdom, denying rest and privacy to her staff, whom she fires on a whim. Sissy has also made sure that she will maintain an earthly presence even after death: except for one dollar which will go to her daughter, the entirety of Sissy's estate will go to a cultural foundation named after herself (12).

Like a *shite* figure, Sissy's life now revolves around her past. "Has it ever struck you, Connie," she says to the Witch, "that life is all memory, except for the one present moment that goes by you so quick you hardly catch it going? . . . Practically everything is a memory to me, now. . . . Four husbands, all memory now. All lovers, all memory now" (46–47). Many of her speeches are monologues about her past in the form of dictated memoirs. Judging the play by traditional Western dramaturgical standards, these speeches are narrative, amateur mistakes that stop the play in its tracks. According to Japanese convention, they are precisely the kind of tactics by which Nō proceeds.

Sissy's life has been as devoted to physical pleasure as it has been to the acquisition of material goods. Not surprisingly, her memoirs—like the one Williams himself would write twenty years later—are largely about the earthly matter of sex, and there is a lot of that to recount, what with four husbands, numerous lovers, wild costume parties where Sissy appeared completely nude as Lady Godiva, and sex-crazed men competing to "dismount me so they could *mount* me" (36). Like earlier Williams heroines, Sissy conflates the gift of the "love of true understanding" with physical passion. While Williams validated this association in Two-River County, Glorious Hill, and St. Cloud, in the Zen world of *Milk Train,* this is a significant mistake on Sissy's part, one for which Williams will hand out no rewards. Her description of her last husband, who, alone of all four, brought her that gift, is merely a recounting of his physical perfection and of sex they had on the first night of their marriage. Alex's body, she tells Blackie, was "god's perfection" (14). That's about all we learn of husband number four (that, and the fact that he died when his "red demon sports car" plunged down a cliff near Monte Carlo).

Sissy's denial of her mortality drives her to embrace desire and egotism all the more closely. What she needs to fight off her depression, she tells Blackie, is a lover. "The dead are dead and the living are living!" (35). Carol Cutrere could not put it better, but in *Milk Train,* this credo proves to be another false one. Where Williams once proclaimed sex, love, and spiritual perfection as rough equivalents, in this play, he mocks that philosophy. In *Milk Train,* such a creed, in the mouth of a dying old woman, may at most be touching—or comically grotesque.

Sissy's memory of Alex has not yet faded into silence when Chris Flanders arrives, bearing his heavy white sack. He is a young man—but not as young as he appears. "He has the looks of a powerful, battered, but still undefeated fighter," Williams writes, while, in the distance, "female voices are heard exclaiming" (19). Sissy will mistake his true gift, which is not his sensual being but his ability to release the ego-driven from life—but who can blame her? He fools us, too, because until now, in Williams's typology, a character like Chris always stood for the victory of earthly desire and its spiritual analogue against the forces of repression.

The next morning, Chris's cue to reappear on the terrace is Sissy's line, *"Meaning of life!"* (60). Accustomed to Williams's long parade of young studs, we're likely to take the combination of Sissy's line and Chris's entrance as a typical Williamsesque tribute to the spiritual ecstasy of physical desire. For an audience in 1963, Chris would seem just another version of Kilroy, Val Xavier, Stanley Kowlaski, and Chance Wayne. As it will turn out, Chris is actually Hannah Jelkes, and his role will be not to supply physical ecstasy but to provide a release from its coils. As Williams told *The New York Times,* the values Chris brings Sissy are "values that her life was the opposite of, an acceptance of what must happen ("Milk Train").

Critics have long associated Chris Flanders with Christian symbols. Gassner calls him a paraclete (76); to Norman J. Fedder he is "Christlike" (803) and Roger Boxhill considers him both a symbol of salvation and a prostitute (146, 149). Philip Armato considers Williams a "Christian playwright" altogether (570), while Gilbert Debusscher, more circumspectly, considers Chris a St. Christopher figure. Debusscher points out that the burden Chris carries summons images of St. Christopher bearing travelers across a river (155).

Williams certainly seems to give us several opportunities to view Chris as a modern St. Christopher transporting Christ across the river. The first time we see him, as he stumbles, torn and bloodied onto Sissy's terrace, he is struggling to carry that heavy white sack. Later, when he tries to explain his need to care for others, she replies skeptically, "Oh, you seem to be setting yourself up as a—as a saint of some kind. . . ." (75).

However, Williams is misleading us again. We had gotten used to associating certain of Williams's young men with Christian martyrs. Sebastian in *Suddenly Last Summer* has received much attention as a symbol for his namesake saint, and Val Xavier, Kilroy, and Shannon have been interpreted as symbols of Christ. As Debusscher says, ". . . commentators . . . have managed to make each play yield its Christ figure" (149).

The St. Christopher metaphor, however, will carry us just so far. Chris's nickname, "The Angel of Death," is, to a dying woman like Sissy, more terrifying than comforting. Debusscher is puzzled, too, that while St. Christopher carried people across a river to safety, Chris Flanders once bore an old man out to sea to his death and now has come to the mountain to escort Sissy to hers. The old man even paid Chris well for his aid, and "The Angel of Death" will appear to steal Sissy's rings as she laboriously breathes her last. Debusscher is forced in the end to admit that the St. Christopher parallel raises more questions than it answers. "Christopher's self-appointed task of helping old people, preferably dying women," he writes, "through the last few days of their existence . . . for a not altogether symbolic reward, prolongs the contrast embedded in the St. Christopher parallel" (155).

While one can view Chris and his heavy burden as Christian symbols, in his sack Chris carries another emblem, a mobile called "The Earth Is a Wheel in a Great Big Gambling Casino." Far from representing anything to do with Christianity, this is a symbol of Zen Buddhism. Indeed, since Williams was employing Nō conventions, Chris makes a much more convincing bodhisattva—one of those beings

who have renounced Buddhahood in order to alleviate the miseries of mankind—
than he does a Christian symbol. The old man in the sea wanted to die; it was no
coincidence that Chris was there to help him. Chris's serial appearances at the
homes of fatally ill women who need to reconcile themselves with death are likewise no accidents. He finds his way to where he is needed.

Sissy, whether she can admit it or not, needs a bodhisattva's help. She is caught
in an existential crisis: clinging to her earthly existence, she is beginning to sense
that it is no longer enough. When she proclaims, *"Meaning of life!"* the bodhisattva
enters—providing a tacit indication as to what life's meaning is, according to Nō:
an illusion to be transcended.

Just as Sissy may be seen as a demon woman still caught in the toils of ego and
earthly desires, Chris is a pilgrim, a holy man who speaks a westernized version of
Zen in a specifically Williamsesque *patois*. He shares with Sissy, haltingly, as if still
searching, an image of the world as experienced by two puppies who huddle together at night for security. They can never be sure of their place in a world of ob-
scurity and illusion. Are they pleasing their master? How can they know, since they
". . . hear so many sounds, voices, and see so many things they can't comprehend!
. . . We're all of us living in a house we're not used to . . . a house full of—voices,
noises, objects, strange shadows, light that's even stranger—We can't understand"
(76). Later, Chris extends the metaphor: "Yes—we all live in a house on fire, no fire
department to call; no way out, just the upstairs window to look out of while the
fire burns the house down with us trapped, locked in it" (107). Chris's speech is an
elaboration of a line from *Aoi No Uye,* in which Rokujō, the mistress who sends her
spirit to torment Princess Aoi, tells the Witch of Teruhi, "I drove out of the Burning House . . ." to attack the Princess. The "burning house" is a Zen metaphor for
the material body from which Buddha lures the untutored—a bit of information
Williams borrowed directly from one of Waley's footnotes (182). As for the windows Chris refers to, he elaborates on their Zen meaning as well: "These upstairs
windows, not wide enough to crawl out of, just wide enough to lean out of and
look out of, and—look and look and look, til we're almost nothing but looking,
nothing, almost, but *vision* . . ." (108).

Critics are particularly bothered about the long scenes between Chris and Sissy in
which, they believe, nothing dramatic happens. While Weales believes that Sissy is
a "potentially a vibrant comic character," she has no one to push against. Chris is
simply too bland and symbolic to be her match, and Sissy's ultimate reversal is ". . .
not presented dramatically or defined in any terms but philosophic generalization"
(66). Fedder agreed: ". . . Chris is a negligible antagonist against the egomaniacal
heroine who does him in at every turn . . ." (803). Robert F. Gross objects that
while Chris and Sissy dominate the play, their relationship is impossible to understand (102). This would seem to be a particular problem in scene v.

At forty-two pages, it is by far the longest scene in the play. If to this point the
play is viewed according to Western practice, then scene v ought to contain the bulk
of the conflict between the antagonists as well as a suitably melodramatic climax,

followed by the concluding action of scene vi. This—we shouldn't be surprised— is precisely what does *not* happen. Instead, Sissy and Chris engage in an extended debate, interrupted by narrative monologues that sum up their lives and philosophies. These monologues are self-contained; they have little or no effect on the action or on the character who hears them. The action, if one can call it that, is elliptical and allusive, as it ought to be in a Nō play, in which the pilgrim is not meant to provide conflict but rather the *occasion* for the *shite* to find release.

If the scene does not produce a climax in the Western sense, it approximates the climactic moment of a Nō play. Here, however, "climax" is not to be understood as the point when the protagonist's fate is irrevocably sealed. Rather, it is the key moment of *revelation*. In Nō, this is the *shite's* long dance, where she reveals her true past and real nature before her spirit can be released. In *Milk Train*, Williams give us his version of a westernized equivalent. First, Chris enters, wearing an outfit Sissy left for him the night before, a kabuki robe, girded by a samurai sword. Just as the *shite* literally unveils himself or herself, Sissy has shed her own Kabuki robe which she had worn the previous evening. It was a gift, she explained to the Witch, given her by Harlan during a reconciliation trip to the East. For the Witch, she had indulged in an unconvincing masquerade of health and optimism. Now, shorn of disguises, she is no more than her own true, frail self.

Among the other new possessions Williams gave Sissy for *Milk Train* is a humble past which she now reveals: born "between a swamp and the wrong side of the tracks in One Street Georgia," she became a dancer at a carnival show where she was billed as the "Dixy Doxy" and, like Gypsy Rose Lee, worked herself up into the big time by displaying not only her anatomy but her wit. It was there, in her teens, where she met and married Harlan Goforth who died intestate a few years later, leaving her everything (67–68). From this humble beginning has emerged a demon of tremendous vitality and even larger ego.

Chris responds with the story of his own recent past and present existential confusion. He has come to doubt his vision of the world, one that has always left him alienated from others. Chris, it seems, needs Sissy as much as she needs him. He is a bodhisattva searching for the kindness of a needy stranger.

Chris's gentle, enforced asceticism proves no match for Sissy's ties to her earthly existence. To prove her vitality to both of them, she attempts to seduce him. He suggests that Death is merely one moment; she replies that she prefers the many millions of her rich life. On learning that an ailing old woman Chris recently visited has died, Sissy is shaken but still refuses to believe that his presence suggests that her own time is near. "Sissy Goforth's not ready to go forth yet and won't go forth until she's ready . . ." she declares (95).

When Sissy finally does find release, in scene vi, it is with little of the grace or dignity that accompanies the true acceptance Chris has urged her to seek. Even in her dying moments, she misunderstands why he has come and what he has to offer— not the pleasant, temporary release of the *petit morte* but the permanent liberation of *morte*. After suffering a hemorrhage, she retreats to her bedroom and arrays herself in her most valuable jewelry. As she dies, she is cataloguing her possessions:

"The chandelier, if the dealer that sold it to me wasn't a liar, used to hang in Versailles, and the bed, if he wasn't lying, was the bed of Countess Walewska, Napoleon's Polish mistress. It's a famous old bed, for a famous old body. . . ." (118).

Sissy's last words to Chris are, "Be here, when I wake up" (116). She still believes she will not die. To her last breath she struggles, fighting Chris off as he helps her to her deathbed. She draws a sharp gasp with each ring Chris pulls from her fingers and dies. After all her struggle, the moment of her death is small—merely one moment among many, as Chris had promised (86). There is no melodrama, none of the theatricality of Lady's death in *Orpheus Descending*, of Chance's in *Sweet Bird of Youth*, just the "boom" of the ocean below and the music of the mobile as it turns in the breeze.

In the "typical" Williams play, Sissy's death—the extinguishing of her ego, the end of desire—might be viewed as tragedy. In this play, however, where Williams frustrates every expectation and repudiates virtually all of his traditional themes, Sissy's death—and Chris' failure to guide her towards acceptance—is a comedy.

Walter Kerr wrote that comedy is the battle between our heavenly aspirations and our earthly desires, where the desires prevail. "Comedy spends its hours counting—blandly, almost without comment—the manacles that cannot be gotten rid of" (Kerr *Tragedy* 146). In the ethos of Nō, the proper action is to shed one's ego and transcend. On one level, Sissy knows this—"Another day, Oh, Christ, Oh, Mother of Christ!"—but she cannot do it. In Japanese theatre, there is no such thing as a Nō play where the *shite* does not unshackle the chains of earth. In Western theatre, chains are comedy's *terra firma*.

Now, Williams, in an abrupt shift from all his previous work, says that a graceful letting go of life may be preferable to struggle and endurance. Because Sissy refuses to learn this lesson, because she insists on clinging to every last second of her life when it has robbed her of every dignity, because she refuses to recognize the terrible changes time has wrought in her—changes which are painfully apparent to everyone else—the play is a comedy.

In fact, we've noticed from the beginning that the play is a comedy and an almost thoroughly grotesque one. Williams is not content to show us Sissy's tenacious hold on life—an attitude he had championed in so many earlier plays—he is going to mock her for it, too. Sissy, an old, ravaged, dying woman reveling in her past sexual glory, is a grotesque. Williams describes the effect of Sissy dancing in her kabuki robe as "a sort of grotesque beauty" (43). She is grotesque when she repeatedly tries to seduce Chris; she is grotesque when, in an utter absence of self-knowledge, she tells the Witch of Capri that she could never marry a dancer because "they love only mirrors" (47). She is grotesque because, blinded by fear and ego, she won't accept the truth of her situation. Williams also suggests that in her self-imposed isolation, atop an almost inaccessible cliff where she no longer has to hear the sound of human voices, she is grotesque.

Sissy is not the play's only grotesque figure, however. The Witch of Capri certainly fits the definition, in her "Fata Morgana" outfit which includes blue-tinted hair, "a cone-shaped hat studded with pearls," and hands like claws, "aglitter with gems" (43). Chris is something of a grotesque, too. When he first appears, his shirt and leather lederhosen have been nearly torn off him by Sissy's pursuing guard dogs. Once, this might have been a "typical Williams" ploy for celebrating male flesh; in this context, the strip-tease act is burlesqued. Bodhisattva or not, there is something hapless about Chris, who has failed as a poet and is trailed by a life of disappointment and anti-climax following his youthful success. Making matters worse, he is bossed about and finally defeated by the demon woman he has come to assist. Williams had adopted many Nō conventions and their Zen underpinnings, but he did not put aside his native note of irony.

Today, it is possible that the grotesque elements in the play, especially the emphasis on the overriding, egotistical nature of desire, can be underlined (although they hardly need to be) by the use of a male actor in the role of Sissy. Indeed, the English actor Rupert Everett has played Sissy twice in a production designed and directed by Philip Prowse, first at the Citizens' Theatre of Glasgow in 1994 and remounted in London in 1997. The latter production also provided a male actor, David Foxxe, as the Witch of Capri. The change of genders did not seem to illuminate the play according to reviewers; indeed, several mention an overabundance of camp and a concomitant lack of sexual attraction between Sissy and Chris (as played first by Greg Hicks and later by James X. Mitchell). The greatest danger, in fact, of a male playing Sissy is that the actor can easily descend into caricature; one critic of the Glasgow production described Everett's Sissy as more a performance than acting (Peter). This is a mistake which takes the play further from its Nō-inspired intent and origins than even the two Broadway productions, which starred, first, Hermione Baddeley and then Tallulah Bankhead as Sissy. For, despite the fact that *Milk Train* is a comedy of the grotesque, it deals with the nature of life, suffering, and death, and so its comedy is also religious.

There is, however, another way of approaching the gender issue, at least in theory. Hale writes that when Williams saw the Grand Kabuki company on his visit to Tokyo and in New York a year later, he was intrigued by the famous *onnagata*, or female impersonator, Utaemon VI. Williams experimented with the idea of the *onnagata* in *The Day on Which a Man Dies* and *In the Bar of a Tokyo Hotel* (366). If Chris is viewed as a Bodhisattva who may appear in both male and female forms, then one is invited to view Chris as a woman—and perhaps Sissy as a man. In this case, the central action of the play, to the extent to which it has one in the traditional Western dramatic notion of action, is that of a gentle, artistic woman nurturing a deeply pained man mired in spiritual crisis brought on by the snares of earthly desire and a fear of death. In *The Night of the Iguana*, the result of that action is positive: Shannon will live and may yet find peace. In *Milk Train*, the action ends in the "man's" death—yet in the play's Eastern cosmology, this is also positive: Sissy will die, and in the release from the life of material illusion, she, too, will find peace. One might go so far to say that, when played by a man, the name "Sissy" acquires a new resonance: for in the face of death, Flora is a sissy, indeed, a comic figure unequal to the vital task before her.

While Williams built *Milk Train*'s themes and structure around many of Nō's dramaturgical conventions, he did not write an "authentic" Nō play if only because he had no intention of alienating a Broadway audience with a form entirely foreign to them. Even the playwrights Williams admired most in the late fifties and early sixties and whose work influenced his own—Beckett, Albee, and Pinter—did not eschew the need to communicate with a Western audience. Nonetheless, when Williams sensed that his familiar forms and themes did not suffice to describe new experience—particularly his doubts about the value of survival—he searched for methods that could express this new material. Nō, he found, brought him closer to an accurate expression of his evolving existential view than anything Western dramaturgy could offer.

Indeed, if *Milk Train* has a serious problem, it is not that Williams went too far in using Nō conventions; it is that he disguised them too much. Those elements which were most obviously Asian—the stage assistants, the bizarre Kabuki robes worn by Sissy and Chris, the music—were the only ones noticed by critics, who criticized them as being superfluous "affectations," while the truly substantive Japanese elements, subsumed in character, theme, and structure, were invisible to Western eyes. *Milk Train* only looks inept, its speeches rambling and its characters disengaged, when viewed from the inadequate perspective of Western dramaturgy. If we change the angle of our perception from Greece to Japan, from tragedy to Nō, then suddenly *Milk Train* reveals all the purpose and power Williams built into it. The problem has never been with the play; it has been with us.

Works Cited

Armato, Philip M. "Tennessee Williams' Meditations on Life and Death." *Tennessee Williams: A Tribute*. Ed. Jac Tharpe. Jackson: UP of Mississippi, 1977, 558–570.
Boxhill, Roger. *Tennessee Williams*. Modern Dramatists. New York: St. Martin's Press, 1988.
Coveney, Michael. Untitled Review. *Observer* 6 November 1994. 3 August 2001. <http://members.aol.com/citzsite/citz/gcmtrain.htm>.
Debusscher, Gilbert. "Tennessee Williams' Lives of the Saints: A Playwright's Obliquity." *Tennessee Williams: A Collection of Critical Essays*. Ed. Stephen S. Stanton. Englewood Cliffs: Prentice-Hall, 1977, 149–157.
Devlin, Albert J., ed. *Conversations with Tennessee Williams*. Jackson: UP of Mississippi, 1986.
Falk, Signi. *Tennessee Williams*. Boston: Twyane, 1979.
Fedder, Norman J. "Tennessee Williams' Dramatic Technique." *Tennessee Williams: A Tribute*. Ed. Jac Tharpe. Jackson: UP of Mississippi, 1977. (795–812)
Gassner, John. "Broadway in Review." *Educational Theatre Journal* 16 (1964): 70–79.
Gross, Robert F. "Tracing Lines of Flight in *Summer and Smoke* and *The Milk Train Doesn't Stop Here Anymore*" in *Tennessee Williams: A Casebook*. Ed. Robert F. Gross. New York: Routledge, 2001.
Hale, Allean. "Tennessee's Long Trip." *Missouri Review* 7 (1984): 201–12.
———. "The Secret Script of Tennessee Williams." *The Southern Review* 27 (1991): 363–375.

Kerr, Walter. *Tragedy and Comedy*. New York: Touchstone—Simon & Schuster, 1967.

——. *Thirty Plays Hath November: Pain and Pleasure in the Contemporary Theatre*. New York: Simon & Schuster, 1968.

Mishima, Yukio. "Introduction." *Five Modern Nō Plays*. Trans. Donald Keene. New York: Alfred A. Knopf, 1957.

"'Milk Train' Gets Second Chance." *New York Times* 18 Sept. 1963: 32.

Peter, John. Untitled Review. *Sunday Times* 6 November 1994. 3 August 2001. <http://members.aol.com/citzsite/citz/gcmtrain.htm>.

Taubman, Howard. "Theater: Tennessee Williams's *'Milk Train'*." *New York Times* 18 Jan. 1963, Western ed.: 7.

Waley, Arthur. *The Nō Plays of Japan*. 1922. New York: Grove Press, 1957.

Weales, Gerald. "Tennessee Williams' Achievement in the Sixties." *Tennessee Williams: A Collection of Critical Essays*. Ed. Stephen S. Stanton. Englewood Cliffs, NJ: Prentice-Hall, 1977. 61–70.

Williams, Tennessee. Production Notes. *The Glass Menagerie*. *The Theatre of Tennessee Williams*. Vol. 1. New York: New Directions, 1971. 123–237.

——. *Orpheus Descending*. *The Theatre of Tennessee Williams*. Vol. 3. New York: New Directions, 1971. 217–342.

——. *The Milk Train Doesn't Stop Here Anymore*. *The Theatre of Tennessee Williams*. Vol. 5. New York: New Directions, 1976. 3–120.

Allean Hale

THE GNÄDIGES FRÄULEIN:
TENNESSEE WILLIAMS'S CLOWN SHOW

Of all of Tennessee Williams's so-called "late plays" after *The Night of the Iguana* in 1961, perhaps the most unusual and most difficult is *The Gnädiges Fräulein*. The German title, almost unpronounceable, seems deliberately off-putting. The dictionary definition is of little help: *"Honorable Miss"* or *Young Lady*—an obsolete form of address used for an unmarried young woman of high standing. One is tempted to speculate that Williams, annoyed with the critics' failure to understand the prediction of change implied in the title of his 1963 play, *The Milk Train Doesn't Stop Here Any More*, was challenging them further, as if to say, "Figure this out!" However, this seems unnatural for a playwright who had spent the best years of his life bringing his innermost concerns to the public. *Milk Train*, anticipated as a comedy about a bawdy ex-showgirl, had turned out to be a play about dying. *The Gnädiges Fräulein*, following it in 1966, defied explanation. The play opened at the Longacre Theatre, New York, on February 22, 1966, and closed after seven performances. The efforts of a superb cast, Zoe Caldwell as Polly, Kate Reid as Molly, and Margaret Leighton, who moved it toward tragedy as the Fräulein, could not save it. Reviews were generally unfavorable, citing the work as evidence of Williams's decline.

In mid-life and in the mid-1960s, Williams was tired of Broadway, which he characterized as mostly musicals. He was aware of how theatre had changed with the infusion of foreign dramatists, and he wanted to change with it. The new drama was spare, not dogmatic, wordy, or plot driven—tendencies he saw in his own writing—but allusive, substituting significant action for imitation of reality. Although Williams was often branded a realist, he had always been drawn towards the surreal, as demonstrated in one of his earliest plays, *Ten Blocks on the Camino Real*. Whether or not he had read Artaud's famous call for a new "theatre of cruelty," which would do away with literary drama to return to theatre as spectacle with its ritualistic, magical, and religious origins, Williams's own manifesto for a "plastic theatre" incorporating all the theatrical arts had been published in 1945 in his production notes to *The Glass Menagerie*. It had helped to change the course of theatre in America, creating a new American style.

Williams was also physically tired. He felt the strain of having to produce another commercial "hit." A year after *Iguana*, the death of his long-time partner Frank Merlo sent him into a deep clinical depression, which he tried to confront through psychoanalysis and pacifying drugs. These medications, prescribed by physicians, were not considered harmful at the time, but today's pharmaceutical manuals would describe them as dangerous drugs. The most dangerous were the mysterious "vitamin" mixtures administered by a well-known society doctor, Max Jacobson. (Rensberger 34). Jacobson, called "Dr. Feelgood," would eventually lose his medical license. Williams would later joke about the sixties after Frank's death as his "stoned age," but the expression had a darker meaning. When Dr. Jacobson first plunged the syringe into his hip, Williams recalled, "I felt as if a concrete sarcophagus about me had sprung open and I was released as a bird on wing" (Williams and Mead 253). It is too simple to say, as Dakin Williams does, that *The Gnädiges Fräulein* was written on speed. Williams had the gift of writing directly from the unconscious. He thought metaphorically and saw the symbolic in everyday life. He had always lived on the edge of reality; unreliable about dates and names, he often retold the same happening in different versions, sometimes with different characters or places. Under the influence of drugs he shed all inhibitions and moved further toward fantasy.

Fräulein, first published in *Esquire* in August 1965, does seem to take off from an amphetamine high. A wildly imaginative farce, it is certainly one of the most remarkable plays in the Williams repertory. It combines elements of circus, music hall, puppet show, and pantomime. Brilliant in itself, it is more amazing as a nightmare captured on paper. "I type very fast," Williams said, "but my mind goes even faster." The action centers on a race: when the boat whistles blow, can the Fräulein beat the predatory birds to the dock and bring back a fish? The play speeds along in an irrelevant, colloquial style: satirical, bitter, but hilarious in a comic strip knockdown way. Williams hallucinates from a familiar setting, the front porch of his cottage in Key West, where clones Molly and Polly act as a chorus in rocking chairs, supplying all the dialogue and narrating the action. But the perspective is warped: the stage floor tilts at a dangerous level; the two rocking chairs seem about to slide off; at times the front window lights up to reveal an incongruous red velvet and gilt Viennese interior. The small cottage has become Molly's "big dormitory" which houses "permanent transients" and is patrolled each night by the Dark Angel, who checks their dog tags and never leaves unattended. The local pelicans have turned into "cocaloony birds," with a stalking "big bird" seemingly borrowed from *Sesame Street*. Bird imagery abounds in Williams's plays; here it is as if the gulls which swooped down on the sea turtles in *Suddenly Last Summer* have become giant birds attacking human beings.

The Gnädiges Fräulein, which Williams translates as "gracious young lady," is a once-renowned vaudeville performer, former member of a famous artistic trio:

the trainer, his trained seal, and herself. She would toe dance between the two while fetching the paraphernalia for the seal's balancing act, which climaxed with him catching a fish in his jaws. Once the Fräulein, overambitious, upstaged the seal and caught the flying fish in her own mouth. The surprise intervention brought down the house, and the successful gimmick was kept in the show until at a final performance the seal turned on her and dealt her a blow that ended her career. Eventually she drifted down to the southernmost Key. Now she is reduced to bringing in her catch each day to earn her place in this boardinghouse. The landlady, Molly, and the gossip columnist, Polly, a sadistic duo, lay bets on whether the Fräulein will survive one more trip. The cocaloonies have already plucked out one of her eyes, which is covered by a large bandage. She appears in a bedraggled tutu, the remnant of her theatrical wardrobe; her hair is a fuzz of pink-orange curls. Like a puppet, she performs on command, delivering her outmoded numbers in a quavering voice. She is pathetically anxious to please, offering her dilapidated scrapbook to any who will look. And she is hopelessly in love with Indian Joe, another tenant who appears from time to time. He is an erotic fantasy: deep red skin, hair blond as a palomino, sky-blue eyes. Dressed like a Hollywood Indian, he embodies Hollywood sex. He wears a breechcloth of deerskin and some strings of wampum and whistles "The Indian Love Call." Polly is equally infatuated with this nonverbal primitive, and the two have a contretemps that ends in a mock striptease as she loses her skirt, exposing polka-dot calico knickers. Zoe Caldwell, who played Polly in a performance that almost ran away with the show, said that Williams asked her to wear whiteface and learn to do pratfalls. "Alan Schneider (the director) didn't have a clue to what the play was about," she said; "we all thought it was crazy . . . surrealist" (Caldwell). Later when she visited Key West and saw the characters who salute the sunset each night on Mallory Dock and the women in stark makeup in the bars, she recognized how Williams had simply taken off from reality. As the two clowns synchronize their chairs and rock with pelvic thrusts, smoking their "Mary Janes," they discuss obliquely life, death, the media, the state of the nation, and satirize Key West as Cocaloony Key. Through them, Williams parodies religious rhetoric, quotes sources as various as Longfellow, Scott Fitzgerald, and the Lincoln-Douglas debates, and draws on popular television shows, comic strips, circus acts in a dazzling display of contemporary American comedy. Their language is especially interesting if considered as automatic writing: unfettered Williams, convoluted, full of comic reversals, repetitions, and rhymes, so noticeably rhythmic it reads like a chant . . . "three fish a day to keep eviction away; one fish more to keep the wolf from the door." Non sequiturs pepper the dialogue, which is mainly repartee based on the playwright's sardonic wit.

MOLLY: I'm dead serious, Polly.
POLLY: It's natural to be serious when you're dead. (225)

The two bring the Fräulein out for exhibition, discuss her past famous career in front of her as if she were a dumb object, taunt her into one last attempt to put on her act, then mock her when it fails. Her situation is critical, as lately she has not brought in many fish. Like timekeepers, they clock her final race from the docks. As she returns, fish in bucket, she is attacked by the swooping birds who shred her garments, pull out her hair and pluck out her other eye. (At the time he wrote this, Williams was blind in one eye).

The fact that the cocaloonies suggested critics made it easy for reviewers to take a biographical approach, denigrating the play as the author's personal complaint and noticing that the Fräulein's history closely resembled the playwright's own. When Molly, convinced that the Fräulein will not return from the docks, dictates to Polly the biographical data that will appear in her obituary, it is a fantasized description of how Williams has seen his life in the theatre: Once the center of a famous trio (perhaps Kazan, Williams, Mielziner?) the playwright, like the Fräulein, was gradually upstaged by newcomers with new acts. There was the "golden age" of acceptance, the "new twist" in "show biz" that brought down the house, finally the failure that rang down the curtain. As the Fräulein had once "mounted a flagpole on the courthouse lawn in the costume of Lady Godiva," Williams felt his own naked exposure in television interviews to a gawking public. In her final drift to the southernmost Key, the end of the United States, Williams projects the possible end of his own career. For a writer to "live" he must keep producing—delivering his "fish," even under attack. If self-pity was beneath the surface of the play, it was redeemed by the author's ability to stand back and examine himself dispassionately. Actually, in this case history of the Fräulein, the serious theme of the play emerges as an allegory on the subject of the artist as such, the human costs involved in the creative act, the destructive power of the critics. Williams brooded over the difference between the way the playwright and the painter were regarded in America. Painters were allowed to change their style or to approach old subjects in new ways. Picasso was not abused for moving from his blue or rose period to cubism. Monet could repeat his haystacks at will; when he grew old and his water lilies merged into one pastel blur, he was increasingly acclaimed. But in America when a playwright revisited old material it was seen as senility.

Asked if she saw the play as being about the artist or the author under attack as he struggled to bring in a new play, Zoe Caldwell said: "no, that sort of thing is for the scholars. The actors just have to act out the lines." The discrepancies between interpretation and action would become an increasing problem with Williams's late plays. Also, as Caldwell added, "It should never have been done on Broadway. If it had been done Off-Broadway—and not under Tennessee's name—people would have said Ho, Ho, a black comedy, and laughed their heads off"(Caldwell).

His old friend Harold Clurman noted that the play was something altogether new for Tennessee Williams (Clurman 221). *Fräulein* is certainly the most experimental of Williams's new-direction plays written after *The Night of the Iguana*. When reviewers compared it to Black Comedy, the playwright declared that he had invented Black Comedy. Others labeled it "Theatre of the Absurd." This Williams denied, saying that he could never see human existence as meaningless. Indeed, he was now much nearer to European drama stylistically, the declamatory style of Brecht, the buffoonery of Ionesco, the cruelty of Genet. Molly and Polly, eternally rocking while they wait, seem first cousins to Beckett's Vladimir and Estragon. In the Broadway season of 1965–66 Williams was more attuned to *Marat/ Sade* than to *You Can't Take It With You*. In *Fräulein* he rejects literary quality and plot for theatricality—the use of ritual, music, mime, lighting, acrobatics, the emphasis on excitement, the unexpected. The dialogue in its irrelevance makes nonsense of meaning and communication. Language is actually destroyed in the hilarious duel between Indian Joe and the giant cocaloony in Scene I where their exchange consists wholly of 'Ugh"and "Awk." (This is perhaps a precursor to Williams's experiments with language which would climax with *In the Bar of a Tokyo Hotel* and further mystify the critics.) Williams compounded the confusion by rewriting *Fräulein* nine years later as *The Latter Days of a Celebrated Soubrette* with Anne Meacham as the star. "Adroit Revival Improves Bizarre Play," reported the *New York Times* (48) of the single Off-Off Broadway performance at the Arts Cabaret Theatre on May 16, 1974. This production exposed yet another level of meaning, suggesting that "Fräulein" might disguise a gay character, male rather than female, picturing the homosexual, rather than the artist, as martyr. This time the caustic chorus was played by two tall thin actors in drag, making the play more like Theatre of the Ridiculous.

In the 35 years since its premiere, *The Gnädiges Fräulein* has been produced perhaps twenty times in New York. When in 1999 a fledgling company called Theater Ten Thousand revived it at the Ohio Theatre, a loft space in Soho, The *Theatre Review Archive* characterized it as a "weird, cockeyed play . . . not the sort of Williams you're used to." But it added, "the dialogue soars splendiferously, even when you don't know what the heck it's talking about" (34).

More than a decade after it was published, the literary scholars began to notice the play. Again the question arose, how to approach it? Foster Hirsch, in his 1979 *Portrait of the Artist,* emphasized the "decline and fall" theme, calling the play "sad, overwrought . . . a decidedly minor work" and suggested that an impotent Williams was having his nightmares in public (78–79). Felicia Hardison Londré in the same year was more perceptive, noting that *Fräulein* represented the indomitable spirit of the artist and, by association, Williams's own perseverance despite critical hostility (167). Arthur Ganz in 1980 saw it only as a failed attempt at absurdist style and an exercise in self-pity (110). Roger Boxhill called it black humor (147) but did recognize it as experimental (149). Gilbert Debusscher of the University of Brussels, titled his 1989 essay "Williams's Self-Portrait Among the Ruins." Ten years later, Annette Saddick in her book on Williams's late plays called it absurdist but noted that its language anticipates a postmodern minimalist style (81). In a paper presented at the New Orleans Scholars' Conference in 2000 at the Tennessee Williams Literary Festival she enlarged on the play's relationship to Artaud and the theatre of cruelty, a thesis expanded in this volume. Philip Kolin in 2001 offered the most imaginative study of the play, suggesting that Williams was influenced by the Hitchcock film, *The Birds,* which came out the same year as *Fräulein* (Kolin, 4–21). This insight may be valid, for Williams, like Shakespeare, borrowed from many sources.

The most enlightening analysis has come from Linda Dorff, in her article on Williams's "outrageous" plays (16–19). With *Fräulein,* she sees the playwright moving into new territory, taking an anti-mimetic approach to critique theatre itself through parody and gross exaggeration. Thus the lack of conflict and plot in *Fräulein* mocks the well-made play; its irrelevant repartee mocks psychological dialogue; the Fräulein's delivery of dated songs may comment on the musicals Williams deplored. This "camp" point of view does not mirror the world, Dorff explains, but "like cubist painting, or pop art, engages in self-conscious play with representations that already exist"(15). In 1966, according to her, such examples of pop culture had not yet reached the Broadway stage and critics failed to recognize it, especially in a "Williams" play. The playwright had discarded the techniques for which he was most famous: poetic language, characterization, and the significant scene.

Art may be another path to understanding this play. Williams painted all his life and used painterly images in most of his work. His production notes for Fräulein call for "a totally unrealistic arrangement of [the] porch" with areas "displaced . . . "as if Picasso had designed it" (217). Dislocation is characteristic of Picasso's cubist paintings, where realistic forms become scarcely recognizable as they are combined, just as in Fräulein the opening monologue uses real sentences but combines disparate subjects in a way which dislocates meaning. Much of the dialogue of the play seems skewed in this way. But where Picasso's aim was to understand his subject from various planes and angles at once, Williams seems to use dislocation to figuratively thumb his nose at meaning. To compare Fräulein to the pop art of the sixties when the play was written may be more apt. As the critic Clement Greenberg defined it, Pop Art broke down the barriers between high art and kitsch (Sandler 3). The witty, cartoonish elements found in painters like Roy Lichtenstein, Robert Rauschenberg, and Philip Guston seem kindred to Williams's play, although he may have been more influenced personally by that icon of "Pop," Andy Warhol. Like Warhol, Williams comments on society. At the time he was writing Fräulein, he knew Warhol and sometimes visited The Factory on 47th street. He and Warhol were judges together at the Venice Film Festival in 1972. (Spoto, 302). One of Warhol's groupies, the transvestite Candy Darling, played Violet in Williams's 1972 play, Small Craft Warnings when Williams played "Doc." If Warhol's endless rows of tomato soup cans were comments on American culture, so was Williams's satire on the Wasp inhabitants of Cocaloony Key and their attitude toward the gays who frequented Key West; Polly's take-off of the newspaper obituary is a masterpiece of satire. Finally, Williams's play should be understood in relation to the decade in which it was written. Although he cultivated the image of his "stoned age," and the play reflects his desperation at that time, he was aware of the trauma and upheaval of the sixties—the race riots, the protest marches, Vietnam, the Kennedy and Martin Luther King assassinations. If The Gnädiges Fräulein has components of sadism and savagery, Williams was living in the same world and writing at the same time as Anthony Burgess's A Clockwork Orange or Kurt Vonnegut's Slaughterhouse Five. The Gnädiges Fräulein is a transition play, marking a turn in Williams's work that would prevail for the next ten years. In an interview with Charles Ruas in 1975 the playwright explained: "Let's say that the work has become darker. It began to become dark in the sixties and it became so dark that people find it painful" (Devlin, 287). He described Fräulein as a "gothic" comedy, so grotesque that it was incomprehensible to people. They didn't see the humor in it but saw their own fears of death.

Two hints by the author himself on how to approach his drama are generally overlooked. The strange title can be explained by the fact that Williams had introduced *Fräulein* as the second half of a double bill called *A Slapstick Tragedy,* suggesting that the two plays, *The Mutilated* and *The Gnädiges Fräulein* be performed together. At first take, the two seem to have little in common except that each concerns a woman with a physical mutilation. There is a connecting link, however subtle. *The Mutilated,* which pictures a prostitute who feels disfigured by the removal of one breast, ends strangely with her seeing a vision of the Virgin Mary. The carryover was to project this Marian image onto the title of the second play. Williams did this by interpreting "unmarried young lady" as "virgin." Since he often used foreign expressions loosely, he may even have confused "Fräulein" with one definition of "frau"(married woman, wife, lady) which, when preceded by "our" *(Unsre)* is further defined as "Our Lady, the Blessed Virgin." The most unlikely of Williams's plays may have a theological strain. In his first draft of this play, the cocaloony birds were pelicans: pelicans are symbols of Christ, as the fish was

Ginny Sims as the Gnädiges Fräulein in the University of Illinois Department of Theatre production at the Krannert Center for the Performing Arts. Courtesy of the University of Illinois Department of Theatre.

Self-portrait as Clown by Tennessee Williams. Courtesy of Richard Leavitt.

the sign of his followers. The Fräulein is described in religious terms: "she is trans-figured as a saint under torture"; and she has a halo: "Her hair is an aureole of bright orange curls." There is even a semi-crucifixion in Scene II (259).

Since *The Mutilated* and *The Gnädiges Fräulein* are seldom produced or read to-gether, this allegorical interpretation goes unnoticed. While it offers no practical approach to producing the play, it does suggest that the title *Slapstick Tragedy* alludes most specifically to *Fräulein*. Williams's own description in the original *Esquire* publication gave the most practical clue to his work: "The style of the plays is kin to vaudeville, burlesque and slapstick, with a dash of pop art thrown in"(95). It was this definition that the theatre department of the University of Illinois-Urbana seized on for its year 2000 Summerfest production.

Summerfest, a program of the Krannert Center for the Performing Arts, offered a repertory series of three plays: a light comedy, a murder mystery, and one more serious or experimental choice. For this, it was decided to combine three one-acts by Tennessee Williams under the title "Tennessee Women," each of which portrayed a woman disenfranchised by society, who nevertheless finds a way to overcome. *This Property Is Condemned* was to be followed by *The Unsatisfactory Supper,* with *The Gnädiges Fräulein* as the problematical number. Twice as long as the other plays, it was unknown and obviously difficult. Producing Director James Berton Harris, who had always wanted to attempt the play, aimed to make it so entertaining that the audience would not be too concerned with puzzling out its darker meanings. Recognizing Molly and Polly as traditional clown names, he was attracted to the circus implications of the text. When a self-portrait of Tennessee Williams as a clown was discovered, it seemed an eerie endorsement direct from the playwright himself and Harris decided to do the play as a clown show. Williams had done the painting when he was institutionalized briefly in the psychiatric unit of Barnes Hospital. It shows the face of a grinning clown with wild red hair. Underneath he has lettered in the words: "Fou? Moi? Au Contraire!"

Williams would often assume the role of clown in later years, confessing to be "an almost compulsive comedian in my social behavior"(*Memoirs,* 83). Frequently he exploited this side of his nature in interviews, "to ham it up and be fairly outrageous in order to provide 'good copy.' The reason? I guess a need to convince the world that I do indeed still exist . . . " His comic sense was the key to his survival—the ability to step back from his pain and laugh at it. Versed in classical theatre, he was well aware of the many clown traditions: the tragic clown of Pagliacci, the medieval jester, Shakespeare's fools, spokesmen for truth in the guise of simplemindedness. Williams had made Kilroy a clown and patsy in *Ten Blocks on the Camino Real,* and now unconsciously he may have recovered an influence as far back as his college friendship with Clark Mills, a distinguished poet who had published a cycle of circus poems which Tennessee knew. Williams's own circus poem, "Carrousel Tune," illustrates his meaning in *Fräulein* (*Winter* 45).

> Turn again, turn again, turn once again;
> the freaks of the cosmic circus are men,
> We are the gooks and geeks of creation . . .

Williams, in thinking of himself as a freak of creation, was extending this label to the *Fräulein* as his portrait of the artist. By viewing the human condition in circus terms, Williams seems to have anticipated a theatre trend of the seventies when theatre and church drew closer together as they had in the Middle Ages. St. Clements Episcopal Church in Manhattan was one of the first to bring drama into the sanctuary, holding regular services while serving as home to the American Place Theatre. A pertinent side note is that St. Clements's vicar, the Reverend Sidney Lanier, a founder of the American Place Theatre, was a cousin of Tennessee Lanier Williams and also one of the producers of *The Gnädiges Fräulein*. The "Jesus Revolution," set in motion by Harvey Cox's book, *The Feast of Fools*, introduced the concept of the sacred clown. Clowns suddenly became popular whether or not their origin was understood. "Clown" originated from the Middle English "clod," meaning the lowest form of bumpkin. The white makeup is a death symbol; in contrast, the clown's colorful costume signifies new life. Two pertinent songs would become a theme for the decade, "What Kind of Fool Am I?" from *Stop the World, I Want to Get Off* (1962) and "Send in the Clowns" from *A Little Night Music* (1973). The sacred clown was best exemplified by *Godspell*, the Gospel of St. Matthew as circus with Christ as a harlequin. In his portrait of the Fräulein with her fright wig, Williams embodies all of the sacred clown tradition.

Producer Harris, who held an MFA in costume design from the Yale School of Drama and had wide experience as a designer on and off-Broadway, designed fantastic circus costumes for Molly and Polly. Molly, a tiny actress, was given huge yellow boots in which she stomped around the stage with her mop. In contrast, Polly, who was tall, wore a tiny hat with a ridiculous stand-up flower which exaggerated her height. Her costume was a mock-pretentious layering of embroidered bodice with lace bib and bow and short flared skirt over billowing polka-dot bloomers. In contrast to the clashing colors of the clown's costumes, the Fräulein was in black and white—a spangled black bodice topping a tutu of white tulle—and for the comic touch fuchsia and black striped stockings and red Converse All Star High Tops instead of ballet slippers. These athletic shoes, popular in the fifties, also set a period note.

Sara Lampert Hoover, the director, a specialist in stage movement and dance choreography, blocked out the script in terms of exaggerating body movement which pantomimed the characters' lines and emphasized the slapstick. Her aim was to have the two clowns work together as a comedy team: a sort of Laurel and Hardy or Lucy and Ethel. In fact Producer Harris remarked that doing *Fräulein* was rather like Abbott and Costello playing *Waiting for Godot*. Characterization does not matter greatly in this play as the actors other than the Fräulein are abstractions or cartoons. Indian Joe presented an immediate problem. In Williams's script, he represents a Hollywood stereotype or Hollywood itself in its commercial emphasis on sex. However, in the politically correct atmosphere of the year 2000, the University of Illinois was involved in a struggle over its football mascot, Chief Illiniwek, represented by a white student whose elaborate Indian dance between halves of the games had become a sacred college tradition. Since this figure was currently under attack by Native Americans and sympathetic student groups, any representation of an Indian on stage might provoke a riot! So in the Krannert production, "Indian Joe" was converted to "Cowboy Joe," who seemed as valid a Hollywood icon. "How" in the script became "Pow," and the tomahawk changed to a gun. The character change worked exceptionally well, and the cowboy, in dazzling white with bared body except for crotch-hugging breeches and fake-fur chaps, white boots, and flowing platinum hair under a white Stetson, was an exaggerated sex symbol. His duel with the Cockaloony was a high spot of comedy. The Cockaloony was in pelican-gray tights with feathers protruding from head and tail and a beak with which he inquisitively explored various stage furnishings. The part was played by a tall actor who made incredibly acrobatic leaps from surface to surface and seemed to fly offstage accompanied by the whoosh of a wind machine. In performance, an interesting discovery emerged in the character of "the Permanent Transient," William, also referred to as "the wino." A comic walk-on in his bow tie and bowler hat, he is Molly's "old family retainer," subject to her beck and call. If Molly represents the Producer and Polly the Media, he is obviously the playwright, Tennessee Williams, making a self-deprecating comment.

Before the play began, the sound of wind punctuated by bird cries built atmosphere. To immediately establish the circus concept, scene designer Lee Boyer constructed the set as a circus-wagon, from the back of which the characters entered onto a platform stage. The wagon was lit fantastically for interior scenes and for the Fräulein's entrance, which was built up by strains of "Vienna, City of Dreams," an effective touch not in the script. The waltz became her *motif* as a string of tiny lights outlined the stage, suggesting the footlights of her days as a star. In sparkling bodice, white tutu, and porcelain white makeup she created an ethereal effect. The "clown" element was retained in her orange wig of corkscrew curls and her incongruous gym shoes—a subtle hint of her comedown since the days she danced *en pointe*. Her appearance suggested one of those cartoonish and cruel portraits by Toulouse Lautrec. Williams had written that the Fräulein should be performed by a singer, someone like Lotte Lenya, and Ginny Sims, a talented professional actress and singer (the only non-student performer) fulfilled that role. Music contributed greatly to her portrayal, as she sang requested numbers off-key, improvised others, and in the poignant final scene sang "Whispering Hope" in true voice as she crept up the stairs with her fish bucket. To counteract the script's treatment of the Fräulein, which is perhaps too cruel for audience consumption, her comic wig could be pulled out curl by curl, and her spilled blood was represented by glitter spangles.

The play proved to be physically dangerous for the actors. With three different staging heights and a run through the audience to maneuver, it was not difficult for the Fräulein, eyes covered with a bandage, to bump into props and seem battered. The actress actually played the part with her eyes shut, dodging the various hazards. (In the New York production Margaret Leighton had crashed into a fence and broken her shoulder.) As rehearsals progressed, the basic problem of the play emerged. In production, the action quarrels with the written content. Williams hinted at this dichotomy in calling his work a "slapstick tragedy." "Slapstick" implies slam-bang exaggerated action and suggests that the play should move fast. However, the script is wordy, with intricate lines, puns and word play, so the speed designed to keep audience attention threatens to obscure the serious meaning. Often the lines are nonsensical, delivered with a chanting repetition which tends to slow the pace. Directing then becomes an exercise in balance and sometimes a decision as to how much a particular line matters. Although bits were deleted here and there, it was found very difficult to cut a Tennessee Williams play. An audience accustomed to following a plot was confused by this almost plotless drama, where the development concerns the Fräulein's daily race to the docks for her catch and the only suspense is whether, under attack by the cocaloonies, she can make one more run. Characterization isn't of primary importance. Aside from the Fräulein, the characters are abstractions or cartoons. In acting the parts, Molly and Polly did manage to present individuality and contrast. Polly, the society editor of the local *Cocaloony Gazette,* is pretentious, superficial, and silly but shrewdly stupid. Molly, keeper of the roominghouse, is tough, manipulative, hard-nosed, sardonic; her speeches are put-downs. The contest between the two does form a slight subplot: Molly trying to get a good writeup for herself and "the big dormitory" from Polly; Polly intent only on a human interest story about the Fräulein for her gossip column.

What is the function of the Fräulein, for example? She is certainly more than "a nutcase in a tutu" as a local reviewer described her. For a play about the Fräulein one might expect her entrance sooner, although it is prepared for at the beginning by Molly sweeping up her blood. The lengthy monologue on her history seems to come rather late in the play. Since she represents the tragic aspect of the drama, it is essential that there be a turnabout from broad comedy on her final race to the docks. Molly is already composing a sob-story and the two indulge in some horseplay with a telescope as they watch. But as suspense mounts about whether she will live to return, their banter turns to awed whispers.

> *The Gnädiges Fräulein appears on the sidewalk in terrible disarray but clinging tenaciously to her tin bucket containing a rather large fish. Great flapping noise of cocaloonies in pursuit. She crashes through the picket fence and scampers around the side of the house, disappears.*
> POLLY: What's this? *(Has picked up some bright orange fuzz.)*
> MOLLY: Oh, my God, they scalped her! (259)

The references to God in this play are usually blasphemous, but in the Fräulein's final speech, telling how she caught the fish that would secure her existence one more day in life's dormitory, her words suggest belief: "I can't imagine how I happened to catch it, it was so dark at the fish-docks. It just landed in my jaws like God had thrown it to me" (261). So the playwright must have felt when in desperation his imagination summoned up a new play. Even the two clowns are aghast at the Fräulein's appearance. By now the cocaloonies have plucked out both eyes and her face is half-covered with a bloody bandage. Her tutu is torn away, her tights are dabbled with blood, but she triumphantly holds forth her fish. The final tableau in tying up the plot brings together the secular, religious, and autobiographical meanings of the play. As the baroque red-and-gold parlor is lighted within the dormitory's gray exterior, I believe it is meant to suggest a theatre space and make us realize that this is a play about theatre itself. Indian Joe, Molly and Polly at the table eating the Fräulein's fish may represent Hollywood, the Producers and the Media consuming the artist's work. The scene also suggests a Eucharist, as the three partake of the Fräulein's offering—the fish symbolizing her broken body and the wine, her shed blood. This reinforces Artaud's idea of the theatre as a sacred space. However, in the small confine of the circus wagon interior, any allegory was inevitably lost, and only the idea of eating the meal came through. Audience interest was on the Fräulein, alone on stage. Like the endings of many Tennessee Williams plays, this one is ambiguous, so the finale must be accomplished by the actress herself. Bucket at the ready, she moves downstage. Confronting the audience, she crouches in starting position as she strains to hear the fishboat whistle that will signal one more gallant run to the docks.

Ultimately the play comes through as existentialist rather than absurd. It reminds us of Brecht's Mother Courage, eternally pulling her wagon, or Camus's Sisyphus, daily pushing his rock up the hill even though he knows it will roll down again. "En avant!" was Williams' battle cry.

Audience reaction varied from night to night. Some even seemed uncertain about the outcome of the play and whether it was time to applaud. Although playing time for *The Gnädiges Fräulein* was less than an hour it was in two scenes, and, with little plot to follow, some viewers found the play overlong. This may have been because it was experienced in contrast to the two brief one-acts preceding it, both realistic dramas, easy to follow. After the intermission, the audience may have been expecting more of the same. Listening to audience reaction, again the most common query seemed to be, as Williams had predicted: "What is the play about?" Viewers tended to react strongly to the play, some nights with laughter and applause, others with silence. One woman left the theatre in tears. On another night six persons rose and walked out. Molly and Polly, who were improvising freely by this time, commented on their leaving and waved goodbye, to the amusement of the rest of the audience. The triple program played from June 16 through July 29 and had eleven performances. In the Studio Theatre, which seated 250, it was a complete sellout. However, director Lampert Hoover, producer Harris, and dramaturge Allean Hale agreed that in another production they might cut some of the more author-indulgent lines.

The Krannert performance is to date the latest of the perhaps two dozen times the play has been performed since its premiere in 1966. *Camino Real,* the other Williams play it most resembles, which in 1946 his agent told him to put away and not show to anyone, had an acclaimed production in 1998 by London's Young Vic Theatre Company and in 1999 at the Hartford Stage. After fifty-odd years audiences seemed to find no trouble in understanding it. Harold Clurman was the one critic who predicted that *The Gnädiges Fräulein* would be "seen and acclaimed in future productions of universities, community theatres and on foreign stages" (222). Will *Fräulein* have to wait fifty years for acceptance? No doubt Tennessee Williams, the clown who saw humor in everything, is saying hopefully: "Au contraire!"

Works Cited

Artaud, Antonin. *The Theater and Its Double*. New York: Grove Press, 1958.

Bigsby, C.W.E. "Tennessee Williams." *A Critical Introduction to Twentieth Century American Drama*. Cambridge: Cambridge UP 1984. 15–134.

Boxhill, Roger. *Tennessee Williams*. New York: St. Martin's Press, 1987.

Caldwell, Zoe. Telephone interview, Caldwell with Allean Hale, Pound Ridge, NY, 2 Jan. 1988.

Clurman, Harold. "Slapstick Tragedy." *The Critical Response to Tennessee Williams*. Ed. George Crandell. Westport, Conn.: Greenwood Press, 1996. 220–222.

Cox, Harvey. *The Feast of Fools*. Cambridge: Harvard UP, 1969.

Debusscher, Gilbert. "The *Gnädiges Fräulein*: Williams's Self-Portrait Among the Ruins." *New Essays in American Drama*. Eds. Gilbert Debusscher and Henry I. Schvey. Amsterdam/Atlanta: Rodopi, 1989. 63–74.

Devlin, Albert, ed. *Conversations with Tennessee Williams*. Jackson: UP of Mississippi, 1986.

Dick, Kay. *Pierrot*. London: Hutchinson, 1960.

Dorff, Linda. "Theatricalist Cartoons: Tennessee Williams's Late 'Outrageous' Plays." *Tennessee Williams Annual Review*. 2 (1999) 13–33.

Ganz, Arthur. "A Desperate Morality." *Tennessee Williams*. Ed. Harold Bloom. New York: Chelsea House, 1987. 99–111.

Hirsch, Foster. *A Portrait of the Artist: The Plays of Tennessee Williams*. London: Kennikat Press, 1979.

Kolin, Philip C. "'a play about terrible birds': Tennessee Williams's *The Gnädiges Fräulein* and Alfred Hitchcock's *The Birds*." *South Atlantic Review* 66.1 (2001): 1–21.

Londré, Felicia Hardison. *Tennessee Williams*. New York: Ungar, 1979.

Mills, Clark. *The Circus*. Prairie City, Il: James A. Decker Press, 1943.

The New York Times. 29 May 1974. 48.

Rensberger, Boyce. "Amphetamines Used by a Physician to Lift Moods of Famous Patients. *New York Times*. 4 Dec. 1972: A1+.

Saddick, Annette. "The Inexpressible Regret of All Her Regrets: Tennessee Williams's *The Gnädiges Fräulein* as Artaudian Theater of Cruelty." Unpublished. Presented at New Orleans Tennessee Williams Festival, 2000.

———. *The Politics of Reputation: The Critical Reception of Tennessee Williams' Later Plays*. London: Associated University Presses, 1999.

Sandler, Irving. *Art of the Postmodern Era*. New York: Icon Editions, c. 1996.

Spoto, Donald. *The Kindness of Strangers*. Boston: Little, Brown, 1985.

Theatre Crafts Magazine. Theatre-Church Encounter issue. May/June 1972, 38.

Theatre Review Archive. "The Gnädiges Fräulein" The New York Theatre Experience, < http://www.nytheatre.com/nytheatre/arch_004,htm > 3Jul.2000

Warhol, Andy, & Pat Hackett. *Popism. The Warhol '60s*. New York: Harcourt Brace Jovanovich, 1963.

Williams, Dakin, and Shepherd Mead. *Tennessee Williams*. New York: Arbor House, 1983.

Williams, Tennessee. *In the Winter of Cities. Collected Poems*. New York: New Directions, 1964.

———. "Slapstick Tragedy." *Esquire* 64.2 (1965): 95.

———. "The Gnädiges Fräulein." *The Theatre of Tennessee Williams*. New York: New Directions, 1970. Vol.7: 215–262.

———. *Memoirs*. New York: Doubleday, 1975.

———. "The Mutilated." *The Theatre of Tennessee Williams*. Vol. 7. New York: New Directions, 1970. Vol.7: 76–130.

Una Chaudhuri

"AWK!": EXTREMITY, ANIMALITY, AND THE AESTHETIC OF AWKWARDNESS IN TENNESSEE WILLIAMS'S *THE GNÄDIGES FRÄULEIN*

> *Is there a more mysterious idea for an artist than to imagine how na-*
> *ture is reflected in the eyes of an animal? . . . It is a poverty-stricken*
> *convention to place animals into landscapes as seen by men; instead*
> *we should contemplate the soul of the animal to divine its way of sight.*
> *—Franz Marc*

> *We believe in the existence of very special becomings-animal travers-*
> *ing human beings and sweeping them away, affecting the animal no*
> *less than the human.* *—Gilles Deleuze and Felix Guattari*

The subject of this essay lies somewhere between the meaningless mono-
syllable of my title and the possibly utopian program of my epigraphs.[1]
This "AWK!" encapsulates the questions raised by the encounter between
art and animality that frames my inquiry. In both its significations, as animal yelp,
or, more familiarly, as marginal notation in red ink, this "AWK!" helps me to ask if
that encounter is always—by definition—*awkward*? And if it is, can something be
made of that awkwardness: a new aesthetic, perhaps, with which to undertake
such visits to the non-human as are envisioned in my epigraphs and which have
traditionally remained out of artistic bounds?

Those seeking to rescue the late plays of Tennessee Williams from critical and
commercial oblivion generally contest the earlier verdicts on these plays as aes-
thetically limited and insufficiently realized. The idea of awkwardness leads me to

propose a different possibility: that what is important and valuable about these plays is precisely their apparent failure. My claim rests on a new conceptualization of failure itself, drawn from an extreme margin of postmodern theory. Reading failure as a productive *crisis of expertise,* a *creative refusal* of mastery and authority, theorists of postmodernism have urged a renewed interest in the values of *not knowing* and *not succeeding.* In *Terror and Experts,* Adams Phillips opposes "curiosity," which is endless and creative, to "answers," which seduce us with their airs of authority while also entrapping us in their false finalities. From this radically altered perspective on artistic accomplishment, the challenge for serious practitioners in any field, artistic or otherwise, is how "to learn how not to know what he is doing" (104).

Williams's experimentalism, while it may have stopped far short of not knowing what he was doing, certainly opened him up to margins and transgressions of all kinds: cultural, aesthetic, sexual, generic. Did it also open him up to that ultimate artistic transgression, failure? One of his plays in particular, *The Gnädiges Fräulein,* suggests an experimentalism pursued beyond the usual motivation of new discoveries en route to new successes. The imagistic, linguistic, and psychological excesses and attenuations of this play could signal an anti-aesthetic that might shed light on other late plays as well. Of all Williams's failed human beings (and these were, of course, his stock in trade: failed artists, priests, lovers, mothers, sons), few are more abject than the eponymous protagonist of this play. Her abjection, moreover, is precise, placing her in another extreme margin of postmodernism: the rethinking of the animal.

Postmodernism comes to the animal as it does to other margins of dominant discourse or to other excluded terms of a hegemonic humanism. As I will discuss in detail below, it comes to the animal as to a figure capable of inspiring and guiding a new journey—a postmodern shamanism, if you like—across the ideological borders with which modernism has kept the human separate from its many "others." While traditional shamans undertook their spirit travels in the company of animal "familiars," postmodern travelers favor odd and ungainly beasts, "unfamiliars" with strange—and strangely powerful—forms. One recent sculpture that exemplifies this kind of "postmodern animal" is John Isaacs's *Untitled (Dodo)* (1994) (Figure 1), courting awkwardness as a strategy, a discourse, and a revisioning of aesthetic values. It belongs to the genre that Steven Baker memorably dubs "botched taxidermies," deliberately messy animal representations that register modernity's alienation from the non-human. Isaacs's Dodo strikes me as a particularly appropriate "animal unfamiliar" to invite along as I venture into the awkward world of Tennessee Williams late plays.

Though little-known and rarely produced, *The Gnädiges Fräulein* encapsulates paradigmatic elements of Tennessee Williams's late plays and extends them to their signifying limits. The play's set—and its setting—are a case in point. Like so many of the late plays, this one performs Williams's drift away from classical dramatic modernism by eschewing the normative domestic interior of dramatic realism. The "big dormitory" of this play is surely the extreme version of the transient spaces in which Williams increasingly located his attempts to stage the kinds of

Fig. 1. John Isaacs, *Untitled* (Dodo). Courtesy of The Saatchi Gallery, London. Photo by Stephen White.

"limit-experiences" which increasingly interested him—and which Raymond Williams calls those "crucial areas of experience [which] the language and behavior of the living room could not articulate or fully interpret" (85). The civic values and kinship relationships once articulated by the stage living room are nowhere to be found in the nightmarish boardinghouse of *The Gnädiges Fräulein,* where shelter itself has become a grotesque balancing act: in this hotel, those who cannot afford a bed can rent "standing room" for the night and try to sleep on their feet like (as one character notes) flamingos!

The play's set is as fractured as its setting. Williams explicitly requires "a totally unrealistic arrangement of assorted props, porch steps, yard, and picket fence . . . as if Picasso had designed it" (217). This literal displacement reflects the play's thematics, which push notions of social slippage and psychological dislocation to their human limits. The characters of *The Gnädiges Fräulein* are so radically transient that they are sliding off the map, barely clinging to the "southernmost tip of terra firma" (219). The long opening monologue riffs on this geographical extremity, quickly thrusting us into the surreal enactment of the play's most original and extreme realization of human extremity: namely, the slide into animality.

The Gnädiges Fräulein tells the story of a former European showgirl now fallen on hard times and struggling to survive in a poverty-stricken town on the Florida shore. Her fate is in the hands of a sadistic boardinghouse keeper named Molly, who gives the Fräulein (we never learn her real name) a roof over her head in exchange for a daily payment of three fish, which the Fräulein scavenges from the rejected catch of passing fishing boats. This grim arrangement is described by Molly for the benefit of Polly, a reporter from the local paper, whom the landlady hopes to persuade into giving her some free publicity for her boardinghouse. In the course of the narration, the Fräulein makes several scavenging forays to the offstage docks, each time returning more damaged and debilitated. In her quest for fish she is, it turns out, in competition with the vicious cocaloony birds, who do not take kindly to having a human rival. They violently attack her every time she ventures out, leaving her, by play's end, horribly tattered, bloodied, and blinded in both eyes. The main action of the play, then, is the cruel disintegration of the Fräulein at the hands of the brutal birds.

With two notable exceptions, critical discussions of *The Gnädiges Fräulein* have focused on this action, reading it as a bitter but unsuccessful satire on the fate of the artist in modern society. A discussion by Linda Dorff brings enormous texture and renewed interest to this reading, arguing that Williams's use of cartoonish characters and actions extends his satire far beyond the autobiographical into the generic and institutional. According to Dorff, Williams used "the two-dimensional aesthetics of the cartoon" not only to construct a parable for "the grotesquely disfigured position of the artist within the frames of the theatre and of the larger American society" but also to parody—in a distinctly *meta*-mimetic mode—the tradition of psychological tragic realism to which he had always had an ambivalent relationship (16). An even more recent discussion of *The Gnädiges Fräulein,* by Philip Kolin, furthers Dorff's method of reading Williams intertextually with other cultural and pop-cultural forms. Exploring the connections between *The Gnädiges Fräulein* and Alfred Hitchcock's roughly contemporaneous film *The Birds,* Kolin locates *The Gnädiges Fräulein* in relation to an apocalyptic streak in Cold War American culture. Both *The Birds* and *The Gnädiges Fräulein* are, writes Kolin, "cultural scripts of fear," which evoke the "lunacy and dread of nuclear attack in the mid 1960s" (6). As the only article to pay sustained attention to what is surely the most unusual feature of this play—the role played in it by other-than-human figures—Kolin's article opens the door for my "animalized" reading. I submit that by "taking [the] animals seriously" (Degrazia), we can discover a transgressive animalizing imagination that complements the pop-cultural imagery and political resonance which critics like Dorff and Kolin have already uncovered in this supposed "failure" of a play.

The Gnädiges Fräulein is, of course, hardly unique among Williams's plays in using animal and bird imagery: such imagery appears in the titles of several of his plays—Not About Nightingales, Sweet Bird of Youth, I Rise in Flames Cried the Phoenix, A Perfect Analysis Given by a Parrot—as well as in key symbolic elements, such as Val's snakeskin jacket and peacock sleeping curtain in Orpheus Descending. Actual animals—represented either diegetically or mimetically—are also memorably troped in several plays, most famously in Sebastian's soul-shattering vision of the carnage wrought by predatory birds in the Galapagos (Suddenly Last Summer). In two other important plays mimetically represented animals provide powerful theatrical (acoustic) imagery as well as central dramatic symbolism: the howling dogs that chase Val at the end of Orpheus and the trapped reptile that gives its name to Night of the Iguana. The animals in these two cases occupy a potent dramatic margin, an unseen but hyper-audible space resounding with danger, cruelty, and violence. This is precisely the space that The Gnädiges Fräulein attempts to enter and inhabit.

While animals and animal imagery are pervasive in Williams's drama, The Gnädiges Fräulein is unique in the Williams canon for its attempt to confront animality on the far side of metaphor. Literalism is one crucial characteristic of postmodern animalizing, the mark of its refusal of modernism's various (and, as we shall see below, constitutive) tropings of the non-human. Another characteristic of the "postmodern animal," writes the author of a book by that name, is its look: the animal that escapes modernism's metaphorizing power is often "a fractured, awkward, 'wrong,' or wronged thing" (Baker 54). There could hardly be a better description of Williams's Fräulein, whose miserable condition, grotesque appearance, and bizarre history put her almost beyond the human pale. Almost, but not quite. The Fräulein is saved from actually embodying animality by the presence in the play—on stage—of an actual (though neither real nor realistic) animal. The Gnädiges Fräulein is one of surprisingly few plays to include an actual animal in its list of active characters (the two most famous others are Ionesco's Rhinoceros and Shaeffer's Equus, which I discuss below). This is not to say that The Gnädiges Fräulein is a play "about animals." Actually, Williams explicitly contested (and bemoaned) the reading of The Gnädiges Fräulein as "a play about terrible birds," insisting that the real subject was "the tragicomic subject of human existence on this risky planet" (Preface 95). Moreover, the animals in it, though literal, are not real. They are an extravagant and preposterous invention: "vicious, over-grown sea birds" (220) who give their cartoonish name to the Key where the action takes place, Cocaloony Key.

In a production note to the play, Williams says that he thinks of the cocaloony "as a sort of giant pelican." He then goes on—puzzlingly—to share the following information about his compositional process: "in fact, all through the first draft of the play I have typed the word "pelican," scratched it out and written over it "co-caloony" (218). What, one wonders, is the significance of this detail? Might it inflect our understanding of the play's central fiction to know that it had its origins in reality? Does the pelican's metamorphosis into a creature of imagination signal other transformations, possibly in the realm of the human, where something might also be getting "scratched out" and "written over"? It is worth remembering, too, that Williams explicitly connects the monstrous pelican of *The Gnädiges Fräulein* to its counterpart in *The Mutilated,* the play with which William paired this one for a double bill he called *Slapstick Tragedy*. In both plays, it would seem, a figure of grotesque animality is needed to fully explicate Williams's genre-bending vision of human extremity "on this risky planet" (Preface 95).

At the limits of their resources, Williams's protagonists are at risk of devolving into non-human creatures. But the social margin they inhabit, like the little planet to which it clings, is also at risk. The play's vision of extremity extends beyond the human, situating human risk on a continuum that traverses (to use Deleuze and Guattari's term) traditional taxonomies just as readily as his set transgresses the boundaries of realism's living room. The play's challenge to modernism lies in this "traversing," directly challenging modernism's "process of purification" (Lykke 16). Modernism rejected anything that unsettled boundaries, rendering "the world intelligible by eliminating and suppressing inconsistencies, impurities, and dissimilarities" (Baker 99). Modernism assigned all beings to one of two camps, the human and the non-human, denying the continuity between humans and others, be they machines, monsters, or animals. In the rhetoric of modernism "animal" became the *opposite* of human rather than its larger context. In this process, the animal turned into a powerful rhetorical device, a figure of *lack* in relation to the plenitude of human identity. This rigidly oppositional construction makes the animal a potent figure for postmodernism's attack on all binarisms. If modernism insisted on using animals to construct its "humanist politics of norms and identities" (Shildrick 2), the animal now offers itself as a powerful tool for postmodernism's challenge to identity-thinking.

In modernism, as an important theorist of postmodernism puts it, "animals must be made to say they are not animals" (Baudrillard 129). Noting that animals were only "demoted to the status of inhumanity" with the triumph of rationalism and humanism, Baudrillard lists the various new roles in which this progress cast animals. Among these is their role as "beasts of somatization" (133): forced to carry a psychological life entirely invented by—and projected onto them by—humans. Humanism constructs itself by denying that humans are animals too, and modernism follows up by *troping* the animal, putting it to work as a metaphor for the human, and denying it its difference. Modernism's constitutive dualisms rest on a compulsive silencing of the animality around us and within us, wresting preeminence for culture by making nature mute. Lurking beneath all the great narratives of modernism is a great animal silence, born of a programmatic misrecognition.

The "failure" of *The Gnädiges Fräulein*[2] is a function of and a thematization of this very misrecognition. The voices raised in this play are precisely the ones which are excluded by the standards of cultural value on which theatrical success has traditionally rested. To scour the play for the latter values—to read it, for instance, as yet another (autobiographical) portrait of the alienated artist—turns up a judgment of clumsiness, or worse.[3] To refuse such metaphorical readings, however, is to find here an altogether different register of expression, another set of voices.

The voices I hear in *The Gnädiges Fräulein* are not animal voices (animals do not have "voices") but rather human voices in search of and in expression of what Alan Bleakley, following and expanding upon Deleuze and Guattari's notion of "becoming animal," has called "the animalizing imagination." The animalizing imagination is emphatically not a matter of giving animals human form, either physical or psychological. Rather, it is the consequence—and bringing to consciousness—of our own animality, and its forms are not actual animals but psychological animals, of great importance to our sanity and our life in the world.

Besides Deleuze and Guattari, Bleakley is inspired in his formulations by Gaston Bachelard, who proffered the "surprising but delightful notion that imagination creates the natural, as a 'biological dream'" (104). In his reading of Lautreamont's animalized text *Maldrodor*, Bachelard discovered evidence that, contrary to common belief, it is not animals who give their shapes to human visions of the marvelous and the monstrous but just the opposite: when human imagination conjures wonders and marvels, they naturally take the form of animals. "The first function of imagination," says Bachelard, "is to create animal forms" (27). The imagination animalizes. The animalizing imagination, then, is a fundamental aesthetic register, furnished with animal forms, shapes, sounds, smells, sensations, and experiences. It allows and invites a mode of expression in which the human animal can acknowledge its participation in animality, can manifest its own animal nature.

As powerful as it is both prohibited and hence transgressive, this imagination furnishes one of the more progressive and promising resources of postmodernism. The animalizing imagination, like the cyborgian imagination theorized most notably by Donna Haraway, belongs to a consciously post-*humanist* and ecologically invested postmodernism. This, in turn, belongs to a "second moment" or "late stage" of postmodernism, in which, as Hal Foster says, the "highs of the simulacral image" are sacrificed for the "lows of the depressive object" (165). Leaving the surface aesthetics of parody and pastiche, this postmodernism replaces early postmodernism's ironic "fragmenting of bodies and texts" and attempts instead to "imagine differently reconstituted communities and selves" (Wheeler, 74). Among the categories with which the new selves and communities are reconstituted are (non-human) animals and species. It is as a manifestation of this discourse that I propose to read *The Gnädiges Fräulein*, arguing also that this "biocentric," posthumanist, stream of postmodernism might provide an as good if not better aesthetic framework for re-evaluating Williams's late plays than even those counter-realisms—expressionism, absurdism, surrealism, etc.—to which these plays resonate so powerfully.

Fig. 2. Broadway premiere at the Longacre Theatre, 22 February 1966, with Zoe Caldwell as Polly, Kate Reid as Molly, and Art Ostrin as the Cocaloony. Photo by Friedman-Abeles. Courtesy of the New York Public Library.

If such a thing as an aesthetic of awkwardness could be said to exist, *The Gnädiges Fräulein* would be its exemplar. Awkwardness permeates the play, systematically distancing it from the accomplished aesthetics of modernism and the purist norms of humanism. This awkwardness is given its fullest representation in the figure of the cocaloony bird, "stalking jerkily about, poking its gruesome head this way and that with spastic motions" (234). In both appearance (see figure 2) and expression, the cocaloony is awkward, in expression literally so, since its "discourse" (no other word will do, yet no other word is more ironic in this context) consists of the single word "AWK!" Taken up and repeated in various tones by the human characters, this "word" is the play's hymn to the animal. Why this animal needs to be so ugly and its hymn so dissonant[4] has to do with its postmodernity.

Williams's bird belongs to that category of postmodern animal art that Baker calls "botched taxidermies," works like John Isaacs's dodo, which use effects of tattiness, messiness, bungling, and deliberate imperfection to draw attention to modernity's "botched" relationship to the non-human world. Like the grotesque bird Williams invented for his play (Figure 2), Isaacs's dodo captures the final moments of a long misapprehension of animals by human beings. At the extreme point of its relationship to human beings, at the point, indeed, of giving up on the thankless task of trying to engage human beings in a genuine sharing of the world, these animals attain their most vivid, most powerful, and most tragic expressivity. Like the cocalooney's tragedy, the dodo's is "slapstick" as well, a matter of jerky movements and ineffective flappings (Isaacs's sculpture incorporates a motor scavenged from a washing-machine) that allows movement but no flight. In these works, awkwardness becomes a strategy for lifting the modernist repression of animality: "tattiness, imperfection, and botched form . . . render the animals *abrasively visible,* and they do so regardless of how the artist thinks about animals" (Baker 62). The last point is especially important. The expression of animality requires strategies that circumvent the artist's unwitting participation in modernity's repression. The postmodern animal must emerge *"regardless of how the artist thinks about animals,"* and awkwardness marks the independence of the postmodern animal from its human frames, its ideological "cages." Thus the cocaloony's "AWK!" has something of the *negative communicative power* that Jacques Derrida seeks in his recent "zoo-auto-bio-biblio-graphy," *L'animal donc je suis.* To invoke animals without falling prey to the rhetorical abuses with which animals have been entrapped within human discourse, Derrida invents the punning neologism *"animot."* This "awkward living word-thing" (Baker, 74) is needed to escape from modernism's trap of subjectivity, yet that same trap prevents one from defining the term other than negatively: the *animot* is *"ni une espece, ni un genre, ni un individu"* (292).

Neither species, nor genre, nor individual, the Derridean *animot* relates to the Deleuzian notion of "becoming-animal" (*"devenir-animal"*). Originally formulated by French philosophers Deleuze and Guattari in a study of Kafka (1975), the concept was later elaborated as part of a vast program of "anti-oedipal" "becomings" (including "becoming-minoritarian, becoming-woman, becoming-molecular and becoming-imperceptible" [Baker 103]). The Deleuzian becoming-animal consists of a "deterritorialization," an escape from the human which is "proposed" by the animal and which can defeat the tyrannies of individual subjectivity and exclusivist human identity upon which modernism stakes its claims. The state of becoming-animal is a state of flux, uncertainty, openness, and experimentation. It counters the forces that Deleuze and Guattari call "Oedipalization": the forces of control, conformity, meaning, interpretation. Becoming-animal occurs outside of metaphor, allegory, imitation, or fantasy: it is "a human being's creative opportunity to think themselves other-than-in-identity" (Baker 125).

The first description of the cocaloonies makes it clear not only that they are inventions, but that they will not escape the fate that Baudrillard diagnosed for animals in modernism—to be captured for symbolization: "they flap and waddle out to the boat with their beaks wide open on their elastic gullets to catch the throwaway fish, the discards, the re-jecks, because, y'see—tell it not in Gath!—the once-self-reliant-and-self-sufficient character of this southernmost sea-bird has degenerated to where it could be justly described as a parasitical creature, yes, gone are the days it would condescend to fish for itself . . ." (220). Parasitical and nearly paralytic, the cocaloonies are a grotesque version of the romantic denizens of many modernist bohemias, best exemplified perhaps in O'Neill's *Iceman*. In this play, however, that kind of milieu, represented by "the big dormitory," is utterly transformed in effect and in meaning by the *actual* presence within it of actual animals. The animal clamor that fills the skies above Cocaloony Key, and the animal forms and features that increasingly appear among and upon its human inhabitants suggest a new framework for understanding human life "on the edge." This framework depends on acknowledging the *continuity* between animal and human nature, of thinking of humans as animals, and of animals (as some recent ecologists have insisted) not with the discounting phrase "non-human" but as *"other-than-human."*

The other-than-human (and, for that matter, the "other-than-pelican"!) makes *The Gnädiges Fräulein* not a play "about animals" but rather an "animalized" play, a play that has anticipated Deleuze and Guattari's notion of "becoming-animal" as a mode of aesthetic expression. In *The Gnädiges Fräulein,* Williams manages to clear a rare dramatic space within which to explore and express the human experience of animality *in and of itself,* not as a metaphor for something else but as an extreme condition of humanity. This level of the play—always ignored—is to be found not only in the miserable present condition of the Fräulien, but also in her remarkable history. The unusual skill she displays in competing with the cocaloonies in their scavenging for fish has an amazing origin. The Fräulein, it appears, once worked as the stage assistant to an animal trainer, helping him show off his trained seal. Then, one day, the Fräulein did something extraordinary. As told to Polly by Molly, drum rolls and all, it is worth quoting in full:

> [Drum.] Scene: a matinee at the Royal Haymarket in London? Benefit performance? Before crowned heads of Europe? . . . *The Gnädiges Fräulein!*—The splendor, the glory of the occasion, turned her head just a bit. She overextended herself, she wasn't content that day just to do a toe dance to music while bearing the paraphernalia back and forth between the seal and the trainer, the various props, the silver batons and medicine ball that the seal balanced on the tip of his schnozzola. Oh, no, that didn't content her. She had to build up her bit. She suddenly felt a need to compete for attention with the trained seal and trained seal's trainer. . . . Now then . . . the climax of the performance. [*Drum.*] The seal has just performed his most famous trick, and is balancing two silver batons and two gilded medicine balls on the tip of his whiskery schnozzle while applauding himself. [*Drum.*] Now, then. The big switcheroo, the surprising gimmick. The trained seal trainer throws the trained seal a fish. What happens? It's intercepted. Who by? *The Gnädiges Fräulein.* NO HANDS. [She imitates the seal.] She catches the fish in her choppers! [Drum.] Polly, it brought down the house! (256)

Perhaps this play merits its putative genre of "slapstick tragedy"; there is a destiny at work here, however grotesque. Things do come full circle, however absurdly. The Fräulein's current method of survival—*acting the animal*—is actually the final stage of a process that began during *an animal act*.

Animal acts occupy a particularly overdetermined position in the human relationship to animals and, in particular, to the kind of rethinking of that relationship initiated by Deleuze and Guattari and now taken up by others. The animal act appears at first glance to be an instance of human beings *appreciating* animals, gathering to marvel at and celebrate their powers. On closer inspection, however, the occasion seems rather to be one of human beings gathering to collectively mark animals *as inferiors*—that is, as creatures capable only of the most superficial mimicry of human skills. Though individual animal acts encode specific attitudes from the vast array of attitudes through which human beings manage their relationships with animals,[5] the fundamental principle of all animal acts is a performance of the superiority of culture over nature. The animal act, in short, is one of the (paradoxical) ways in which human beings distinguish themselves as uniquely creative creatures, capable of play and display of a kind that animals can only imitate, clumsily and hilariously. By forcing animals to perform as quasi-humans, the animal act actually stages the animal's otherness, its "bestiality." In the animal act, the work of mimesis is to mark the animal's ontological distance from the human. As such, the animal act is an ideal site for performing the constitutive fiction of humanism, the fiction that humans are not animals.

When the Fräulein disrupted the animal act (a disruption already prepared by Williams, I think, in the unlikely claim that such an act was being presented to the "crowned heads of Europe"), she was intervening in something rather more significant than a successful sideshow. She was initiating a transgression to protest against the injustice of her decline from success, youth, and beauty. Shorn of dignity and hope within the established social terms of her milieu, she resorted to animalizing. The Fräulein's impulsive and outrageous reaction to her social marginalization was, we learn, the first step in a process—an alarmingly logical process—that has ended up in a life on the very margins of humanity. When the Fräulein disrupted the animal act, she was indexing the transgressive awkwardness that she now inhabits.

For all its bizarre inventions and grotesque images, nothing makes this play more original than the fact that its exploration of "becoming-animal" is narrativitized, recognized, and explored *as an autonomous process.* The point I want to make here can perhaps be made most clearly by comparing *The Gnädiges Fräulein* to two other well-known modern plays: Eugene Ionesco's *Rhinoceros,* and Peter Shaeffer's *Equus.* Both plays centrally involve what we might call (invoking Bottom, that early figure of animal-becoming in drama) a "translation." But only *Equus* can be said to exemplify to any degree the Deleuzian concept we are pursuing here. *Rhinoceros,* with its troping of the rhinoceroses (as cowards, conformists, fascists, or all of the above) is the antithesis of "becoming-animal"; in it, animals are one-dimensional signifiers whose value is exhausted by whatever reflection they can supply for certain loathsome human traits. By contrast, both *Equus* and *The Gnädiges Fräulein* offer a more "biocentric" perspective: the animal nature of the animals is more important than their human qualities, and the human characters discover and confront this otherness in the course of a long and painful process. In *Equus,* however, the animalizing potential of the horse, although it is experienced by the boy, is, for the audience, contained and limited by the authoritative discourse of the psychiatrist, Dr. Dysart. While he does not reduce the animal to a small set of human meanings (as Ionesco does), Shaeffer nevertheless does not allow the meaning of the horse to appear (or not appear) from the act of becoming-animal itself. The psychiatrist, true to his trade, supplies symbols and interpretations, thereby curtailing that full-scale "traversing" and "sweeping away" of human beings that distinguishes the Deleuzian "becoming-animal."

The world of *The Gnädiges Fräulein* is conspicuously devoid of any authoritative discourse. Indeed the play's characters all suffer various degrees of grotesque discursive failure: Molly and Polly frequently lose their "concentration," breaking off many topics in mid-sentence. The Fräulein herself communicates only by reciting memorized program notes and song titles from her soubrette days, and her most memorable utterance is an elongated "AHHHHHHHHHH!"—"expressing," Molly explains oxymoronically, "the inexpressible regret of all her regrets" (248). The play's only other "speaking characters" are Indian Joe and the Cocaloony Bird, both of whom restrict themselves to monosyllables like "How," "Pow," "Wow," "Ugh," and "Awk." Of course Molly and Polly, as their twinned names suggest, are loquacious, parrotty creatures, but their theories about the strange goings on of the humans and animals around them lack authority or eloquence (asked why the Fräulein uses a lorgnon even after the cocaloonies have gouged out both her eyes, Molly proclaims: "Habit! Habit! Now do you get the point?" [247]).

With no one in the play capable of successfully capturing the animal for symbolization (as Ionesco did the rhinoceros and Dysart the horse), a space is cleared for a different kind of literary animalizing, "affecting the animal" as Deleuze and Guattari say, "no less than the human" (237). *The Gnädiges Fräulein* is "traversed" by animality, as is the Fräulein herself. Having allowed herself that one desperate act of animality in the past, the Fräulein now performs it routinely, as a very means of survival. While once it was impulsive, extraordinary, and spectacular, her becoming-animal is now necessary and quotidian. Flapping her arms like wings as she dashes offstage to battle the cocaloonies, the Fräulein is a figure of the animalizing imagination, journeying into otherness. She returns, shaman-like, from the wilderness, bringing nourishment for all. The play ends, astonishingly, with a feast, a ritual incorporation that "invites a participatory animality as emotional response" (Bleakley xii). The invitation is accepted: the other characters are "swept away" (as Deleuze and Guattari say): Molly moos like a cow, Polly awks, and Indian Joe struts like a cocaloony. The slapstick tragedy ends not with death or defeat but with perseverance. Though blood-soaked and blinded, the Fräulein keeps flapping her skinny arms like wings, awkwardly performing the awkwardness of survival on "this risky planet."

Notes

1. This essay is dedicated to the memory of Linda Dorff, passionate Williams scholar and treasured friend, and to her beloved bird, Popcorn.
2. The original production closed after seven performances to terrible reviews and hostile audience response. (Schneider, 370). Martin Denton estimates that the play has received no more than twenty New York performances since it was written (quoted in Kolin, 2).
3. Richard Gilman called the play a "witless arbitrary farce," and John McCarten said it was "spectacularly undisciplined" and "too outlandishly horrible to be tolerated" (quoted in Kolin, 2).
4. The play begins with the sound of " a loud swoosh above . . ." after which a character says: : "Was that two cocaloony birds that flew over or was it just one cocaloony bird that made a U-turn and flew back over again. OOPS! Birdwatchers, watch those birds! They're very dangerous birds if agitated and they sure do seem agitated today!" Throughout the play, characters have to periodically crouch down as the birds "swoosh" overhead, and the Fräulein's many entrances from the direction of the docks are accompanied by "terrific flapping and whistling noises" (243). A reviewer of the first production wrote that the "whistling, whooshing, cackling flight" of the cocaloony birds sounded "like a half-spent rocket dragging a loosely screwed wooden caboose along neglected tracks (Nadel 30).
5. For an illuminating analysis of the complex ideological agendas underlying animal acts, see, for example, Elizabeth A. Lawrence's essay on rodeo (in Willis).

Works Cited

Baker, Steve. *The Postmodern Animal*. London: Reaktion Books, 2000.

Bachelard, Gaston. *Lautreamont*. Dallas: The Dallas Institute Publications, 1986.

Baudrillard, Jean. *Simulacra and Simulation*. Michigan: The University of Michigan Press, 1994.

Bleakley, Alan. *The Animalizing Imagination*. London and New York: Macmillan Press and St. Martin's Press, 2000.

Deleuze, Gilles, and Guattari, Felix. *A Thousand Plateaus: Capitalism and Schizophrenia*. Trans. Brian Massumi. Minneapolis: University of Minnesota Press, 1987.

Degrazia, David. *Taking Animals Seriously: Mental Life and Moral Status*. Cambridge: Cambridge UP, 1996.

Derrida, Jacques. "L'animal que donc je suis (a suivre)." *L'Animal autobiographique: Autour de Jacques Derrida*. Ed. M.-L. Mallet. Paris: Galilee, 1999.

Dorff, Linda. "Theatricalist Cartoons: Tennessee Williams's Late 'Outrageous' Plays." *The Tennessee Williams Annual Review* 2 (1999): 13–34.

Foster, Hal. *The Return of the Real: The Avant-Garde at the End of the Century*. Cambridge: MIT Press, 1996.

Kolin, Philip. "a play about terrible birds: Tennessee Williams's *The Gnädiges Fräulein* and Afred Hitchcock's *The Birds*." *South Atlantic Review* (Winter 2001): 1–22.

Lawrence, Elizabeth A. "Rodeo Horses: The Wild and the Tame," in Willis, R., ed. *Signifying Animals*. London: Unwin Hyman, 1990.

Lykke, Nina. "Between Monsters, Goddesses, and Cyborgs: Feminist Confrontations with Science," in *Between Monsters, Goddesses, and Cyborgs: Feminist Confrontations with Science, Medicine, and Cyberspace*, eds. Nina Lykke and Rosi Braidotti. London: Zed Books, 1996.

Midgely, Mary. *Beast and Man: The Roots of Human Nature*. Ithaca: Cornell UP, 1978.

Nadel, Norman. "Bizarre, Grim 'Slapstick Tragedy.'" *New York World Telegram* 23 (Feb 1966): 30.

Phillips, Adam. *Terrors and Experts*. Cambridge, Mass: Harvard UP, 1996.

Schneider, Alan. *Entrances: An American Director's Journey*. New York: Viking, 1986.

Shildrick, Margrit. "Posthumanism and the Monstrous Body," *Body and Society*, 11/1 (1996).

Williams, Raymond. *The Politics of Modernism*. London: Verso, 1989

Williams, Tennessee. *The Gnädiges Fräulein. Dragon Country: A Book of Plays*. New York: New Directions, 1970. 215–62.

Willis, Roy. Ed. *Signifying Animals*. London: Unwin Hyman, 1990

Wheeler, Wendy. *A New Modernity? Change in Science, Literature, and Politics*. London: Lawrence and Wishart, 1999

Gene D. Phillips, S.J.

TENNESSEE WILLIAMS'S FORGOTTEN FILM: *THE LAST OF THE MOBILE HOT-SHOTS* AS A SCREEN VERSION OF *THE SEVEN DESCENTS OF MYRTLE*

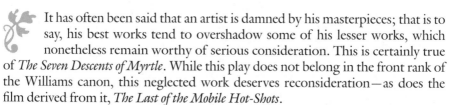 It has often been said that an artist is damned by his masterpieces; that is to say, his best works tend to overshadow some of his lesser works, which nonetheless remain worthy of serious consideration. This is certainly true of *The Seven Descents of Myrtle*. While this play does not belong in the front rank of the Williams canon, this neglected work deserves reconsideration—as does the film derived from it, *The Last of the Mobile Hot-Shots*.

The Seven Descents of Myrtle began its artistic life as a short story, "Kingdom of Earth." Williams wanted to retain the title for the play until producer David Merrick prevailed upon him to change the title to *The Seven Descents of Myrtle* for the Broadway production.

The short story, like the eventual play, centers on Chicken, a brawny manual laborer who deeply resents that the old family homestead has passed to his half-brother Lot. Lot is a legitimate descendant of their father while Chicken is not. To Chicken's great chagrin, Lot brings home a buxom ex-showgirl and part-time whore named Myrtle as his new wife. Chicken had counted on inheriting the property as soon as his gravely ill half-brother died of tuberculosis, and now it appears that everything will go to the eleventh-hour widow.

Lot's marriage proves to be no obstacle, however, since Myrtle succumbs to Chicken's animal magnetism on the very same night that the frail Lot succumbs to T.B. So Chicken gets Lot's land and his wife, too. Having long ago discarded any aspirations for attaining the Kingdom of Heaven, Chicken is willing to settle for inheriting the Kingdom of Earth.

Tennessee Williams and Herbert Machiz, stage director.

The Seven Descents of Myrtle inherited not only the basic situation of the short story—embellished, of course, with more material to make a longer play—but also much of Chicken's philosophy about contenting one's self with earthly rather than heavenly salvation. But there are some significant differences between the short story and the play. For example, in the short story, Chicken is erroneously thought to have been the child of his father and a black mistress; in the play there is no doubt that this is the case. Another difference between the story and the stage play is that in the latter, Lot is a transvestite homosexual with a deeply rooted Oedipal complex, as well as a consumptive.

These new facets of Lot's personality intensify the already strong contrast between the two half-brothers: Chicken is the lusty, resourceful heterosexual stud, and Lot is the impotent, ineffectual homosexual. Chicken, we learn, earned his nickname because once during a flood he subsisted on the roof of the house by biting the heads off chickens and drinking their blood. Lot, on the other hand, is not capable of such survival tactics and is coughing up what little blood he has left in his disease-ridden body, which, in turn, symbolizes the weakness of his neurotic psyche as well.

Myrtle and Lot arrive at the old homestead just as a flood warning is being issued. Even the dull-witted Myrtle quickly surveys the lay of the land and realizes that her new husband married her for the sole purpose of following his dead mother's orders to keep the socially unacceptable Chicken from coming into his own. The whole situation has a biblical tinge, starting with the concept of the two half-brothers contending like Jacob and Esau over their birthright and continuing on to the Deluge which, in the framework of the Old Testament, will, one hopes, cleanse this little patch of earth and its inhabitants. When Lot dies clad in his mother's finery, it is clear that not the meek but the strong will inherit the earth but, in this case, justifiably so.

Lot and Myrtle take up residence in his mother's room, and as his life ebbs away he seeks solace in his memories of her by systematically transforming himself into her and ultimately relinquishing his own identity entirely. By play's end he has doffed his own identity and donned hers along with her clothes and mannerisms. Lot dies wearing one of his mother's faded frocks, a symbol of a bygone past; like his mother, Lot has become a prisoner of the past, totally out of tune with the present.

It is no surprise that in the course of the play Myrtle periodically liberates herself from the suffocating insulation of the elegant bedroom which she shares with her increasingly remote husband (Lot's Kingdom of Heaven) and goes down to the kitchen to talk to the more vital Chicken (Chicken's Kingdom of Earth). Myrtle is the only character who moves freely between the territories that the two half-brothers have staked out for themselves: from the chilly and ultra-refined bedroom with its decorative fringes and ornate brass bed, where Lot withdraws more and more into his fantasies of the past, to the warm and homey kitchen, where Chicken busies himself with practical exigencies of the present.

Inevitably, Myrtle's attention to Chicken's vitality and virility and corresponding revulsion to Lot's languor and effeminacy escalate into a sexual interest in her half brother-in-law. Indeed, the playgoer can detect quite early on that to Lot, Myrtle can only be a coddling mother, nursing him in his last illness, while to Chicken there is hope that she can be a real wife.

Indoors the two men are rivals for the property and for Myrtle while outdoors a flood is threatening the area. At the finale Chicken exhumes the family skeleton and acknowledges that he is not only a bastard but that he was the child of his father and a black mistress. With that, as one critic put it, Lot, the levee, and the play simultaneously collapse.

Withal, Chicken sees in the durable Myrtle a survivor like himself, since she has come through several scrapes in the course of her checkered career as one of the four members of a combo called the Mobile Hot-Shots. She is the only one of the girls still alive, the others having become victims of sex crimes, drugs, or suicide. Myrtle has kept her head above water through the vagaries of her sordid experiences, and there is every reason to believe as the curtain descends that with Chicken's help she can continue to do so, not only as they prepare to climb atop the roof of the house to wait out the Deluge but in the face of whatever catastrophe, personal or public, they may have to face in the future.

Having finished writing this play about survival, Williams now had to face fire and flood in the form of mounting the production for the New York theater. The cast consisted of Estelle Parsons (Myrtle), Brian Bedford (Lot), and Harry Guardino (Chicken). When the play opened on March 27, 1968, most of the critical fraternity thought it a predictable encounter among three superficial characters, and it ran for only 29 performances.

On the contrary, *The Seven Descents of Myrtle* is a rather delightful minor work of Williams, an unpretentious three-character play conceived on a small scale which works on that level for those who are willing to accept it for what it is and not expect it to be a fully orchestrated large-scale work. It is true that we have seen Williams's shy, neurotic homosexual, his good-hearted whore, and his self-assured stud before, but never have they been mingled in such a lighthearted, heady brew—despite the darker corners of the human psyche into which the play at times intrudes. Myrtle's witless attempt to seduce Chicken into giving up his inheritance claims by donning her gaudy Hot-Shot costume as if she were some sophisticated *femme fatale* working her wiles on a country bumpkin, is worth the price of admission or a re-reading of the play.

For his part, Williams always thought of the play as fundamentally a comedy and refers to it in his autobiography as "my funny melodrama" (40). He consequently suspected that many critics and playgoers alike erred in taking the whole thing much too seriously. When Warner Brothers purchased the film rights, he looked to the movie version as a second chance to launch his work and this time properly. The motion picture adaptation, rechristened *The Last of the Mobile Hot-Shots,* seemed particularly promising because several individuals associated with other Williams films were participating in the venture. The director was Sidney Lumet, who directed *Orpheus Descending;* the screenwriter was Gore Vidal, who had written the screenplay for *Suddenly Last Summer;* and the cinematographer was James Wong Howe, who photographed *The Rose Tattoo,* for which he won an Academy Award.

A major casting decision was choosing a black actor, Robert Hooks, to play Chicken in the film, rather than a white, as on the stage. *Variety* observed that Harry Guardino took the part of Chicken on the stage, "thus providing a surprise story element when it was revealed that the scorned half-brother was really black." In the movie, however, "even that angle has been snuffed out" by having Chicken played by a black actor. On the contrary, Harry Guardino, a hefty Italian type, was totally miscast as the half-breed, half-brother in the Broadway production, whereas Robert Hooks's performance is far more believable in the film. The story concerns the confrontation between a Negro and his poor white trash half-brother, after all, and how the girl gets caught in the middle between them while they are trying to make mutual adjustments that go beyond the color bar.

James Coburn agreed to play Lot, named Jeb in the movie (after some initial hesitation about tarnishing his screen image as the masculine hero of some super-spy flicks like *Our Man Flint*) because he liked Gore Vidal's adaptation. "Gore Vidal has kept all the good things in Tennessee's play and improved on the bad," he baldly stated to Rex Reed. Williams did not agree. As he remarked to this writer, "Gore Vidal wrote the script, he said, out of friendship for me. With friends like that . . ."[1] Coburn refused to play Jeb as a transvestite because, he said, he drew the line at playing someone quite so weird: "I'm making him impotent, but not a transvestite. This way he has more significance."

It is difficult to see how Jeb gains more significance by canceling the transvestite dimension of his personality. Actually the reverse is true. In the play Lot's attachment to the decaying mansion is rooted in neurotic identification with his mother, an identification that leads him at first to want to preserve what is left of the tattered elegance of the old Southern mansion so dear to her, then to assume her clothing, and with that, finally, her personality. By removing this Oedipal content from Jeb's character in the movie, his desire to hold onto the plantation becomes much less frantic and pathetic.

Instead of Jeb donning his mother's dress in the movie, he has Myrtle wear one of his mother's Mardi Gras gowns while he puts on a Confederate officer's jacket. But the effect is ludicrous in the film whereas in the play it is sad that Lot is driven to masquerade in his mother's clothing for reasons much darker and deeper than mere nostalgia for an era that is gone with the wind—which seems to be his sole motive in the movie. The Jeb character, as Williams conceived him, is both psychologically and physically weak, a wretched individual whose psyche is being devoured by his obsessions as surely as his body is being eaten away by disease. (One might say that the Jeb character in the play begins by enjoying his fantasies and ends with his fantasies enjoying him.) Jeb is therefore less complex and less interesting in the film and has less "significance," to use Coburn's term.

Of course Jeb is still impotent in the movie, as Coburn pointed out in his interview during shooting, and this malady is still indicative of his inability to be productive in any way. Unlike Chicken, Jeb has no interest in cultivating the fruit-ful farm land attached to the plantation but is preoccupied with refurbishing the ramshackle house "to look just the way it did in 1840!" As a radically empty human being, he will never be capable of siring a son to inherit the plantation any more than he will be resourceful enough to carry out his plans to restore the dilapidated domicile to the former glories of its antebellum splendor.

There is some hint in the movie that Jeb cherishes Oedipal feelings toward his dead mother, for there are several fragmented flashbacks shot in slow motion which punctuate the film, depicting his mother in the same ball gown that Jeb had Myrtle try on. At first his mother is seen far off, walking through a meadow. Each time the brief flashback is repeated, she advances a little closer to the camera. The last time she appears, the shots of her are intercut with those of a black servant woman suckling a white baby in the kitchen of the mansion, and Jeb's mother is seen to turn her back and walk away in the opposite direction.

What these images portend is anybody's guess, but the intention of the direc-tor might be to imply that Jeb found his mother a remote and domineering woman, who turned him over to a servant for the nurturing and maternal care which she should have given him, and in so doing denied him the maternal love for which he still thirsts—and which he now looks to Myrtle as his mother figure to provide for him.

Another set of fragmented flashbacks, also shot in slow motion and scattered through the film, are designed to portray how Jeb's impotence made him jealous of his half-brother Chicken and precipitated the rift between them that is perpetu-ated in their rivalry for the family inheritance. Jeb and Chicken are seen as enlisted men frolicking with a variety of camp followers in these flashbacks; in the last one of this series, the camera shows a garish peroxide blond astride Chicken on a rum-pled brothel bed. As she turns round and bursts into derisive laughter, the camera pulls back to show Jeb, standing nearby wrapped in a sheet and painfully, shame-fully looking at the pair. His impotence has reduced him to voyeurism and self-hatred as well as to sexual jealousy of Chicken, one infers. It seems too that accord-ing to this set of flashbacks, he has married Myrtle, a voluptuous hooker like the ones which he had known in the army, with the conscious hope that such a super sex object could stimulate him to producing an heir—though subconsciously, ac-cording to the other group of flashbacks, he really chooses Myrtle to mother *him,* not any child that they might have.

These two sets of flashbacks, which are shattered like so many pieces of a broken mirror in the film, are intended to give some hints to the sources of Jeb's unhappy childhood and youth, once the viewer has assembled them into some kind of meaningful coherence. But even after doing so, the average moviegoer would not have anything more than murky insinuations about the nature of Jeb's physical and psychological problems. *Variety* complained that the flashbacks are filmed with "tinted film stock and slow motion," just so that nobody misses the fact that they are flashbacks; the reviewer added that this "repeated gimmick . . . is clubbed to death."

By contrast the straightforward presentation of Lot in the play as a transvestite homosexual, who has never had any sexual interest in the female of the species at all beyond fathering an heir to beat his half-brother out of the family property, is much more satisfactory than the hazy and elliptical delineation of his character in the movie. In short, Coburn should either have consented to playing the Jeb character as it was developed in the play or let someone else play the part.

At any rate, Chicken's big revelation to Jeb at the end is that he is the bastard son, not of their father as in the play but of their mother. During one of the previous floods, it seems she was sequestered on the roof of the house with the black handyman; and that situation was the occasion of the conception of Chicken. Changing the erring parent from the father in the play to the mother in the film makes Jeb all the more miserable when he learns that his adored mother was guilty of infidelity. Otherwise, making his mother rather than his father, the adulterous party, does not change the outcome of the story; it is pellucid from the beginning of the film that the sickly, impotent Jeb will never be able to rise to the occasion of generating an heir, especially once Myrtle starts consorting with Chicken. In the end, Jeb has a final fit, coughs up blood, and dies.

In the last analysis, the film has some definite merits, beginning with the direct presentation and expansion of Myrtle's long expository speech in the play of how she came to marry such an unlikely bridegroom as Jeb, and it is hilarious. During the credit sequence Jeb is seen hitting the sidewalk as he is tossed out of a bar. He reels into the packaged liquor store next door to the bar and comes out with a six pack of beer, which he consumes while wandering aimlessly into the waiting line for a daytime TV show. He is standing just behind Myrtle and becomes her partner in a volleyball game on stage (on a mud court, no less!) which will determine the couples competing for the chance to be married on the air the following week. Jeb and Myrtle win and he agrees to wed her on the show because, as we learn later, he realized that this was his last chance to provide himself with a son and heir.

As the last credits are superimposed on the screen, Myrtle, decked out in a mini-skirted bridal dress, marries Jeb on TV, and the prologue draws to a close. Myrtle is still sporting her incongruous wedding outfit as they partake of their wedding breakfast at a drive-in before setting off for Jeb's family home with all of the electrical appliances which the TV station gave them as prizes. These gadgets will be as out of place in the backwoods of Alabama as Myrtle herself will be until she becomes acclimated to her new home, more through the auspices of Chicken than of her husband.

Once arrived at the plantation, called Waverly in the film, the script settles down to playing out the rivalry between Jeb and Chicken within the confines of the circumscribed setting dictated by the logic of the play. The two men are isolated from the world by the remote location of the estate and isolated from each other by occupying their respective turfs within the house: Jeb in his mother's bedroom upstairs and Chicken in the kitchen downstairs, with only Myrtle to mediate between them.

Because the decayed plantation house is the key setting for the entire film, most of the movie was shot on location in just such a rotting house near Baton Rouge in the swampland of Louisiana, which helps immensely to create an authentic atmosphere for the story. Furthermore, the three characters marooned in the broken-down house are photographed at times in confined spaces like the bedroom or kitchen; as Frank Cunningham notes, these "images of enclosure" imply that they are imprisoned together and must confront each other at close quarters in order to cope with their conflicts.

The final shot of Chicken and Myrtle atop the roof of the house, clinging to the chimney as the flood waters rise round them, symbolizes the union of races as the pair face the future together. This spacious shot, Cunningham comments, "discloses Myrtle and Chicken's tentative safety" and implies that they must stick together to survive (242). These visual images are marks of Lumet's craftsmanship.

Among the other merits of the film are the visual touches by which he telegraphs information to the audience without resorting to dialogue. We know, for example, that Myrtle is a frivolous young woman who avoids facing the unpleasant side of reality when, during the long ride to Waverly, she quickly shuts off the car radio report of flood warnings for the very area to which they are traveling. That Jeb is no more realistic than she is, moreover, is suggested by his wearing tinted glasses as he drives along telling Myrtle about his romantic plans for restoring Waverly. He obviously prefers to see the world from behind rose-colored glasses which soften the harsh realities of the present for him so that he can more easily bask in his reveries of the past.

In contrast to Jeb's rosy picture of Waverly are the realistic shots of the estate which Lumet uses as an ironic comment on what Jeb has been saying. The viewer is introduced to Waverly by a close-up of a weather-beaten sign which looks as if it will collapse at any moment, signaling the disrepair of the house and grounds that Jeb hopes to restore to their appearance in 1840. Later the tarnished chandelier is photographed through a cracked mirror to indicate the gap between the rundown state of Waverly and the way that Jeb prefers to think that things are or, at least, can be. The deteriorating mansion, with the help of these images, becomes symbolic of Jeb's own disintegrating life.

The Last of the Mobile Hot-Shots is a finely crafted and well-acted motion picture, and while one does not deny its definite drawbacks, one still can only speculate why it ranks as a critical and commercial failure, despite the credentials of the original author, scriptwriter, director, photographer, and stars, and the fact that it was made by a major studio. Warner Brothers gave the film only token distribution after the poor critical and box office reception of its premiere engagement in New York in 1970. Because the film industry's censor and his advisory board gave the movie an X-rating, it was then relegated to the grind circuit, to play in soft-core porno houses and finally be shelved by the studio, which never sold it to television. It seems, then, that the combination of poor notices and an X-rating (which misled many moviegoers in those days into assuming that it was a trashy film) conspired to label *Hot-Shots* as box office poison. *Time* did not help matters by calling the film "not so much a version as a perversion" of Williams's play though the reviewer was correct in criticizing the cumbersome plot line of the movie as a strain on the average filmgoer's patience (167).

The basis of the X-rating (persons under 17 not admitted) was primarily the scene in which Chicken seduces a very willing Myrtle. The film follows the play's stage directions (692) in having Chicken perched on the kitchen table directly in front of Myrtle, who is sitting in a chair close to him; at this point the scene fades out. This suggestion of fellatio is just that: something to be inferred by a perceptive adult viewer and is in no way blatantly stated. The consequent X-rating accorded to the movie seems unduly harsh, therefore, particularly in the light of the kind of adult material which soon became acceptable in the R category (persons under seventeen must be accompanied by an adult), as the rating system—which was less than a year old when *Hot-Shots* opened—continued to evolve. Because the censor tended to be less stringent as time went on, the film's X was changed to a more benign R when the film was finally released on videocassette in 1994.[2] It is obvious from a comparison of the original release print of the movie (available at the Library of Congress) with the videotape of the film that the picture received an R rating without any alterations in the movie.

At first glance the project seemed well suited to Lumet. Louis Giannetti and Scott Eyman describe the typical Lumet film as one in which "a group of characters come together," who are usually caught "in a vortex of events they can neither understand nor control" but which they must nevertheless resolve. "Nearly all of the characters in Lumet's gallery are driven by obsessions or passions," they continue; "the protagonists, as a result of their complex fixations, are lonely, often disillusioned individuals" (298–90). This description in various ways fits all three of the principal characters in *The Last of the Mobile Hot-Shots*, while the authors' concluding remark surely applies to Jeb in particular: "Lumet's most emotional characters present a grim vision of idealists broken by realities."

Since Lumet seemed to have an affinity for the material, why did he not produce a better film? Asked this question, Gore Vidal replied in correspondence, "*The Last of the Mobile Hot-Shots* was fine in rehearsal, but Sidney Lumet hates and misunderstands humor. The camera was always a mile away during key dialogue scenes. Lynn Redgrave was not understandable, but it was not her fault. 'More terror!' he kept saying." Lynn Redgrave's southern accent was not comprehensible at times as Vidal notes; it seemed, as *Time* put it, to be a mixture of two Birminghams: Alabama's and England's. And Lumet's insistence that she often speak her lines several decibels louder than what was called for was a further drawback for the English actress. Indeed, *Variety* dismissed her delivery of her lines as "caterwauling."

Giannetti and Eyman astutely point out that "Lumet's casts are not always compatible in terms of acting styles, particularly when he mixes American and British . . . actors in the same movie," as he did in the present film. "Individual performances may be fine in their own right, but they sometimes fail to mesh with the

Lynn Redgrave in *Last of the Mobile Hot-Shots*.

others, fail to elide into an ensemble effect. This problem occurs in such movies" as *The Last of the Mobile Hot-Shots* and other films.

As far as Lumet's attempts to elicit terror from her, which Vidal also mentions, he apparently wanted to give the impression that there is a real possibility of Chicken abandoning her with her dying husband to the flood waters when the levee finally gives way and that Myrtle and the audience should both find this a real source of terror. But actually it is obvious from the development of Chicken's personality in the course of the story that he is only toying with Myrtle when he playfully threatens her in this manner, and even if she takes him seriously, the audience should not.

Lumet's too-literal interpretation of this facet of the story lends support to Vidal's contention that comedy is not this director's forte. In an interview with Guy Flatley which Lumet gave after making *Hot-Shots,* the director confessed that he felt unsure of himself in dealing with comedy and pointed to a film he made the year before *Hot-Shots* called *Bye, Bye Braverman.* That movie centered on four friends reminiscing about a deceased buddy and had the same serio-comic flavor as *Hot-Shots. Braverman,* Lumet recalled, was an instance of how he tends to flounder when working with this kind of material. *Bye, Bye Braverman,* he said, "went off just enough to spoil it. And it was my fault." The same can be said, to a great degree, of *The Last of the Mobile Hot-Shots* as well.

As Stephen Bowles and John McCarty state, Lumet is "most vulnerable when attempting light entertainment" (398). It is highly ironic that Williams sold *Myrtle* to the movies to get a second chance to prove that the play really had a substantial comic dimension to it, for it wound up being directed by a filmmaker who was unable to highlight satisfactorily those very comic aspects of the script which Williams contended had not been fully exploited in the stage production.

Vincent Canby noted that the movie "is haunted by ghosts of earlier, more memorable Williams characters who are easily identifiable." Thus Myrtle has the strength of Stella in *A Streetcar Named Desire* and "carries on in non-stop, expository monologues that could have been tailored for Baby Doll." In short, Canby suggests that, when one compares the present film to earlier Williams movies, it is to the disadvantage of *The Last of the Mobile Hot-Shots* (38).

Given the risks attendant on turning over a play to a studio for filming, why did Williams willingly allow his works to go before the camera? There were, of course, the handsome fees which he received for the film rights. "I must admit that I could not easily have lived without the movie-sales" of the plays, he said in correspondence. "There are no unmixed blessings or afflictions that I know of." In addition, there is always the chance that this time around maybe the chemistry of the various creative and technical artists involved will coalesce into producing a motion picture of genuine worth. In the case of *The Last of the Mobile Hot-Shots,* given the first-rate talent involved in the production, the film merits the attention of anyone seriously interested in the plays and the films of Tennessee Williams.

Notes

1. Unless otherwise indicated, the remarks of Tennessee Williams quoted in this essay are from the author's meeting with him at the Cannes International Film Festival in 1976.
2. *The Last of the Mobile Hot-Shots* may be purchased from Movies Unlimited, 3015 Darnell Road, Philadelphia, Pennsylvania 19154–3295. Telephone: (800) 668–4344. $19.99.

Works Cited

Some material in this essay appeared in a completely different form in Gene Phillips, *The Films of Tennessee Williams* (Cranbury, N.J.: Associated University Presses, 1980). In preparing the present essay, I have consulted numerous research materials not available when the book was published.

Bowles, Stephen, and John McCarty. "Sidney Lumet." In *Film Directors Encyclopedia*. Edited by Andrew Sarris. Detroit: St. James Press, 1998, pp. 297–99.
Canby, Vincent. "*The Last of the Mobile Hot-Shots.*" *New York Times,* January 15, 1970, p. 38.
Cunningham, Frank. *Sidney Lumet: Film and Literary Vision*. Revised edition. Lexington: UP of Kentucky, 2001.
Flatley, Guy. "The Kid Actor Who Became a Director: Sidney Lumet." *New York Times,* January 20, 1974, sec. 2:11.
Giannetti, Louis, and Scott Eyman. "Sidney Lumet." In *Flashback: A Brief History of Film* Revised edition. Upper Saddle River, N.J.: Prentice-Hall, 2001, pp. 324–27.
"*Last of the Mobile Hot-Shots.*" Variety, December 31, 1969, n.p.
"Ménagerie à Trois." *Time,* January 19, 1970, p. 67.
Reed, Rex. "Flint, Meet Georgy Girl: *The Last of the Mobile Hot-Shots.*" New York Times, June 8, 1969, sec. 2:15.
Vidal, Gore, Letter to the author, February 9, 1976.
Williams, Tennessee. *Kingdom of Earth (The Seven Descents of Myrtle)*. In *Plays: 1957–80*. Edited by Mel Gussow and Kenneth Holdich. New York: Library of America, 2000, pp. 623–705.
———. Letter to the author, October 23, 1975.
———. *Memoirs*. Garden City, N.Y.: Doubleday, 1975.

Works Consulted

Corrigan, Timothy. *Film and Literature*. Upper Saddle River, N.J.: Prentice-Hall, 1999.
Crandell, George, ed. *The Critical Response to Tennessee Williams*. Westport, Conn.: Greenwood Press, 1996.
O'Connor, Jacqueline. *Dramatizing Dementia: Madness in the Plays of Tennessee Williams*. Bowling Green: Bowling Green State UP, 1997.
Roudané, Matthew. *The Cambridge Companion to Tennessee Williams*. New York: Cambridge UP, 1997.
Williams, Tennessee. "Kingdom of Earth." In *Collected Stories*. New York: New Directions, 1985, pp. 368–78.

Terri Smith Ruckel

UT PICTURA POESIS, UT POESIS PICTURA:
THE PAINTERLY TEXTURE
OF TENNESSEE WILLIAMS'S
IN THE BAR OF A TOKYO HOTEL

When not on loan to various academic and civic galleries as part of the acclaimed Roger H. Ogden collection, an original Tennessee Williams oil on
canvas perches enigmatically on a second-story wall of Mr. Ogden's New
Orleans estate. In all likelihood, the painting, *Many Moons Ago* (Figure 1), so titled
for the words inscribed across the bare chest of its young male subject, attained
membership in the exclusive collection as a result of the fame of the dramatist/art-
ist. And since Mr. Odgen allows the collection to be loaned by the individual
work, the borrower need not request the entire collection but may be interested in
selected works for individual showings. One might suspect that the Williams
painting seldom leaves its spot, considering that Williams's reputation with a pen
eclipses any repute he has earned with a paintbrush. Williams scholars might be
more likely to have seen the painting in publications dedicated to the appreciation
of art, such as Randolph Delehanty's *Art in the American South: Works from the
Ogden Collection.*

In addition to *Many Moons Ago,* numerous other Williams paintings grace private collections—although as is true of the plays, arriving at a definite number of
the paintings may be hard to calculate—still others are in museums and art galleries located in cities including New York, Key West, New Orleans, and Austin. In
1995 alone, the Rare Book and Manuscript Library at Columbia University acquired from the Williams estate, "[Sixty-six] miscellaneous pieces of artwork,
among them paintings by the playwright" ("Tennessee Williams Collection"). Significant works in Williams's extensive art portfolio include *The Faith of Gatsby's
Last Summer,* a painting that recalls the optometrist billboard described in *The*

Fig. 1. Many Moons Ago. Oil on Canvas by Tennessee Williams, Roger H. Ogden Collection. Copyright 2002 by the University of the South. Printed by permission of the University of the South, Sewanee, Tennessee.

Great Gatsby; On ne peut pas comprendre toujours, a memory portrait of his mother; *Jai trouve parmi les fleurs,* a nude portrait of one of Williams's important male companions, Robert Carroll; and *Un beau mec,* "an expressionistic piece of a child on a tricycle, one of Tennessee's rare portraits of a pre-pubescent"(Plumley 801).

Despite the fact that dozens of Williams's paintings exist, his artistic achievements and their impact on his plays have not received much, if any, critical acknowledgment. One exception is the work of William Plumley, who offers some discussion about Williams as a painter and notes the playwright's revealing confession about "the relationship of [his] painting to his first published story" (803). The unfortunate result of not reading his paintings coincides with another problem—the widespread lack of acceptance of Williams's later plays, about which Philip C. Kolin says, " . . . once considered derivative or opaque, are among his most innovative works produced on the American stage"(ix). Ironically, one reason for this juxtaposed set of misapprehensions has been simple ignorance of how Williams's literary works and his painterly achievements grew from a common source: Williams's compulsive yet continually developing artistic vision fused with his "keen response to the social and political crises of a tumultuous era and his restless experimentation . . . to push style, dramatic form, and language to their limits" (Savran 132). Careful attention to the commonalities between Williams's paintings and his later plays helps to highlight Williams's experimentation with dramatic form and opportunely provides a productive, fruitful way to read Williams's later works.

In this essay, I want to connect art and literature even more to locate the palette of painterly techniques that ties Williams's paintings to his later writing, most especially to *In the Bar of a Tokyo Hotel.* An investigation of Williams's plastic art portfolio affords a natural segue to a grasp of the painterly qualities in his literary localities. This nexus, a journey into the interdisciplinary aesthetics of *ut pictura poesis* ("as is painting, so is poetry," from Horace, *Ars Poetica*), an interartistic theory reinvigorated by semiotics and the postmodern age, works especially well to obtain insights into what might be Williams's most misunderstood later play. Seen as pure visuality, in a painterly form, *In the Bar* becomes the performance of the painted word, not as the play is often regarded, the repression of language or, worse yet, merely Williams's own personal murmurings about his melancholy life.

Williams himself made explicit connections between his writing and the plastic arts. "When I write," said Williams, "everything is visual, as brilliantly as if it were on a lit stage" (qtd. in Devlin 334). When Williams painted, he related his paintings to his plays, often, reports Plumley, painting "the characters as he imagined them" (791). Especially during the later years, Williams routinely coupled the two arts, synchronously working on paintings and plays. *Jai trouve parmi les fleurs,* his nude portrait of Robert Carroll, to whom Williams dedicated *Moise and the World of Reason* (1975), was completed sometime between *Moise* and the release of William's collection of poems, *Androgyne, Mon Amour* (1977). The painting appeared on the poetry volume's dust jacket. *The Faith of Gatsby's Last Summer* was created while Williams was writing *The Red Devil Battery Sign* (1976). Williams's production of *In the Bar* (1969) predates these paintings as it does *Many Moons*

RUCKEL | *Ut Pictura Poesis, Ut Poesis Pictura* 83

Ago (1980), the memory portrait of long-time friend, Fred Nicklaus, though the time span separating the works is of no consequence to their connectedness. Williams scholars have long been aware of Williams's chronic tendency to revise as he "re-visioned" his work. Kolin asserts that Williams "repeatedly fused one work into another and often transformed earlier works" (xi). *In the Bar* and several of Williams's paintings—*Many Moons Ago, The Faith of Gatsby's Last Summer,* and *On ne peut pas comprendre toujours* testify to such fusions. The affinities that exist amongst these texts are unmistakable.

Recognizing the intertextualities of *In the Bar* and these paintings obliges a new critical approach to the play. In fact, reading *In the Bar* in light of Williams's paintings offers a view of the play that neither abases autobiography nor wallows in it. A visual reading counters the barrage of negative reviews that immediately followed the premiere and harshly codified the play as "Williams's aesthetic impotence" ("Torpid Tennessee" 18), as "an unabashed confession" that might "serve the author as therapy" (Clurman 709), and as Clive Barnes alleged, "too personal . . . too painful, to be seen in the cold light of public scrutiny" (54). Envenoming their critique of the play's autobiographical weariness, critics of *In the Bar* have zeroed in on Williams's anomalous use of dialogue, pointing censoriously to the incomplete lines and fragments, shouting down his dramatic technique, and calling it "an attempt to convey a sort of nervous inebriate inarticulateness" (Clurman 710).

Even within the recent, revisionist effort to reevaluate Williams's later work, *In the Bar* has not received the praise it merits structurally and poststructurally, though Allean Hale laments *In the Bar's* assessment as "Williams's monumental failure"(Hale 363). Hale and David Savran offer the two most viable readings of the play. Hale sees *In the Bar* as Williams's "real tribute to Japan . . . his polished rewriting of the 'occidental noh' play" (370) and links the play's structure to the Noh form. Savran provocatively reads *In the Bar's* fragmentary dialogue and plot as evidence of Williams's repressed frustration over his concealed homosexuality and as "the result of a pivotal change in his public status: his coming out" (136). Further, Savran contextualizes *In the Bar* with the history of the late sixties— everyone was "coming out" in one way or another during the sexual revolution and the series of other protest movements, and Williams, "Finally empowered to speak directly after so many years of (self)censorship . . . could only stutter, only hammer out a broken and lacerated speech" (137).

More recently, Annette J. Saddik positions *In the Bar's* collapse of linguistic structure as being "outside the constructed boundaries of sanity" (87). Ruby Cohn almost unilaterally narrates her interpretation of *In the Bar* with her own painterly aesthetics, calling Williams's predictable Broadway failure "spare and monochromatic" (236) and "a critique of art" (237). Yet Cohn stops just short of espousing *In the Bar's* visual functionality when she says, "Before and after *[In the Bar of a] Tokyo Hotel,* Williams dramatized the tyrannies of art in theatrical rather than painterly terms" (238). Cohn's reference to "painterly terms" and the fact that she does not complete, nor valorize sufficiently her aesthetic connections, highlights the potential for an explication of the painterly texture of *In the Bar.*

In the Bar's connections with painterly aesthetics commence in the barroom of an unnamed Japanese hotel that serves as the play's setting. Characteristically described as Williams's dark portrait of an artist, *In the Bar*'s plot revolves around the collapse and death of Mark Conley, an artist who has "discovered color" and is breaking through to "a new style." Conley, a successful yet maniacal American artist, who "has narrowed his life to his painting" (Cohn 237), occupies rooms at the hotel with Miriam, his tragic, sex-starved wife, who has resorted to promiscuity as a means of emotional survival. Considering that Mark cloisters himself in his room, crawling on a canvas nailed to the floor, much of the play's action directly focuses on Miriam, her flirtation with and attempted seduction of the Barman as well as her confrontation with Leonard, Mark's gay agent, who arrives from New York at Miriam's request. Weary of life with her insane artist husband, Miriam sends for Leonard in hopes that he will escort Mark back to New York and into a mental hospital. She proposes having Mark committed so that she will no longer be deprived—of sex, of reason, of life. Traumatically, Mark dies at the play's conclusion, and Miriam, free now to go her own way, stands frozen in her spot of light and dejectedly offers, "I have no plans. I have nowhere to go" (53).

Williams presents this one-act play in two parts, and for almost all of Part One, Miriam sits at a "small round table." In fact, this play extraordinarily recommends itself in its likeness to plastic art, since the entire play takes place in one setting and has very little action—moments occur during the play when all action ceases and the characters are frozen in dramatic frames. For instance, as the play opens, the Barman stands behind the bar, in a pin-spot of light. All action is briefly but painterly suspended until he "raises a metal shaker, a few moments after the rise of the curtain" (3). Later in Part One, Miriam invades the Barman's most personal space; she deliberately situates her hand on his crotch. Their subsequent dialogue volleys back and forth for ten lines before she releases him. Except for the rhythm of their words, no physical movement takes place. The Barman is frozen in his compromised position; the dramatic focus is on the plastic moment.

Comparable plastic moments occur consistently throughout *In the Bar* and afford opportunities for making painterly connections between the play and the paintings *Many Moons Ago, The Faith of Gatsby's Last Summer,* and *On ne peut pas comprendre toujours.* Though making the connections requires a symmetrical reading of the play and painting, even the most novice student of painterly aesthetics should have no trouble navigating the plastic spaces. Since in most cases, an iconograph involves a single scene, and therefore one "theatrical" set constructed onto a single two-dimensional space, the plastic spaces of the paintings are confined. Likewise, the plastic space of *In the Bar* is confined to one theatrical set. Aside from this significant fact, however, other, perhaps even more meaningful iconographic similarities exist between *In the Bar* and Williams's painterly works.

Many Moons Ago is set against a backdrop of brightly colored geometrical shapes, and the entire scene is devoid of recognizable objects. *In the Bar*'s set is also sparse, though Williams's stage directions call for spotlights taking various shapes, such as these from the play's first moments: "a small area of intense light"

(3) polishes Miriam and the round table at which she sits. The Barman is displayed in "a pin-spot of light" (3) that narrowly illuminates the bar, itself a shape. That bamboo bar is streaked with the natural vertical lines of the wood. Finally, there is the "arch of a door leading offstage" (7). Circles, arches, lines and bars—painterly tools—create *In the Bar*'s expressionistic backdrop—the entirety of what Williams's aesthetic sense would allow for his "new creation." *In the Bar* would indeed make it possible for "his real concerns to appear in a stark and raw form" (Kroll 133). On the canvas of *In the Bar*'s simple set, Williams creates shapes with light and lines, carrying artistic creation back to its earliest, simplest elements, which is the essence of expressionism. Reaching beyond his earlier, mimetic dramas, Williams is striving for an expressionist method. He wants to "destroy the space that normally surrounds objects"(Feldman 226) in order to reduce the psychological distance between audience and subject by eliminating that which could distract from the subject. Absent from *In the Bar* is the prodigious amount of props which Williams typically details in copious and explicit production notes. Critics have long emphasized Williams's use of visual imagery in such plays as *Camino Real, The Rose Tattoo,* and even *The Glass Menagerie,* but that imagery depended largely on the use of elaborate sets, the extensive use of props and special effects. Unlike these earlier plays, *In the Bar* opens on a stage appointed with nothing but the bare minimum necessary for communicating his art.

Williams employs the same expressionist use of space in *The Faith of Gatsby's Last Summer* and *On ne peut pas comprendre toujours. Gatsby's Last Summer,* set on a moonlit beach, would seem at first glance to have nothing in common with *In the Bar of a Tokyo Hotel.* However, by beholding both play and painting from within their creator's expressionist vision, both works can be read as one. At first glance a seascape, *Gatsby's Last Summer* presents just one piece of dominating furniture, just as *In the Bar* features the bamboo bar center stage. The vertical lines of the gazebo's supports, the optometrist's bar-shaped sign, and the circle of the moon all provide the same shapes that Williams employs for *In the Bar*'s setting. These shapes create a space for the drama Williams wants to display, whether as painting or play; he uses these simple shapes to avoid distracting the audience from that drama.

The optometrist's sign hangs improbably in thin air above and just behind the gazebo's roof, which therefore seems to be adorned by other "circles"—the optometrist's unblinking eyes. *In the Bar* also takes place beneath unblinking eyes, those of the Barman who, like "an oriental idol"(3) watches everything and is the only character who is virtually ever-present. Like Williams's optometrist, Williams's Barman seems to hang in the air, unmoved by any emotion even when Miriam grabs his crotch. As one reviewer noted, the Barman is "a model of stoic restraint"("Torpid Tennessee" 75). By suspending both the optometrist and the Barman above the dramatic conflict, Williams makes them passive judges, the omniscient audience of what takes place. Williams supplies his own audience to witness the anguish of an artist struggling with his art.

Not only does Williams use circles, lines, and bars, but he uses them in a way that effectively shines a spotlight on that which he would impress upon his audience, such as the bottle at the center of *Gatsby's Last Summer* or the purple flowers on the Miriam's table of *In the Bar*. Just behind Gatsby and to his left, a small round tray offers a bottle of wine. The tray itself is really only a suggestion formed from a circular patch of white that pushes the bottle to prominence, confidently occupying the painting's very center. The spotlights of *In the Bar* obviously have the same effect of focusing attention on one subject or another. Williams attains a similar effect by flattening the perspective of the painting so that the seascape, almost completely obscured by the other oversized elements of the painting's composition, seems to shove those elements to the foreground. The objects are relegated to positions where the audience will find it difficult to ignore them.

In fact, not only the details but the painterly settings as a whole offer Williams a medium for his expressionist vision: neither *In the Bar* nor *Gatsby's Last Summer* requires their settings in the least. Both the beach and the bar are so totally without character that they make for a sterile space in which Williams can explore and exhibit without distraction the psychological realities which are the true subjects of his expressionist creations. In much the same way, the staged set of *On ne peut pas comprendre toujours* modestly features a royal poinciana (an ornamental flowering tree) and one small round table—the scene reminiscent, if not symbolic, of some tropical café. Indeed, the painting's set is tantamount to *In the Bar's* set—both are located in tropical bars. The simplified pictorial structure of all of these canvases suggests the expressionist technique of flattening space, of reducing line to an "arbitrary or decorative element" (Feldman 226), so that the artist might focus on expressing the unconscious.

Just as the sets of *Many Moons Ago, The Faith of Gatsby's Last Summer,* and *On ne peut pas comprendre toujours* mirror the sparse set of *In the Bar,* the characters in all three paintings might pass for the characters of *In the Bar*. Mark and Miriam Conley, *In the Bar's* protagonists, present somewhat of a conundrum for the reader or the spectator. Should the vigorous and bold Miriam be the central focus of the canvas or is the artistically perceptive Mark located at center stage? Miriam, "whose desires are far more complex and volatile than those of her tormented husband" (Savran 137), taunts Mark with her retort, "I can't be caught" (14). Miriam's passion pulls the reader's/spectator's thoughts away from Mark, the heroic artist who passively whines, "I can't interrupt my work here before I've controlled it"(19). Miriam, whose sanguine sexuality would extend into the audience the "hand of a woman who burns"(13), is juxtaposed on the canvas of *In the Bar* with Mark, the melancholy and unstable creator whose gifted hand is "too tremulous to lift a glass to his mouth" (15). Literati would no doubt argue for Miriam's dominance in the play's plot and see Miriam "as the primary point for the reader or spectator's interpellation into the text," as Savran has argued (137). And yet, from a painterly perspective, since both members of the "marital dyad" stand center canvas, neither one of them may be moved to the margins, and thus the painterly texture of the play demonstrates the expressionist's desire to "undertake the thoughts and feelings of more than one individual" (Lind 140).

Williams dramatizes multiple points of view in his paintings as well, featuring central male subjects whom Williams has positioned in proximity to female subjects. A man bedecked in a hot pink suit is center stage on the canvas of *The Faith of Gatsby's Last Summer.* Seated underneath the shelter of the gazebo, he clasps his hands protectively over his groin. To the immediate right of the canvas, a woman's specter-like head, including a substantial portion of her upper torso, hangs suspended in the sky over blue waves of water. Her penetrating gaze is directed at the man alluding to similar plastic moments from *In the Bar* such as Miriam's ogling of Mark when he makes his bar appearance in Part One. Disgusted with his physical impotence as well as with his painterly appearance, Miriam sneers: "Then go in my room. Here's my key. Throw that fantastically decorated suit out the window" (21). A male and female couple are also center stage on the canvas of *On ne peut pas comprendre toujours,* which features a woman dressed in contemporary attire sitting across the table from her gentleman caller. The plastic composition of this painting also imitates several *In the Bar* scenes, in particular, those scenes when Miriam shares the small round table with Mark or with Leonard.

In like manner, *Many Moons Ago* features a stunning young male figure at center stage, with a sad-looking young woman standing close and behind the man so that his bare torso eclipses her genitalia, a portion of which remains bare as do her breasts. Analogous to Miriam, the young woman's sexuality is exposed for public view. From the background, her downcast eyes and the white-silvery colors that form her body make this female figure appear otherworldly, especially in opposition to the male figure, whose body is touched with muted oil pastels. Williams leaves us no doubt as to the painting's title, since it is inscribed across the foreground, much of it across the male's bare chest. In spite of the title's intrusion, however, we can still clearly see the man's nipples, which appear as highlighted and moonlike, circles of light.

In a corresponding visual scene from *In the Bar,* the emotionally explosive Mark Conley first appears on stage with "vivid paint stains on his unpressed suit" (13). Much like the young man touched with paint in *Many Moons Ago,* Mark's suit, hands, and hair are paint splattered. As a further similarity, the emotionally challenged Miriam first appears on stage "in a small area of intense light. She is glossily handsome" (3). The light and the "attractiveness" link Miriam to the surrealistic woman of *Many Moons Ago* as does the look of dejection that both women wear.

In these visual fields, both for the paintings and for *In the Bar,* the male and the female are closely positioned and appear to be competitive; their juxtaposition looks ominous. But the spacing of the male and the female on the canvases as well as the blocking of Mark and Miriam on stage, indicates that Williams's design extends beyond the obvious message of sexual rivalry. In painting, when a line "encloses a piece of space, it creates a shape" (Feldman 35). The shape that Williams created on the canvases of *Many Moons Ago, The Faith of Gatsby's Last Summer,* and *On ne peut pas comprendre toujours* melds together the form of the male as well as the form of the female; the two become one. Only light and color separate them. Tracing the outline—the outward lines of the shape—locates only one mass.

Throughout *In the Bar,* Williams uses the same illusion of line and shape to connect Mark and Miriam. In both play and painting, Williams presents the male and the female as connected; they share the same space on the canvas. Williams, the painter, has created an illusion of lines "by juxtaposing contrasted shapes and areas of color" (Feldman 36).

Mark and Miriam take on form-united shape in several scenes of *In the Bar.* Near the end of Part One, when the Barman serves Mark a second drink because Mark has spilled the first, Miriam orders, "Don't touch it. I'll lift it to your mouth" (16). Like the multi-armed Hindu god, Shiva, Miriam and Mark are joined—their forms overlap each other just as they do in Williams's paintings. Mark comments about his painting that there is "no division between us at all any more! The oneness, the!" (17); his words also point out the blocking of the two characters on stage as Miriam picks up the cocktail and pours it down Mark's throat. When Mark's hysteria begins to increase and he shakes the table, Miriam grabs the other side, and the round tabletop locks them into a circular embrace. Again, only light and color separate Mark and Miriam. The lines converge together to create one mass on the stage. When Miriam holds a mirror to Mark's face and shouts for him to look at himself, these stage directions follow: "She holds her large mirror but he stares above it at her" (18). Williams's visual intention is quite clear: Miriam and Mark are the same person, one shape that might be construed as two, an illusion created by the innovative artist and his use of "Color, color, and light!" (24)—a notion that Mark continues to articulate throughout the play. Miriam also voices the couple's oneness when she asks, "Are we two people, Mark, or are we. . . . One!" (30). In an interview in 1975, Williams reiterates these lines from *In the Bar* in his version of Mark and Miriam as two sides of one person. "One side was a man driven mad by the passion to create, which was frustrated, and the woman, as he described her, was a compulsive bitch" (qtd. in Devlin 294).

By the end of Part One, Mark's ugly confrontation with Miriam shifts to physical violence. *"He seizes her shoulders. She staggers to her knees; he lifts her and flings her through the arch, out of the bar"* (30). Following Miriam's removal from the stage, which seems like an amputation performed to separate female from male, Mark crosses to center stage and sits in a chair reciting his fragmented line, "I will stay here until my wife returns from" (31), after which the stage lights are dimmed and Mark sits on in darkness, perhaps a foreshadowing of the play's end. At the close of Part Two, with Mark dead and his body removed from the stage, Miriam is similarly frozen in her spot. She has "no plans" and "nowhere to go." The stage darkens and she is left without light. Both endings are like halves of a portrait, in which the two characters might be rejoined as one shape on the canvas, comparable to the joined spaces that grace the canvases of *Many Moons Ago, The Faith of Gatsby's Last Summer,* and *On ne peut pas comprendre toujours*

Not only the localities of scene and subject play a principal part in conversations about painting and theater: light and color play a vital part as well. Williams, who unfailingly looked at life and drama with his painter's eye, used color and light extensively to further stamp his expressionistic style on the canvas of *In the Bar.* In his paintings, he laid patches of color here and there until forms emerged, not un-like the way he arranged splotches of color and narrative on the canvas of *In the Bar*. Miriam, dressed exotically—a description which certainly translates into the use of bright colors—begins her on-stage reign wearing a "hat crowned with blue-black cock feathers" (3). Later in Part One, Williams slings a colorized action onto the canvas when the Hawaiian Lady crosses the stage. "She wears a dress printed with large flowers" (8). During other painterly moments, Mark appears with paint splotches on his suit and in his hair; Miriam complains to the Barman about the "purple flower on the red table" (20), and Williams bursts color through the dia-logue with Mark's testaments to the power of color: "What I'm saying is—color isn't passive, it, it—has a fierce life in it" (24). He concludes the artistic sermon with a revelation: "I know the last things," Mark testifies, ". . . the imperishable things are color and light" (24).

In fact, imperishable light plays an influential role all through *In the Bar*. Williams's painterly love of light ushers in the play's opening scene as Miriam ap-pears in a small area of intense light. While still sitting in this light, she brings out a mirror to catch and to reflect light, in her own way creating a "circle of light," which the Barman accuses of blinding his eyes and burning through his clothes. "For light in your eyes be grateful," professes Miriam to the Barman (5). And fi-nally, Miriam attributes Mark's absence/death as the "mistake of deliberately mov-ing out of the [light]" (53). The painterly "circle of light" that Williams created on the canvas of *In the* Bar is endorsed by Nancy Tischler as "the image of the brief, intense and heroic moment of the human struggle—as man fights furiously to be a hero, swaggering in the spotlight, only to disappear into the darkness" (140).

Without question, Williams's plastic theatre directly corresponds to the scenery and subjects of his painterly compositions, to the color and light and plastic space of his painting, something he emphasizes in *Will Mr. Merriwether Return from Memphis?* when Louise says: "In painting, there's such a thing as plastic space" (121). In his *Memoirs*, Williams makes clear his convictions about the power of the visual image:

> The work of a fine painter, committed only to vision, abstract and allusive as he pleases, is better able to create for you his moments of intensely perceptive being. Jackson Pollock could paint ecstasy as it could not be written. Van Gogh could cap-ture for you moments of beauty, indescribable as descent into madness. (250)

In the Bar celebrates the work of the painter and examines the interdependence of the artist and his art as well as anatomizing how that interdependence affects the artist's relationships with the people around him. In an interview just prior to *In the Bar*'s May 11 premiere in 1969, Williams claimed that when he wrote *In the Bar*, he was writing about artist Jackson Pollock: "I knew towards the end," declared Williams, "that Jackson Pollock was crawling around naked on the floor with a spray gun, just spraying canvas and just streaking it over the canvas with his fingers" (qtd. in Devlin 294). Much like *In the Bar*'s artist gone mad, Pollock tragically died at the end of a reportedly stormy relationship with his wife. Described as the archetypal "action painter," Pollock is known for transforming his canvas "into a modern-day arena wherein an epic struggle between man and material might unfold" (Rosenberg 213).

Like Pollock, Williams also wrestled with the idea of connecting action and performance with canvas, of fusing art and artist. *In the Bar* substantiates this connection when Miriam confronts Mark with his own struggle: "When I looked in your room and saw you crawling naked over a huge nailed down canvas, I thought, 'My God, it's time . . .'"(17). In light of the connections between Williams's literary work and his painterly work, the time has come for a recognition of Williams's artistic fusion of art and artist.

Much earlier in his career, even before his acquaintance with Pollock or the artistic concept of "action painting," Williams had expressed his own artistic impulses about conjoining performance with canvas. One of Williams's letters to Donald Windham concomitantly reads like stage directions and painting instruction: ". . . you should cover the bed with a large white piece of oil-cloth. The bodies of the sexual partners ought to be thoroughly, even superfluously rubbed over with mineral oil or cold cream" (37). Here, Williams clearly confirms his innovative idea to paint with expressionistic action—to write on the canvas with physical experience. Williams concludes his obvious meditation on performance and art with a note about lighting instructions. "The sun," writes Williams, should be "directly down on the bed" (Windham 37). Regrettably, Williams's painterly concepts go unnoticed, and such statements, as do his dramatic works, consistently stimulate more comment about his preoccupation with sex and with his own inscription of his personal life within his art than with his patent determination to create the visual. Nonetheless, much like Pollock, Williams wants to create a canvas that reflects the struggle between man and the performance of creation, and he attempts this visual creation on the dramatic canvas of *In the Bar*.

Asked about his interpretation of *In the Bar,* Williams once replied: "The theme was creation" (qtd. in Devlin 294). Williams himself strove with energy against stubborn media that resisted expression at the moment of creation. Plumley observes that "Many of [Williams's] canvases have thick globs of paint smeared through the image as if the form he was seeking would not come to life quickly enough" (800). *In the Bar* voices Williams's very personal interpretation of artistic frustration, and his own artist's voice speaks directly through Mark: "I've understood the intimacy that should, that has to exist between, the, the—painter, and the—I! It! Not it turned to me, or I turned to it, no division between us at all any more! The one-ness, the!" (17). Like Mark, Williams's struggle is with his media.

To settle this struggle, Williams uses the canvas of *In the Bar* to move beyond the spoken word as dialogue by employing the expressionist painter's method. His theatricalized images become painterly images; his theatrical spaces become painterly spaces. Williams redirects the dramatic emphasis from language to image in the plastic space of *In the Bar*. As he does, he creates what Stephen Baker claims are the "indispensable elements of performance," the spaces in performance art that are in between the "unconscious actions of which human life consists and the conscious activity we would identify as performance" (7). Performed dialogue is conjoined with performing image. *In the Bar is* suffused with these plastic spaces and the coupling of dialogue with image just as spaces and images are manifest in the performance frames of *Many Moons Ago, The Faith of Gatsby's Last Summer,* and *On ne peut pas comprendre toujours*—spaces that serve to delineate/illuminate/explicate the visual mastery Williams so artfully exploits.

Regrettably the efficacy of William's art(s) has often been misunderstood. During the last two decades of his life, Williams produced a miscellany of divers art forms. Between *The Night of the Iguana* and his death in 1983, he wrote at least twenty-five more scripts for public theatre, most of which were experimental, most of which were disappointing to those expecting reincarnations of Williams's earlier masterpieces, nearly all of which triggered negative press. As critics were panning Williams's plays with gleeful ire, his career closed with yet another experimental work, *Something Cloudy, Something Clear,* which like *In the Bar,* was seen by the critics as too autobiographical. Led by Williams scholars such as Philip C. Kolin, more recent criticism emphasizes Williams's postmodern dramatic techniques. Kolin reads *Something Cloudy* as "a triumphant closure to Williams's exploration of non-linear dramaturgy" and as Williams's "postmodern investigation of the playwright and his art" ("*Something Cloudy*" 38). Throughout this highly confessional and yet self-reconstructive period, Williams also painted when "the brush provided something that the pen could not; unguarded, raw exhibition" (Plumley 792). Williams settled any competition between his brush and the pen with *In the Bar.* Much like *Something Cloudy,* it, too, investigates "the playwright and his art." Williams alluded to this relationship between his painting and his writing as he described his feelings about New Orleans. "He talked of the city and the moon being like sisters, which is a great romantic image, the image of young longing. He says of them that they have learned to understand each other and speak to each other in a wordless way . . . sisters aging gracefully together" (Rasky 39). Indeed, like sisters, Williams's paintings and *In the Bar* speak to each other in this wordless way.

Works Cited

Baker, Stephen. "Disorder of the Lights Perhaps an Illusion." Studies in the Literary Imagination 24.2 (Fall 1991): 7–28.
Barnes, Clive. "Theatre: *In the Bar of a Tokyo Hotel,*" New York Times 12 May 1969, 54.
Clurman, Harold. "Theatre." *The Nation.* 2 June 1969, 709–10.
Cohn, Ruby. "Tennessee Williams: The Last Two Decades." *The Cambridge Companion to Tennessee Williams.* Ed. Matthew C. Roudané. Cambridge: U of Cambridge P, 1997.
Delahanty, Randolph. *Art in the American South: Works from the Ogden Collection.* Baton Rouge: Louisiana State UP, 1996.
Devlin, Albert J. ed. *Conversations with Tennessee Williams.* Jackson; UP of Mississippi, 1986.
Feldman, Edmund Burke. *Thinking About Art.* Englewood Cliffs: Prentice-Hall, Inc., 1985.
Hale, Allean. "The Secret Script of Tennessee Williams." *Southern Review* 27:2 (1991): 363–76.

Kolin, Philip C. "*Something Cloudy, Something Clear:* Tennessee Williams's Postmodern Memory Play." *Journal of Dramatic Theory and Criticism* 12 (Spring 1998): 35–56.

——. Preface. *Tennessee Williams: A Guide to Research and Performance*. Ed. Philip C. Kolin. Westport: Greenwood Press, 1998, ix–xiii.

Kroll, Jack. "Life Is a Bitch." *Newsweek* 26 May 1969, 133.

Leavitt, Richard F., ed. *The World of Tennessee Williams*. New York: G.P. Putnam's Sons, 1978.

Lind, Ilse Dusoir. "The Effect of Painting on Faulkner's Poetic Form." *Faulkner, Modernism, and Film: Faulkner and Yoknapatawpha*. Eds. Doreen Fowler and Ann J. Abadie. Jackson: UP of Mississippi, 1979.

Plumley, William. "Tennessee Williams's Graphic Art: 'Two on a Party.'" *Mississippi Quarterly: The Journal of Southern Culture* 48:4 (1995): 789–805.

Rasky, Harry. *Tennessee Williams: A Portrait in Laughter and Lamentation*. New York: Dodd, Mead and Company, 1986.

Rosenberg, Harold. "The Concept of Action Painting," *Artwork and Packages*. Chicago: University of Chicago Press, 1969, 213.

Saddik, Annette J. *The Politics of Reputation: The Critical Reception of Tennessee Williams's Later Plays*. Madison: Fairleigh Dickinson UP, 1999.

Savran, David. *Communists, Cowboys and Queers: The Politics of Masculinity in the Work of Arthur Miller and Tennessee Williams*. Minneapolis: University of Minnesota Press, 1992.

"Tennessee Williams Collection Acquired." *Columbia University Libraries Newsletter* June 30, 1995, 1.

Tischler. Nancy M. *Student Companion to Tennessee Williams*. Westport: Greenwood Press, 2000.

"Torpid Tennessee." *Time,* May 23, 1969, 75.

Williams, Tennessee. *In the Bar of a Tokyo Hotel*. 1969. *The Theatre of Tennessee Williams,* Vol. 2. New York: New Directions, 1981. 2–31.

——. *Memoirs*. Garden City: Doubleday, 1975.

Windham, Donald, ed. *Tennessee Williams's Letters to Donald Windham—1940–1965*. New York: Hold, 1977.

Felicia Hardison Londré

THE TWO-CHARACTER OUT CRY
AND BREAK OUT

Two dramatic characters—a brother and sister—are confined by fear inside a house where their parents died in an apparent murder-suicide. Two other dramatic characters—a brother and sister acting team who portray the first pair of characters—find themselves physically confined inside the theatre that contains the stage setting for their play. Two actors portray those four dramatic characters in any production of Tennessee Williams's *Two-Character Play* (1967, 1975) or its 1973 incarnation titled *Out Cry*. All four characters wrestle with the theme of confinement that so obsessed their author. Meanwhile, actors must struggle against the long-prevailing critical confinement of the play to a condition evoked in Jack Kroll's review of *Out Cry:* "Lamentably, Williams has turned a theater into a prison for audiences."

Williams was working on *The Two-Character Play* throughout his "stoned age," a period of deep depression stemming from the death of his companion Frank Merlo in 1963 and culminating in his involuntary three-month confinement at Barnes Hospital, St. Louis, in autumn 1969. "Confinement has always been the greatest dread of my life," Williams wrote in his *Memoirs;* "that can be seen in my play *Out Cry*" (233). It can also be seen as early as his 1939 play *Not About Nightingales,* which is set in a prison, and in *Stairs to the Roof* (1945), subtitled "A Prayer for the Wild at Heart That Are Kept in Cages" (xii). Similarly, his late play *Clothes for a Summer Hotel* (1980) deals with Zelda Fitzgerald's confinement in an asylum.

Confinement for Williams, however, was not only about physical constraint but also about being trapped by his own past successes that had defined him as a playwright. As a maturing playwright, Williams often felt critical and commercial pressure to force his talents to fit within some paradigm based upon the works that had catapulted him to the front ranks of American dramatists in the 1940s. In a 1972 interview, he commented on the changes in his work since the 1960s: "I think that I'm growing into a more direct form, one that fits people and societies going a bit mad, you know? . . . I'm very interested in the presentational form of theater, where everything is very free and different, where you have total license" (Devlin *Conversations* 218). Thus, *The Two-Character Play,* which a London critic (Lewis) called "defiantly non-commercial," was for Williams an evasion of the artistic straitjacket.

To the fear of physical and artistic confinement, one might add a third concern: fear of being trapped in a role. Fixed identities restrict the fullness of human contact, as suggested by references throughout Williams's work to "solitary confinement" within our "separate skins." Interviewing Williams for *Playboy* in 1973, C. Robert Jennings asked: "Isn't it true that until 1970, you had never talked openly about your homosexuality?" Williams verified that he had unexpectedly, and with some embarrassment, come out on national television when David Frost asked him pointblank if he were homosexual. Although the studio audience had applauded his frank admission, "I cover the waterfront," he "became socially ostracized in Key West." But the long-term result was a release from confinement: "I don't care what anyone knows about me anymore. I just don't give a shit, which gives me a new sense of freedom" (Devlin, *Conversations* 232).

Williams often referred to *The Two-Character Play* and *Out Cry* as among his most important work and his most personal. The interviews and feature stories collected in *Conversations with Tennessee Williams* (Devlin) provide examples. In 1970, he called *The Two-Character Play* "my best play since *Cat.* Maybe better" (164). And: "If I live, it'll be my best play, but that doesn't mean it will run more than three weeks" (179). In 1973: "I think *Out Cry* is my most beautiful play since *Streetcar,* and I've never stopped working on it. I think it's a major work. I don't know whether or not it will be *received* as one. It is a *cri de coeur,* but then all creative work, all *life,* in a sense, is a *cri de coeur.* But the critics will say I am excessively personal and I pity myself" (239). And: "*Out Cry* is a major play, as I've said. This morning I wrote the best fucking scene since 1961, baby" (249). In 1974: "I think it's my best play since *Streetcar Named Desire.* But they (critics) don't understand it, but they will one day." Asked by the interviewer "what's so great about it?" Williams replied: "It's a very personal play. It's my own human outcry" (255). In a 1979 roundtable, he referred to the original London version: "When I wrote it in 1967, I was so crazy I didn't know where I was. When you're really crazy you do some of your best work, you know" (308). In *Five O'Clock Angel,* Maria St. Just recalled that *Out Cry* and *Camino Real* "were Tennessee's two favorite plays" (230). In his *Memoirs,* Williams noted that *Out Cry* "was especially close to the marrow of my being, wherever that is" (228). And further: "I considered *Out Cry* a major work and its misadventure on Broadway has not altered that personal estimate of it" (233).

The critical response to both plays in the 1970s largely bore out what Williams had predicted. Virtually every review of the Broadway production of *Out Cry* connected the play's content with aspects of Williams's own life. Douglas Watt began his review by saying that "it is difficult to disassociate" the play "from what we know of the author's own mental turmoil during the 1960s." According to T. E. Kalem: "Here, the man who suffers and the mind which creates are no more separate than a drunk and his crying jag." Martin Gottfried claimed that "the sister is plainly a homosexual-substitute" and condemned the script's "embarrassing use of the theater as a confessional, autobiographical medium and therapy." The television reviewer Leonard Harris admitted to purveying a "lay psychoanalysis of Tennessee Williams." Edwin Wilson's otherwise sensitive review fell into the same trap: "It is a matter of public record that Williams has been battling a number of private and public ghosts in recent years." He then catalogued Williams's "breakdown," his dramatic self-referentiality, and his sister's institutionalization. In other words, the reviewers of the 1973 production were bringing to bear too much of what they knew about the author in their attempts to get a handle on the play. The two decades since Williams's death have not entirely distanced us from that tendency, as evidenced in a 1999 feature article by Steven Leigh Morris: "Part of the thrill of watching any Williams play today is decoding the clues to his tormented life and sexual yearnings."

Despite some lingering critical fixation on the personal element in Tennessee Williams's plays, it is possible that audiences now have enough objectivity to see Williams's most personal works on their own terms and to assess whether they are viable without a biographical context. Further, it is clear from Williams's own remarks that he regarded his plays' grounding in his own experience as a strength and an impetus to seek new forms. The unconventional form of *The Two-Character Play*, *Out Cry*, and his other late plays reflected the emotional "frenzy" that unbalanced him from the 1960s, Williams told interviewer Charles Ruas in 1975. He explained: "I'm quite through with the kind of play that established my early and popular reputation. I am doing a different thing, which is altogether my own, not influenced at all by other playwrights at home or abroad, or by other schools of theatre. My thing is what it always was, to express my world and experience of it in whatever form seems suitable to the material" (Devlin, *Conversations* 284–5). In 1981, Williams told Dotson Rader: "My work is *emotionally* autobiographical. It has no relationship to the actual events of my life, but it reflects the emotional currents of my life" (*Paris Review* 165). The artistic release that Williams struggled to achieve in the 1960s, bolstered by his personal liberation after 1970, found an expression in the various versions of *The Two-Character Play* and *Out Cry*.

The Two-Character Play premiered at London's Hampstead Theatre Club (December 11, 1967). New Directions published that version in 1969 in a limited edition of only 350 copies. As *Out Cry*, the play appeared at Chicago's Ivanhoe Theatre (July 8, 1971), at New York's Lyceum Theatre (March 1, 1973), in print (1973), and at the Thirteenth Street Repertory Company Off-Broadway (June 17, 1974). Further revised, it was presented as *The Two Character Play* at the Off-Broadway Quaigh Theater in New York (August 14, 1975); at the Showcase Theatre, San Francisco (1976); and at Callboard Theater, Los Angeles (February 22, 1977). The 1976 version published in volume 5 of *The Theatre of Tennessee Williams* must be regarded as the definitive text for purposes of critical analysis, but it is interesting that The Library of America (2000) anthologizes instead the 1973 text of *Out Cry*.

The rarity with which either *The Two-Character Play* or *Out Cry* was given major productions during the 1980s seemed to confirm the critical dismissal of "a disaster" (Kroll). Yet there were occasional studio productions, and both plays began to find international audiences. In 1979 Kim Stanley directed a production of *Out Cry* that ran a week (7–16 August) at the Van Dam Theatre in New York. In 1982 Austin Pendleton and Barbara Eden-Young performed *The Two-Character Play* at New York's Open Space. It was performed in Italian at the Todifestival in Perugia in September 1988. Elizabeth Ashley and Keir Dullea gave a staged reading of *Out Cry* at the University of North Carolina, Chapel Hill, on 26 February 1996. A Russian translation of *Out Cry* premiered in St. Petersburg on 27 November 1993, directed by Volya Vaha.

A spate of productions since 1999 can be referenced on the World Wide Web, giving rise to the possibility that what Williams saw as "my most difficult play" (Colt 7) might at last be coming into its own. San Francisco director Jay Leo Colt had commented in 1982: "In twenty years, I venture to predict, the play will be slotted habitually in repertories" (6). Indeed, in my own 1979 book on Williams, I wrote that "the play has not yet found general acceptance in the theater, but it may need something like the seventeen-year gestation that *Camino Real* had before audiences caught up with it" (192). Twenty-five years after the publication of *Out Cry*, its 1998 production by the Mixed Company at the Phoenix Center for the Performing Arts, directed by David Barker, was nominated for the ariZoni Theatre Best Play Award. *Out Cry* also had 1999 productions by Company One at the Boston Center for the Arts, at the Petit Hébertot in Paris, and at Hobart and William Smith Colleges (Geneva, New York). In 2001 it was produced at the University of North Dakota (Grand Forks). *The Two-Character Play* had productions by Zoo District at Artshare Los Angeles in 1999 and by the Walnut Street Theatre in Philadelphia in 2001.

If these instances do herald a resurrection—a breaking out of the critical limbo within which both versions of the play had been on hold—one must question why the earlier *Out Cry* (1973) gets chosen by theatre artists more than twice as often as the later *The Two-Character Play* (1976). Because *Out Cry* is the more marketable title, one cannot overlook the possibility that the 1976 published text might get performed under the 1973 published version's title without risk of much outcry from literary purists. But let's assume that the titles are directly indicative of which version was presented. Indeed, for the Paris production of *Out Cry*, the husband and wife acting team Robert Symonds and Priscilla Pointer claim to have "studied six extant versions of the play and delved into Williams' biographies, private correspondence and unpublished notes on an early production to discover, they said, 'the play that the author had hoped to complete'" (Grogan).

It was also *Out Cry* that was chosen over *The Two-Character Play* as the focus of a 1979 research seminar on dramatic form at the University of Wisconsin-Madison; the seminar culminated in a staged reading and led to a 1981 production. The rationale for that choice, according to one of the faculty leaders of the seminar, Esther M. Jackson, was that "the dilemma interpreted in *Out Cry* derives not so much from causes which are psychological as metaphysical. It is a poetic work, one which shares with certain of the dramas of Samuel Beckett, Jean-Paul Sartre, Harold Pinter, and Edward Albee a vision of an absurd universe" (6). In other words, the 1973 text offered the opportunity to explore more pronounced—or less "inhibited"—departures "from traditional uses of theatrical form" (80).

My own sense of the two plays is that on the page they are fairly equal contenders; the reader of both published versions will get from each an impression of the whole that will not differ substantially in terms of content or literary style.[1] When it comes to staging, however, the differences can add up significantly, both in terms of artistic choices made by the production team and audience reception. As Williams repeatedly revised the work—generating many more versions than the three that saw print during his lifetime—he certainly responded primarily to discoveries made in rehearsal and performance. Yet one detects also in comparing the 1973 and 1976 published texts some alterations that seem to respond to points made by the reviewers. For example, Richard Watts wrote that *Out Cry* was "too long," especially in the second act. The second act of *The Two-Character Play*, even though set in a larger typeface than the 1973 edition of *Out Cry*, is four pages shorter. Seeing *Out Cry* as "schizophrenia given dramatic shape," Douglas Watt mused whether the brother and sister characters "are one and the same person," while Martin Gottfried thought it was "difficult to tell the difference between *Out Cry* and the play within it." In Mel Gussow's words, "the two characters are too similar, not conflicting halves of a personality so much as one person talking to himself" (3). In *The Two-Character Play*, we find clearer distinctions between Clare and Felice as well as between the brother and sister acting team and the characters they portray in the inner play.

Williams recognized that early versions of the play were too long, as evidenced in his letters to Maria St. Just (220) and in his *Memoirs* (80). He worked on tightening the script during the autumn of 1970 in Bangkok and felt that he had a much improved version, now titled *Out Cry*, with which to go into rehearsal at the Ivanhoe Theatre in Chicago. George Keathley, director of that production, was surely the right person to nurture a work that had already been undergoing revisions for three years to the point that it had lost its shape. Indeed, when Williams later reread the limited edition of *The Two-Character Play* published in 1969, he saw "a simplicity and freshness that is now lost" (St. Just 250).

Having worked with George Keathley for fifteen years at Missouri Repertory Theatre (1985–2000), I know that his greatest strength as a director was clarity of storytelling; he could underscore the narrative throughline and bring out the immediacy of motivation in the most arcane writing. Keathley also knew how to leaven a drama with light moments. While rehearsing *Out Cry*, however, he soon saw that his challenge lay not so much in the play as in the playwright. In the summer of 1971, Williams was both vulnerable and volatile. In a letter to Maria St. Just, postmarked 23 July 1971, Williams recounted "one of my really apocalyptic rages" (232). Several eyewitnesses have reported the cruelty with which he broke off relations with Audrey Wood, his agent of many years (Wood 199–201; St. Just

231; Keathley). Keathley was concerned enough to seek help for Williams; he went to Claudia Cassidy, the Chicago *Tribune* drama critic whose appeals to her readership had saved *The Glass Menagerie* from closing prematurely in 1944 and had allowed it to move on to Broadway. Keathley and Cassidy spent about two hours in her apartment, discussing ways to help the tormented artist.[2] Perhaps it was Keathley's visit that prompted a letter from Cassidy that seems to have meant a lot to Williams: "Yesterday a sweet letter from Claudia which I'll have duplicated and sent to you. She says she is still haunted by the play and its 'unsparing magic'" (St. Just 232).

Donald Madden and Eileen Herlie proved to have been well cast as Felice and Clare, and the Chicago production was strong enough to get *Out Cry* optioned for Broadway. Williams's own assessment is recorded in a letter dated August 4, 1971: "At last, the night before leaving Chicago, I saw a truly beautiful performance of OUT CRY. All the comedy came through . . . , and [Herlie] was in exceptionally good (strong) voice, several people came up to me afterwards and said they considered it my best play. It is far from that, since one does not write his best play at sixty, but out of the Chicago gig I feel there has come, at long last, a closely knit and effective piece of theatre which would be a knock-out in the hands of [Margaret] Leighton and [Paul] Scofield" (St. Just 244).

During the year and a half before *Out Cry* opened at the Lyceum Theatre, produced by David Merrick, Williams was both working on his *Memoirs* and acting the role of Doc in *Small Craft Warnings*. His *Memoirs* are sprinkled with references to the process of working on the script with a new director, Peter Glenville. Notably, he comments: "Glenville has restored a lot of material that I excised with remarkable cunning during the Chicago gig. Now I must cut it out once again whether Peter approves or not" (80). His letters to St. Just remained upbeat about the production almost up to its opening (282). St. Just herself believed that the casting of such young, attractive actors as Michael York and Cara Duff-MacCormick undercut the play by robbing it of "its pathos and desperation" (282). By the time of the pre-Broadway run in Washington D.C., Williams's relationship with Glenville had seriously deteriorated. He felt that the director had not only made everything too literal in the visual design, but that Glenville had taken liberties with the script by incorporating bits "from all the versions," while Williams felt that he was "not being allowed to cut and revise as I should" (Devlin *Conversations* 289–90). "At the interval on opening night at the Lyceum," Williams recalled, "I heard someone descending from the balcony with me observe that the play had been better in its Chicago tryout the year before, and I turned to the stranger and said, 'Thanks, I agree'" (*Memoirs* 233).

The Broadway production's "failure" (291) was devastating to Williams, but he plunged ahead with further revisions for the 1973 published edition. He described that process in his *Memoirs:* "I was able, between production and publication, to edit out the material that impeded its flow, and to improve that opening monologue which had been mangled by dissension between author and director" (233).

Still Williams continued to revise the script as he worked with the 1975–76 productions that led to its 1976 publication as *The Two-Character Play*. He told a 1975 interviewer: "One of the great improvements now is that the play has been reduced to its proper size. Between a third and a fourth has been cut out" (290). That brings us back to the question of why theatre artists today seem to prefer the 1973 text over the later one, especially since the 1975–76 productions of *The Two-Character Play*, though not particularly high-profile ones, had been well received.

Several distinctions between the 1973 and 1976 published versions are significant with regard to staging the work. For example, the opening stage directions of *Out Cry* evoke greater menace and unreality than the merely "dismaying shapes and shadows" of *The Two-Character Play*. The *Out Cry* opening further calls for a sound score of underground "mechanical sounds suggesting an inhuman quality" (7). Thus the nightmarish quality of the frame-story setting for *Out Cry* reifies the characters' fear. There is more in this version to stimulate the imagination of the stage designer to give scenic form to projections of the characters' psyche. On the other hand, some critics would argue—as does William J. Free— that "the reduction of the dramatic symbolism" is "the most striking improvement" in *The Two-Character Play*. Free prefers that play's description of a setting that is "obviously a theater, not a demonic figment of someone's imagination" (827). Despite the intrinsic appeal of heightened theatricality in the *Out Cry* treatment, *The Two-Character Play* arguably holds stronger dramatic validity by its contrast between the "realism" of the theatre backstage and the artifice and incompleteness of the inner play's setting. A "realistic" frame-story setting gives the actor and actress a recognizable foundation from which to make their forays into make-believe or madness, rather than—as *Out Cry* might be said to do—launching them from pre-existing madness into a different level of escapist fantasy.

In *Out Cry* the actor playing Felice gets to begin with a physical action—he attempts to push away the enormous statue that dominates the dark area of the stage—as opposed to the later version in which he begins by talking to himself about his unfocused fear. Clare's entrance in *Out Cry* is heralded by a flash of humor in response to Felice's line "I yelled my head off." Her quick comeback is: "Oh. Decapitated?" (9). In contrast, *The Two-Character Play*'s incarnation of Clare enters as if she were a warmed-over Blanche DuBois, projecting a grand manner despite her disheveled hair and tawdry tiara. So many more funny lines as well as literary references intersperse *Out Cry* that one almost suspects that Williams achieved his tightening in *The Two-Character Play* by rejecting both laughs and literati.

Out Cry sometimes employs its metatheatricality more skillfully. Felice tells the live audience to "Imagine the curtain is down" before he establishes their functional reality as a component of the play when he comments on them to Clare (9). When he shouts to Clare, "Will you quit shouting with an audience out there?" (10), he effectively subsumes the live audience into the play's audience. *The Two-Character Play* fails to achieve that degree of audience complicity. That is, it does not adequately set up the convention of the live audience doubling as a component in the narrative: Felice's earliest direct reference to the live theatre audience is when he says "They're coming in" (313), though the actual audience is aware of having been settled in their seats for some time already.

On the other hand, *The Two-Character Play* makes better use of the piano for metatheatrical effect: Clare asserts herself as a collaborator in the creation of the inner play by insisting on cuts in the script whenever she strikes a note on the piano (324), and she strikes a chord on the piano to bring Act One to an end (339). The act ending in *Out Cry* had put the emphasis more explicitly on the possibility that Clare—either Clare the actress or Clare the character in the inner play or both in one—is mentally unbalanced: "Felice! There is a gunman out there. A man with a gun pointed at me." So Felice tells the real audience: "I am afraid there will have to be an interval of about ten minutes while my sister recovers. You see, she is not at all well tonight" (37). *The Two-Character Play* maintains tension between the two at the end of the act as they exit arguing over the length of the interval to be taken.

The criticism that *Out Cry* was weighted down by its heavy-handed symbolism seems to crop up less often in commentary on *The Two-Character Play*. In fact, the same repertoire of symbols and imagery used in *Out Cry*—doors and windows, light and dark, the statue, astrological signs, sunflowers, soap bubbles, opal ring, revolver—reappear in *The Two-Character Play,* but perhaps seem to operate with greater subtlety in the context of the more pronounced narrative throughline. According to Douglas Watt's review of *Out Cry,* the program included a quotation from the Song of Solomon: "A garden enclosed is my sister . . . a spring shut up, a fountain sealed." Although both published versions of the play use only the first six words as epigraph, the water symbolism of the complete verse is interesting with reference to the specified locale of both inner plays: "a deep Southern town called New Bethesda." In the Bible, Bethesda was the name of a pool where Jesus healed a man who had been paralyzed (John 5:9). In the dialogue of *Out Cry,* New Bethesda is mentioned several times, as if to emphasize the symbolism of the name, but most of those dialogue references have dropped out of *The Two-Character Play.* In *Out Cry* then, the epigraph's identification of the sister with an enclosed source of water coupled with the Biblical allusion of the inner play's locale seem to point to an interpretation of the sister as healer, which could certainly inform an approach to production.

From a dramaturgical point of view, the challenge posed by both scripts is that they do not give their audiences much to cling to or identify with in terms of what's at stake for the protagonists. For one thing, fear of confinement is a rather abstract obstacle on which to build dramatic conflict. It is a passive, psychological source of conflict rather than an active, dramatic one. Further, most viewers will latch onto the dilemma of the "real" people, the actor and actress Felice and Clare, as opposed to the characters of Felice and Clare in the inner play, where those characters' problems are distanced as the stuff of "only a play." Granted the concerns and leitmotivs of the inner play skillfully echo those of the larger situation and granted Williams was experimenting with a form intended to communicate emotional texture rather than traditional dramatic action, theatregoers still crave a story and characters that relate on some level to their own lives. When Felice and Clare get "lost in the play" that Felice has written for them, they remove themselves from the most immediate throughline of action and thus from the audience's active identification with them. In this respect, Williams's giving Clare in *The Two-Character Play* the initiative of the note on the piano as a cue to move out of the inner play, even momentarily, indicates that he recognized the problem. The ability of the actress to control the situation in which her character finds herself probably serves to keep the inner-play action more dependent upon the dominant narrative.

These concerns are counterbalanced by the brilliant theatricality of Williams's use of the telegram in both *Out Cry* and *The Two-Character Play* though the device surely packs more punch in the later play. Early in the action of both, Felice shows Clare a telegram from their acting company: "Your sister and you are—*insane!*" Two stagehands had stayed just long enough to put up part of the setting for Felice's "The Two-Character Play" and then deserted them as did the rest of the company (OC 17; 2CP 321). In Act One of both versions, Felice and Clare are jolted out of the theatrical reality of their performance of Felice's "The Two-Character Play" and back into their own personae when they spot the telegram on the set. Felice crumples the telegram and tosses it out the window, and they resume the performance (OC 28–29; 2CP 329). The payoff comes near the end of Act Two when the actor and actress Felice and Clare—realizing that they cannot leave the cold, dark theatre—prepare to escape into the warmth of their art and get lost one last time in a performance of Felice's "Two-Character Play." In *Out Cry* Felice goes out the door of their setting "to get the telegram from the company," returns with it, and places it on the table (68–69). In *The Two-Character Play* the sequence builds more dramatically to the telegram as a stunning metatheatrical touch that suddenly rattles every convention we had bought into about the play's levels of reality. First Felice turns on the taperecorded musical underscoring. Then he convinces Clare to take off her coat as a way of getting into "the feeling of summer" in the inner play. Then it is Clare who directs him: "Put the cablegram back on the sofa!" (366–367), which he does.

In the more poetic ending of *Out Cry,* the revolver is de-emphasized. Felice holds a position looking out the window of the set while Clare crosses to get the revolver from beneath the sofa pillow. But she doesn't even pick it up. Instead she crosses to him, and they stand together as the lights fade on them in a stage death transcending reality (71–72). The final action is considerably more protracted in *The Two-Character Play:* Clare takes up the revolver, holds it at arm's length, aims at Felice, and hesitates. He says: "Do it while you still can!" She drops the revolver and asks if he can do it. Felice picks it up, aims at Clare, and "tries very hard to pull the trigger," but drops the revolver. They reach out toward each other, then embrace and disappear in total darkness (369–370). This version's ending caps what has been throughout the action a clearer balance of responsibility between the two characters in the creation of both the framing play and the inner play.

Setting aside the demands of the stage, there are various ways to analyze the literary values of both plays and allow them to break out of the categories—"confessional, autobiographical" theatre (Gottfried), "an enigma" (Watts), "a Pirandellian exercise" (Watt)—to which they have been consigned or "confined." Biographical criticism necessarily begins with the brother-sister relationship, which evokes that of young Tom Williams and his sister Rose, and would also relate the theme of confinement to Williams's unhappy period of employment at the shoe company as well as to his incarceration at Barnes Hospital. Those who are overwhelmed by the enigmatic quality of the plays[3] might well consider the references to madness and insanity in terms of the mutuality of form and content; that is, the breakdown of conventional dramaturgy reifies the mental state of the brother and sister in the inner play, as well as that of their creators (author Felice and both characters as performers) in the framing play, and perhaps by implication that of the creator of the whole, Tennessee Williams. To see Pirandellian influences in *Out Cry* and *The Two-Character Play* is to focus on the plays' frequent switching of levels of reality and to explore their many metatheatrical devices. In an article published as this one was going to press, Kalliopi Nikolopoulou intriguingly suggests that Williams adopted a symbolist aesthetic (which implies minimalization of the material elements of theatre) as a means of expressing in *Out Cry* the ineffability of the reality of death. In Nikolopou's interpretation, the play's "dramatic stasis" (132) arises from its "negative poetics" (133), exemplified in the possibility that the play can be "read inside out" (123) with the inner play as the reality and the outer play as a strategy of endless improvisation to put off closure: "in refusing to depict death as a literal part of the action, *Out Cry* unfolds as the supreme game of putting death into words and yielding meaning out of nothingness" (135).

My own literary interpretation, which might not translate into anything playable on stage, rests more upon *Out Cry* than upon *The Two-Character Play* and takes its cue from the very title. Although Williams referred to the play as his own "human outcry," he clearly conflated his own humanity with his artistry. The play is the outcry of the artist whose creative drive is a kind of madness, a *furor poeticus*. Just as Ibsen reflected on his own artistic trajectory and accomplishments through the character of the mature architect in *The Master Builder*, so the mature Williams necessarily drew upon his record of past achievements and familiar themes. We cannot know with certainty whether the house's having had its electricity cut off intentionally conjures association with *The Glass Menagerie* and the "threadbare rose in the carpet" deliberately evokes *The Rose Tattoo* or whether such touches simply occur as part of Williams's unconscious repertoire of images. Yet the abundance of such allusions, both obvious and oblique, implies some awareness of self-referentiality on the part of the artist (and, indeed, some confidence that his reading and/or theatrical public knows his canon well enough to pick up on some of them). Linda Dorff notes that "nearly every Williams play contains some form of staircase," and cites *The Glass Menagerie* and *A Streetcar Named Desire* for their stairs leading "down into ever deeper levels of inferno" (116). In *Out Cry* "these stairs go nowhere, they stop in space" (14); "the—stairs don't go upstairs, the steps—stop in—space!" (56). The incompleteness of this staircase, like the incompleteness of the entire setting for the play-within-the-play, recalls one of Williams's obsessions as an artist, one that is explored extensively in *In the Bar of a Tokyo Hotel*: fear of incompletion. The theme also finds expression in *Out Cry* through Felice's twice forgetting his lines and by the admission that his *Two-Character Play* never had an ending. The *mise en abyme* for that interpretation of *Out Cry* would be Clare's recollection early in the play of climbing five flights of stairs to visit a destitute old painter and finding him "seated in *rigor mortis* before a totally blank canvas" (11).

If *Out Cry* is indeed about the concerns of the artist for his artistry—or, in other words, if it is an exemplar of the old dictum that "the subject of art is art"— one would have to signal Felice as representing the artist, the creative consciousness. His alter ego Clare is his art, so close as to be virtually inseparable from himself. Felice threatens to leave Clare and even makes the attempt but tells the audience: "Impossible without her. No, I can't leave her alone. I feel so exposed, so cold" (55). Shortly after, she says: "Oh, what a long, long, way we've traveled together, too long, now, for separation" (59). Felice often refers to her beauty, her "face of an angel" (33, 48, 59) as if she were his muse.

The stage setting of the house in New Bethesda—a place of summer light and warmth, but also the site of a lurid murder-suicide—represents the world of the theatre, where Williams's art has been brought to life over the years. As Felice says, "And behind me I feel the house. It seems to be breathing a faint, warm breath on my back. I feel it the way you feel a loved person standing close behind you." But a few lines later, he says: "I realize, now, that the house has turned into a prison" (55). The theatre was for Williams a place of creative self-realization as well as a place of confinement when his artistry encountered obstacles to its fullest expression. In *Out Cry,* the house is surrounded by "sacred flowers" (39); it has a door that sometimes stands open and is sometimes locked (48); it is a place of "unexpected collisions" (29). For Felice and Clare as inhabitants of the house in the inner play, there are threats all around: "those vicious boys" (45), "voices from the street" taunting them as "loonies" (49), neighbors who "gave their son a slingshot to stone the house!" (57). If the house represents the theatre, it is surrounded by philistines and even under attack by critics.

The New Bethesda house is an incomplete stage setting on a larger stage "in a huge mausoleum of a theater somewhere that seems like nowhere" (16). On that darkened stage in a cold, confining theatre facility, the Felice and Clare of the framing play embody the vulnerabilities of the artist and his art in a harsh world. The artist's turmoil and inspiration, whether based on actuality or on something lurking within his psyche like the "huge, dark statue upstage" (7), come out of that darkness. When Felice first addresses the audience in that theatre in Part One of *Out Cry* (23), there is no indication of any hostility on the part of the spectators. At the end of the act, however, Clare says in a tone that is "completely real": "Felice! There is a gunman out there. A man with a gun pointed at me" (37). By the end of Part Two, the audience has left—"en masse!" (60). Felice and Clare's realization that they are trapped inside the building "in this frozen country" (66) suggests that without an audience for one's art, the world is a prison. Still the art and the artist cry out. Whether the artist's out cry is heard or not, the artist finds refuge in the art itself. Felice and Clare get "lost in the play" (71) and conclude that "magic is the habit of our existence" (72).

Proceeding from this understanding of *Out Cry* as the artist's poetic reflection on his art, many lines of dialogue take on resonances that are pertinent to Williams's sense of his place in American theatre. Felice's opening speech about having tried to conceal his "feeling of confusion" followed by his expression of fear both relate to Williams's awareness that his work no longer had the mass appeal of his early plays. Some observations on the plight of the artist are stated quite literally: "you know that artists put so much into their work, that they've got very little left over for acting like other people, their behavior is bound to seem peculiar" (18), and "if we're not artists, we're nothing" (22). Other lines refer metaphorically to the creative process: "Sleepless people love rummaging. I look through pockets that I know are empty" (27); "people are attracted by a sudden disturbance in a house that seemed vacant" (34). Felice hints at the plight of the artist who wishes to innovate: "it's wise to be cautious about things you've never—" (31). Clare tells him: "I'm sorry but you'd allowed yourself to lose contact with anything that seemed real" (47).

Both *Out Cry* or *the Two-Character Play* are rich explorations of the nature of art and the creative drive of the artist. Both are deserving of further exploration on the stage as well as on the page. It will be interesting to see which play emerges over the long haul as most frequently engaging the sensibilities of the artists whose souls will inhabit the two characters and whose voices will echo Williams's outcry.

Notes

1. Drewey Wayne Gunn's capsule assessment in his 1980 bibliography (p. 83) expresses a different view. He refers to the 1969 edition, the unpublished 1971 manuscript, the 1973 and the 1976 editions: "The first version was performed in 1967. It lacked much of the symbolism of later versions and was without an intermission. Its structure is more satisfactory, but its development is less interesting. The second version was produced in 1971. The third version is perhaps the worst play Williams has ever written; the fourth, produced in 1975, is among his most interesting. In both these latter scripts the play within the play remains almost the same; it is the characters themselves and their response to their fate which have changed so radically. Both plays are too long, however."
2. As Keathley was leaving, Cassidy generously gave him one of the three remaining pieces, the elephant, from the original glass menagerie that had been used on stage in *The Glass Menagerie* in 1944–45. The entire collection of twelve glass animals had been given to her at the end of the run. Keathley continued the tradition of generosity upon his retirement in August 1999, presenting the piece to his successor at the helm of Missouri Repertory Theatre.

3. The opening two sentences of Richard Watts's review of *Out Cry,* for example, incorporate the words "puzzling," "baffling," "enigma," "cryptic," and "riddle." The third sentence adds "befuddlement."

Works Cited

Colt, Jay Leo. "Dancing in Red Hot Shoes," *The Tennessee Williams Review* 3, no. 2 (Spring/Fall 1982), 6–8.

Devlin, Albert J., ed. *Conversations with Tennessee Williams.* Jackson: UP of Mississippi, 1986.

Dorff, Linda. "Babylon Now: Tennessee Williams's Apocalypses," *Theater* 29, no. 3, 115–121.

Free, William J. "Williams in the Seventies: Directions and Discontents." In Tharpe, 815–828.

Gottfried, Martin. Review of *Out Cry. Women's Wear Daily* (5 March 1973). *New York Theatre Critics' Reviews* 344.

Grogan, Molly. "The Theater," *The Paris Free Voice* (accessed 16 May 2001). < http://parisvoice.com/99/june/html/theatre.cfm >

Gunn, Drewey Wayne. *Tennessee Williams: A Bibliography.* Metuchen, NJ: The Scarecrow Press, Inc., 1980. Second edition, 1991.

Gussow, Mel. "Catharsis for Tennessee Williams?" *New York Times* (11 March 1973), Sec. 2, pp. 1, 5.

Harris, Leonard. Review of *Out Cry,* WCBS TV2 (1 March 1973). *New York Theatre Critics' Reviews* 356.

Jackson, Esther M. "Tennessee Williams' OUT CRY: Studies in Dramatic Form at The University of Wisconsin, Madison," *The Tennessee Williams Newsletter* II, 2 (Fall 1980), 6–12.

Jennings, C. Robert. "Playboy Interview: Tennessee Williams." In Devlin, 224–50.

Kalem, T.E. "The Crack-Up." *Time* 101 (12 March 1973), 89. *New York Theatre Critics' Reviews* 344.

Keathley, George. Personal conversations, 1986–2000. Telephone message from Key West, 18 September 2001.

Kroll, Jack. "Prisoners' Base." *Newsweek* 81 (12 March 1973), 88. *New York Theater Critic's Reviews* 344.

Lewis, Peter. Review of *The Two-Character Play. The Daily Mail* (London, 12 December 1967).

Londré, Felicia Hardison. *Tennessee Williams.* New York: Frederick Ungar Publishing Co., 1979.

Morris, Steven Leigh. "The Kindness of Strangers: Tennessee Williams on every streetcorner," *LA Weekly* http://www.laweekly.com/ink/99/37/theater-morris.shtml(accessed 16 May 2001).

Nikolopoulou, Kalliopi. "Le Jeu Suprême": Some Mallarmean Echoes in Tennessee Williams's *Out Cry.*" *Tennessee Williams: A Casebook,* ed. by Robert F. Gross. New York: Routledge, 2002, 121–138.

Parker, R.B. "The Circle Closed: A Psychological Reading of *The Glass Menagerie* and *The Two-Character Play." Modern Drama* 28:4 (1985), 517–534.

Rader, Dotson. "The Art of Theater V," interview with Tennessee Williams. *The Paris Review* 81 (Fall 1981), 145–196.

St. Just, Maria. *Five O'Clock Angel: Letters of Tennessee Williams to Maria St. Just 1948–1982.* New York: Viking Penguin, 1990.

Tharpe, Jac, ed. *Tennessee Williams: A Tribute*. Jackson: University of Mississippi Press, 1977.

Watt, Douglas. "'Out Cry' Is Williams Puzzler." *New York Daily News* (2 March 1973), 50. *New York Theatre Critics' Reviews* 343.

Watts, Richard, Jr. "Tennessee Williams' Enigma." *New York Post* (2 March 1973), 30. *New York Theatre Critics' Reviews* 345.

Williams, Tennessee. *Memoirs*. Garden City, NY: Doubleday and Co., Inc., 1975.

———. "Notes for *The Two Character Play*" (dated March 1970, with a Contributor's Note by Thomas P. Adler), *The Tennessee Williams Review* 3, no. 2 (Spring/Fall 1982), 3–5.

———. *Out Cry*. New York: New Directions, 1973. Also in *Tennessee Williams: Plays 1957–1980*, ed. by Mel Gussow and Kenneth Holdich. New York: The Library of America, 2000.

———. *Stairs to the Roof*. New York: New Directions, 2000.

———. *The Two-Character Play*. *The Theatre of Tennessee Williams* Vol. 5. New York: New Directions, 1976. 301–370.

"Williams Drama Baffles Critics." *New York Times* (13 December 1967), 54.

Wilson, Edwin. "A Writer's Cry of Desolation," *The Wall Street Journal* (6 March 1973), 30. *New York Theatre Critics' Reviews* 345.

Wood, Audrey, with Max Wilk. *Represented by Audrey Wood*. Garden City, NY: Doubleday and Co., Inc., 1981.

Philip C. Kolin

"HAVING LOST THE ABILITY TO SAY: 'MY GOD!'": THE THEOLOGY OF TENNESSEE WILLIAMS'S *SMALL CRAFT WARNINGS*

The events surrounding the genesis, opening, and subsequent stage history of *Small Craft Warnings* are filled with the same symbolic sensationalism that attaches to Tennessee Williams himself. These events—some bizarre, others coincidental, perhaps a few even providential—help to situate Williams's play in its critical and cultural contexts. Like so many other later Williams's plays, *Small Craft Warnings* has been shrunk to a *roman à clef*. Emerging from the evocative one-act *The Confessional*, which premiered Off-Broadway in January 1972, *Small Craft* opened on April 2, 1972, Easter Sunday night, the week that Williams (born on Palm Sunday in 1911) celebrated his 61st birthday. It premiered at the Truck and Warehouse Theatre in the Bowery (East Fourth Street), where each morning as Williams attended rehearsals he was greeted by the derelicts congregated around the theatre (O'Haire 35)—the real-life counterparts to the legion of the lost portrayed in *Small Craft* as well as those drifters from the California bars of the early 1940s that Williams frequented. Monk's bar in *Small Craft* offered the same blue-collar ambience as did the area surrounding the Truck and Warehouse. (Ironically, *Small Craft Warnings* was restaged in 1976 in the "center of the main bar-room" of Morgan's Old New York Bar and Grill with the patrons becoming "part of the set" [Frank].) The critics at once linked the drinking in *Small Craft* to Williams and his theatre. Alluding to the playwright's addiction to liquor (and drugs), Harold Clurman assaulted Williams for peddling old wares as new fare: "This . . . is not the Williams of today, whatever his spiritual condition may now be. The play is an encapsulation of past history. We can only hope that when the playwright gets the residue of his toxic affections out of his system (I refer to the plays of his period of exhaustion), he can give a fresh voice to whatever his recovery may dictate" (540). John Simon was even more combative: "It is, clearly, the play of a man who has lost all sense of give and take with life, except for dimly recording the mumblings in barrooms from Tokyo to New Orleans." Simon concluded that: "The result was self-parody" (84).

In June of 1972, *Small Craft* moved uptown to the New Theatre where Williams himself entered the script by playing Doc, a drunken, disbarred physician strung out on booze and Benzedrine, as Williams himself frequently was (Lux). Marilyn Stasio recorded of actor Williams: "At first, his presence is disconcerting; not because of his obviously untutored acting skills, but simply because he is there, that great playwright, exposed to the eye and so terribly vulnerable" (9). During

Tennessee Williams as "Doc" in *Small Craft Warnings*. Richard Freeman Leavitt Collection / University of Tennessee.

part of his three-month acting stint, Williams extended his vulnerability to audiences after performances of *Small Craft*. Ads running in the *New York Times* enticed potential ticket buyers with this langiappe: "Mr. Williams will appear in person on stage at the end of each performance this week—to discuss with the audience the play or any other topic which might interest the spectator" (2–7 June 1972). Several critics accused Williams of crass commercialism, doing anything to hype his new play. Signi Falk, for one, claimed that "Plays like *Seven Descents of Myrtle* and *Small Craft Warnings,* padded extensions of the past, were perhaps written to make money" (128–129). Quoting from Williams's preface to *Small Craft,* "Too Personal," C.W.E. Bigsby psychoanalyzed: "As he explained, having, in his own mind, just emerged from a period in which he retreated from public view and in a sense reality itself, he had an almost insatiable hunger for recognition of the fact that he [was], indeed, still alive, both as man and artist" (115). Williams's public presence also extended "to countless press and broadcast interviews, and [he] even turned up one night recently delivering the weather report on WNEW-TV's Channel 5 New Show" ("Tennessee Williams Acting"), no doubt because of the metaphor he chose for the title of his new play.

Williams was not the only sensational presence in the play. When *Small Craft* moved to the New Theatre, a press release from Gifford/Wallace, the public relations firm representing the theatre, announced that "The show is much 'lighter' in its present form, has had substantial re-writing during its run with the author on stage. The 'new look' deserves a new look" (Trenkle "Dear Critic"). Joining the new, lighter script was the drag queen Candy Darling, who replaced Cherry Davis in the role of Violet, the nympho barfly who makes a living by masturbating men underneath barroom tables. Diva Candy contributed to the sexual titillation for which Williams was infamous. "With the help of Andy Warhol, who named her 'Girl of the Year, 1969,' this leggy blonde with heaps of talent and taste in wedgies has climbed to the very bottom of the heaps and stands out today as America's most glamorous and misunderstood drag queen" (Howell 9). Celebrating the sexual, the outrageous, Candy further underscored Williams's perceived penchant for the grotesque, the sensational, the irreligious. Candy was "an actress who began life as a boy" and whose mother always wanted him/her to appear in a Tennessee Williams play (Dick Brunkenfeld). Commenting on the "confessional" technique Candy and others used to spill their guts in *Small Craft,* Benedict Nightingale ascerbically lampooned Williams himself as an inept priest/playwright: "His characters are often true and touching; but he himself resembles the kind of indolent confessor who shrugs his shoulders and dispatches the sinner to say a couple of 'Hail Marys' after meals" (209).

As is unfortunately clear from its critical reception over the last 30 years, *Small Craft Warnings* has been classified largely as a dramatized script of Williams's life—his camp sensibilities, his addictions, his outrage, his chimeras, his regressions, his need for self-disclosure. Reviewing a revival by the Worth Street Company in New York in 1999, Les Gutman again read Williams the man as the script. "There's no doubt Williams met some variations of each of these creatures many times over the course of his own lifetime of bar-hopping. Several he probably became acquainted with while staring in a mirror." Critics have attempted to see almost every one of the major characters in *Small Craft* as a Williams's psychic look-a-like. Conceivably, each character became a chapter in Williams's self-canon. The scenario goes as follows: like Doc, who was unable to practice medicine (his trade), Williams was separated from audiences in part through his excesses in booze and drugs and in part because of hostile critics and profit-crazed producers. No doubt directors and producers wondered if Williams, like Doc, would ever come back? Elyse Sommer conjectured that Bobby was "Williams's younger alter ego." Like Bobby, Williams yearned for travel and surprises. Quentin, another putative surrogate for the playwright, worked as a screenwriter as Williams did at MGM. Reviewing the revival of the play at the Jean Cocteau Repertory in 2001, Michael Sommers claimed, "One suspects that Quentin's rueful observations mirror the playwright's own feelings as he neared the end of his life." Leona and Violet also might be recuperated as the two sides of Williams's psyche—the Stanley and Blanche hemispheres. Like Williams, both feverishly seek desire, though in different voices. Of all the characters, though, Monk, the hospitalier of the sick and the outcast, may best symbolize the quintessential Tennessee Williams, attracting and sheltering derelicts in New Orleans, New York, and Key West. According to Norman J. Fedder, Monk is "Williams's alter ego" (808).

This line of customary critical inquiry is reductive, circular, and obviates *Small Craft* as a playscript. For too long speculation about Williams, not analyses of the plays he actually wrote, empowered critics to deny his later works the status of major, bold achievements. Critics have used biography as both filter and flagellum. The script of *Small Craft Warnings* deserves a life of its own. Which is not to deny Williams's plea "for a playwright to put his own persona into his work" ("Too Personal" 5), but even he wisely qualified and adjusted such a declaration. Commenting on his "defense of the personal kind of writing," Williams admitted: "Now I assure you it can be overdone. It is the responsibility of the writer to put his experience as a being into work that refines and elevates it and that makes of it an essence that a wide audience can somehow manage to feel in themselves: 'This is true'" ("Too Personal" 6). As Nicholas Pagan proposed a decade ago, maybe it is the work that shapes the life and not the other way around. Accordingly, we need to de-center Williams as the dominant text and move to assigning agency to the script as the meditation between culture and audience, idea and consumption, belief system and representation. In doing so, I want to show that in *Small Craft Warnings* Williams in fact "refines and elevates" the deepest spiritual values that shaped his life through his work to produce one of the most Christian (theological) plays in his canon.

Williams repeatedly and consistently saw himself as a Christian writer. As biographer Lyle Leverich correctly pointed out, "a religious undercurrent, a struggle for faith, can be found throughout Tennessee Williams major works. His self-proclaimed role as that of a rebellious puritan grew out of a little boy's search for

God" (591). In his *Memoirs,* Williams shared an epiphanic experience he had while on a European tour with his grandfather, the Rev. Mr. Walter Dakin. While visiting a cathedral, he powerfully felt the presence of God. "I had no doubt at all that the hand of our Lord Jesus had touched my head" (21). Again from the *Memoirs,* Williams defined writing in Christian terms as the "passion to create which is all we know of God" (242). Baptized a Roman Catholic in 1969 by Jesuit Father Joseph LeRoy, Williams confessed, "I've always been religious . . . I was religious as an Episcopalian and I'm still religious as a Catholic. I pray a lot, especially when I'm scared" (qtd. in Phillips 565). In an interview with Dotson Rader in *The Paris Review* (1981), Williams similarly professed: "I was born a Catholic really. I'm Catholic by nature. My grandfather was an English Catholic" (qtd. in Devlin 333). He added: "My work is full of Christian symbols. Deeply, deeply Christian" (qtd. in Devlin 334).

Unfortunately, Williams's highly symbolic Christian beliefs have not been given attention in *Small Craft Warnings,* where they translate into something far more elevated than the bar mumblings of a decadent writer. Except for a brief reference by John MacNicholas to the sacrament of confession in *Small Craft,* critics have avoided the productive intervention of Christian ideas, ideologically and structurally, in the script. Yet most significantly, *Small Craft* movingly ends with one of the most positive engagements of man/woman with God through others. The play is charged with key theological issues relating to God, life and death, love, and responsibility as Williams sees them. There are also plenty of *mea culpas* to go around. As Leona asserts, "all of you are responsible" for the protection of human life (37). *Small Craft* is a Tennessee Williams's parable—a ministering (dramatic) sacrament—on loneliness, love, redemption, and salvation. Its primary goal is to announce and to celebrate epiphanies—in the "kingdom of earth" (47)—at Monk's. In fact, *Small Craft* presents an eschatological finale of sorts to the previous decade of Williams's work. Many of the plays of the 1960s and early 1970s are activated through Christian sympathy and symbology. *Night of the Iguana* (1961), for example, interrogates the dark night of the soul; *The Mutilated* (1966), perhaps Williams's most prophetic play, invokes the Blessed Mother as the *dea ex machina* bringing order and revelation. And two other plays preceding *Small Craft—The Milk Train Doesn't Stop Here Anymore* (1964) and *Kingdom of Earth* (1967)—delve deeply into the human predicament, on the loss and the resurrection of faith, *sub species aeternitatis.*

As a drama of souls, *Small Craft* appropriately begins with a set suggesting landscapes invested with key spiritual significance. Williams's ecosystem is far more complex and tight—theologically and psychologically—than critics have been willing to concede. As the opening stage direction points out, *"The scene is a somewhat nonrealistic evocation of a bar on the beach-front in one of those coastal towns between Los Angeles and San Diego"* (11). The setting is highly revelatory; it is on the margins, a "between" place, between water and land, between safety and terror. Characterizing Williams's set as "spiritual" and "otherworldly," Scott Shattuck, who directed *Small Craft* at the Jean Cocteau Repertory in 2001, observed that "Williams takes the terra firma right out from under the feet of his characters, leaving them to seek their footing on sea or mist" ("Dreaded Fog People"). Many of Williams's later plays similarly use a coastal setting to allegorize spiritual conflicts—*Night of the Iguana, Gnädiges Fräulein, Milk Train, Something Cloudy, Something Clear.* Monk's bar is between the city of the angels to the north and a fiery diablo to the south. It is a half-way world, neither saved nor yet completely lost; it is "barroom purgatory," as John Lahr observed (60). A weather broadcast heard in the bar confirms such symbolization: *"heavy seas from Point Conception to the Mexican border"* (15). The souls in Monk's are under warnings from birth to death in their purgatorial, quotidian lives. South of the Border could evoke great passion or terror for Williams (Kolin "Compañero Tenn"). Mexico, to the south, is clearly a menace in *Small Craft*. As Leona warns Bobby: "Mexico is dangerous country for you, and there's lonely stretches of the road" (49). Significantly, one of Monk's most loyal friends "died in Mexico City" (51). No wonder Leona wants to drive her trailer far north, to Sausalito, to escape storms, loneliness, annihilation. Caught between heaven and hell, sea and land, Sausalito and lonely roads, Monk's refugees are forced to live and work out their salvation in the trepidatious liminal world where faith and companionship offer the only solace.

Two major design elements of the set—the fog and the *"ocean sounds outside"* (34)—complement the apologetics of the script. The sound of the ocean, heard several times throughout the production, is analogous to the cathedral bells in *Streetcar*—"they're the only clean thing in the Quarter" (410). Taking advantage of the ocean (water) as healing, cleansing, and life-giving, *Small Craft* powerfully closes with the "boom of the ocean outside" (73), the a sound of resolution and purification. Associated with the sea is *"a large varnished sailfish, whose gaping bill and goggle eyes give it a constant look of amazement"* (11). Suspended over Monk's bar, the fish is *"hooked and shellacked and strung up like a flag . . . over much lesser creatures that never, ever sailed an inch in their . . . lives"* (25). The fish, a traditional symbol for the Christ, is indeed the flag for redemption at Monk's. Its large eyes symbolically pierce every one of Monk's patrons, and its "look of amazement" exhorts the necessity of surprise central to the recuperation of souls, which is at the crux of *Small Craft Warnings.*

But the fog may be the signature element of *Small Craft Warnings:* it sits, permeates, isolates, freezes. Fog represents stasis, suspension, the sense of nothing happening, the perfect signifier for the lack of dramatic action, or story, that many critics complained about but have misread in the play. A typical critical response is that of Michael Smith: *"Small Craft Warnings* is without drama; there is hardly any structure of events to keep things moving along; the first act is a monologue punctuated with outbursts of boozly emotion and self-accounting; the second a series of attenuated exits" (61). A somewhat more benign view of such inactivity comes from William J. Free who identified this characteristic as the only novel feature of *Small Craft Warnings:* "The newness in *Small Craft Warnings* is the note of boredom and weariness with life, or more accurately, a delicate tonal quality to that weariness seldom encountered before" (819). Yet both readings neglect/omit the theological.

The fog is a key vehicle to identify and to characterize the liminal state of the lost—the "between" people—Williams is spiritualizing. The fog rolling in is a perfect symbol for the morass in which Monk's lost souls flounder. It is not the enshrinement of wisdom but the absence of direction. The curtain separating union and isolation, life and death, heaven and hell, comfort and corruption, the fog is the perfect atmospheric metaphor for those "who have lost the ability to say: 'My God!'" (47). Aptly enough, Monk's customers are known as "the fog people." So many times throughout *Small Craft* characters go into the fog—and danger—outside. Leona "disappeared in the fog" to report Doc (38); she also warns Bobby to stay inside and not travel: "On a bike, yeah, too late, with the dreaded fog people out" (48). But despite Monk's protection the fog seeps into their souls. "Or is everything foggy to you, is your mind in a cloud?" Leona asks Violet. Diagnosing Steve's malady, Leona claims, "The fog is in your head, which is as thick as the fog on the beach." The vulnerable human vessels in *Small Craft Warnings* sail in fog, tossed between belief and extinction. The fog is an integral part of the catechesis for the lost who need to learn about self through experiencing others and God.

In this fog-encased setting Williams portrays the postlapsarian world not just as "the rag and bone shop of the heart" (W. B. Yeats's 'The Circus Animals' Desertion') but in its most theologically elemental, base sense a marketplace of the flesh. The selfish or isolated world Monk's patrons inhabit is a cesspool—putrefying, corrupt and corrupting. Williams emphasizes the fallen "kingdom of earth" (47)—echoing Genesis 3:17 ("Accursed be the soil because of you")—primarily through the olfactory sense, the stench and stain of the human body and its excrements. Monk says it poetically: "I always leave the doors open for a few minutes to clear the smoke and liquor out of the place, the human odors, and to hear the ocean" (73). But Doc is more blunt, to the point: "The toilet still overflows," and *"his pants cuffs are wet"* (63) to prove it. Perhaps in no other Williams play does the putrefaction of the flesh more harrowingly symbolize the postlapsarian condition. The verbal and physical references to the "human odors" significantly contribute to the purgatory of smells and sounds in which Williams's characters are immersed. Williams's repellent imagery points to how far Monk's patrons have fallen but also, benevolently, how far they can rise. In a 1968 interview with Mike Wallace, Williams affirmed, "I would rather think of my characters in terms of their spiritual honesty, sympathy . . . than in terms of their failings" (qtd. in Phillips 564).

Moreover, what is most disgusting, impenitent in terms of Williams's theology in *Small Craft Warnings*, is that so often desire is linked/attached to these "human odors," interpellating scatological erotics into the audience's moral consciousness. *Small Craft* is saturated with the cropo-erotic. The play mines the sites of desire and shows how each is fouled with connections to bodily discharges. Worms, urine, feces, vomit, tears, sweat—all greet and taint those in need of salvation at Monk's. *Small Craft* turns desire inside out, de-romanticizing its physical sites to emphasize the loneliness and rejection, associated with the depravity of the heart, the ultimate sin for Williams. Recalling the Chicano woman to whom he made love, Doc reveals: "She had worms . . . diet of rotten beef tacos . . . [and he said]

'Bring me a sample of your stool for lab analysis.' She didn't know what I meant . . . I finally said 'Senorita, bring me a little piece of your shit in a bottle'" (13). Doc's desire is rooted in the soiled humanity of this "wet leg" woman: "Dewormed the lady and laid her in place of payment." Later, Doc again juxtaposes feces and the death of desire: "to put out the panic light in dying-out eyes . . . absorbent cotton [is] inserted in the rectum to hold back the bowels discharged when . . . the being *stops*" (35).

Violet, the play's nymph, is also attacked for her bodily uncleanliness, the dirt that clings to and defines her humanity as well as her quest to fulfill desire. Describing Violet's hands, which she uses to grope men, Leona zeroes in on the shame and baseness of Violet's condition: "The red enamel had nearly all chipped off the nails and the fingernails, black . . . like she'd spend every day for a month without washing her hands after making mud-pies with filthy motherless kids . . . it's awful, the degradation a woman can sink down into . . ." (24). Violet is the soiled earth mother, the fallen Eve, the personification of the "unclean, [the] unsanitary." The red enamel represents the blood; the black nails, the corrupt flesh that dissolves. Her "human touch" stains. Her hands—both the loci of and commodity for men's desires are crusted with earth. Williams connects desire to elimination when Leona voices her disgust with Violet: "She lives like an animal in a room with no bath that's directly over the amusement arcade" (20). Again, the excretory and the amatory are joined. In several other places, desire and defecation link Violet to washrooms. Steve confesses that "She gave me the clap once and tried to tell me I got it off a toilet seat. I asked the doctor . . . and he said yes, you can get it that way but you don't" (28). Desire is never far from the shades that hide latrine windows: "You can't stay all night in a toilet, Violet," warns Steve. Unlike the hot baths that refreshed and protected Blanche DuBois in *A Streetcar Named Desire* or the bathroom retreat from scrutiny that Brick sought in *Cat on a Hot Tin Roof,* the toilet at Monk's bar offers neither haven nor solitude. It is the emblem of pain, human existential horror. "Is she howling out the ladies room window," asks Leona about Violet (22).

Doc, Violet, and Steve are not alone in Williams's exposure of the gross anatomy of desire, linking their fallen state to human excretory functions. If Doc, Violet, and Steve are associated with urine and feces, Leona, too, couples desire and bodily discharge as Williams radicalizes the symbolic sites of desire through inversion and transposition. When Violet complains that she is "sick at my stomach," Leona delivers the following lament on wounded, aching desire: "You're lucky you're sick at your stomach because your stomach can vomit, but when you're sick at your heart, that's when it's awful because your heart can't vomit memories of your lifetime. I wish my heart could vomit, I wish my heart could throw up the heartbreaks of a lifetime . . . " (30). A lower organ—the stomach, the gut—usurps the power of a higher one, the heart, in *Small Craft Warnings,* destabilizing again traditional and romantic desire. Comparing wounded desire to vomit shows the extent to which hurt and loneliness level a creature made in God's image. Except for her brother, Leona never finds the one "beautiful thing" in order "To save the heart from corruption" (34). Her tears, a signifier of the emotion/passion of desire, are also reduced to the banal, the gustatory. "She was crying in the stew to save on salt," mocks Bill (17).

Into this world comes the sacred. Questions about God are central to *Small Craft Warnings*, for the Deity is invoked frequently throughout the play, as Williams in fact claimed he did throughout his canon. When Leona asks, "Is life worth living in here?" she voices one of the chief reasons why the broken vessels in Williams's play reach out to God. However diverse their desires, Monk's customers are starving for some type of salvation. But, as the script confesses, these habitues are a collection of individuals at various stages of spiritual awareness and faith. Their images of God are diverse, scattered, some annihilating. A few of Monk's patrons are filled with faith while others wander in an inner wilderness. But all of them are trying to connect, however feebly, with a presence larger than themselves. "Souvenir," Leona's favorite record that she plays on the juke box — "Remembering" — is an appropriate theme song for *Small Craft Warnings*. Each character would like to be awakened to the sacred in the ideal if not the real world. Each would like an encounter with God, a souvenir of Him. Some receive; others retreat; still others deny.

The jaded screenwriter Quentin delivers a long confessional on how his life is untouched by surprise resulting in "having lost the ability to say: 'My God!'" His voice is that of the embittered agnostic, the disappointed searcher. "I've asked all the questions, shouted them at deaf heaven til I was hoarse in the face, and gotten no answer, not the whisper of one, nothing at all." Having repeated his questions so often, his mental image for God is "A big carved rock by the desert . . . monumental symbol of worn out passion and bewilderment in you, a striped stone paralyzed sphinx that knows no answers that you don't but comes on like the oracle all the time waiting on her belly to give out some outcries of universal wisdom . . . and say[s] 'Oh well,' . . . and go[es] back to sleep another five thousand years" (47). Quentin looked for God, and when his questions went unanswered he succumbed to cold resignation, a soul-less denial. Interestingly, Quentin's search — imagistically — is in the desert, underscoring his spiritual dryness; he is in a wasteland, a wilderness, as in Deuteronomy 32:1–12. Spiritually, he has a *"fever that is not of the flesh"* (26). There is no rebirth or reawakening for Quentin at Monk's. The paralyzed sphinx is Quentin listening to himself. Leona characterizes Quentin to Bobby as someone who "wants to escape" (48). And, significantly enough, he enters with Bobby but leaves without him, alone. Of all Monk's patrons, Quentin is the least faith-filled, the most lost, the least able to love. Williams's searing portrait of Quentin (his homoeroticism aside) reinforces what he declared in an interview in the *Village Voice:* "Homosexuality isn't the theme of my plays. They're about human relationships. I've never faked it" (qtd. in Bell 58).

Doc moves up the ladder of faith from where Quentin wallows by admitting there is a God, but he projects an image of Him that is distant, unavailable, uncaring. To his credit, Doc acknowledges and defends "the holy mysteries of birth . . . and death" (36), rightly calling them "miracles" (35). Yet he slips into spiritual apathy reflected in his personification of God: these miracles are "dark as the face of a black man, a Negro, yes. I've always figured God is a black man with no light on his face. He moves in the dark . . . like a Negro miner in the pit of a lightless cool mine, obscured completely by the relevancies and irreverencies of public worship . . ." (36). If Quentin's faith is in the desert, Doc's is down a mine shaft, an apt metaphor for clandestine medicine, shadowy image, and failures, his retreat. Doc forgets that with God there is no darkness. (The mine is also an appropriate signifier in terms of the birth and death canals that Doc had been describing earlier.) God as the uninterested coal miner fits Doc's sense of isolation, blind-alley life. Like Quentin's paralyzed sphinx, Doc's miner deity offers no answers, allows no encounters with the divine. Doc's true self, rather than Williams's, is unmasked in this allegorization. Closer to Williams's own views is his characterizing a merciful, powerful God through Black characters, e.g., the Porter in " The Last of My Solid Gold Watches" (Kolin "'Night, Mistuh Charlie'") or Uncle Pleasant in *Orpheus Descending*. A youthful, early skeptic in Williams's *The Fugitive Kind* (written in 1937)—the young revolutionary Leo, who is expelled from college for seditious actions—is the one who demands comparison with Quentin. Like the screenwriter, Leo depicts God as uninterested in or even fed up with the mortal condition. "Tonight's God's night of sleep . . . He's tired of looking at the nasty mess we've made of ourselves. He's pulled down a big white shade to cover us up. Our stink can't reach his nostrils" (130). Again, consistent with his desire to focus on Christian symbols, the stench of sin was on Williams's mind in his early work just as it had been in his later plays.

Bobby and Violet experience God through a purely physical but no less meaningful encounter. God is real for them because they can feel His presence in others. With their faith rising higher than Quentin's or Doc's, both of them are opened to an epiphany, a healing surprise. Symbolically born in Goldenfield, a place in and of the sun, Bobby innocently encounters the divine spark of joy and beauty in "a sketch of Michangelo's David" that he finds in "a back room" of a flower shop (run by a gay man) "decorated Chinese, with incense and naked pictures." He finds "drying up flowers rattled in the wind and wind-chimes tinkled" (49). Aside from the homoerotic imagery and context, Williams invests in Bobby's epiphany both Christian and Eastern mythologies. Bobby comes to God through the pleasure of sight, sound, and touch. Accordingly, David is the perfect patron for young Bobby—the virile singer of sacred hymns, the poet-priest who chased after God's own heart, a Williams's sexualized saint. Bobby leaves Monk's ready for the surprise of the Pacific, the healing ablutions of water. "I've got a lot of new adventures, experiences to think over . . . " (50).

Like her flower name, Violet is planted in physical soil. (Imagistically, Violet is linked to Alma Winemiller in *Summer and Smoke* since both describe themselves as a water plant, a lily [69].) Violet is half plant, half water, a wacky combination at Monk's but not so extreme she cannot express her faith. She is part mystic, part sacrificial victim. Flowers are often a central symbol in Christian belief, combining Violet's pain and joy, e.g., the Rose of Sharon, "lilies of the field," yet she is most closely associated with the Book of Lamentation—*"Violet's lamentation begins"* (19)—in her paroxysms, all-encompassing religious faith, and her relationships with and to God. *"Her lips are pursued in sorrow so that she is like travesty of a female saint"* (29). Her religious rituals are painful; she "utters an apocalyptic outcry" (20) in fleeing from Leona. Expressing her ultimate gratitude to Leona, *"She sways and sobs like a religieuse in the grip of a vision"* (55). Sex for her is a prayer, a religious credo. "She's got some form of religion in her hands . . . " (52), quips Leona mockingly, yet a truthful expression nonetheless of her saving passion. Resignedly, she tells Monk at the end of the play that Violet's behavior of groping men under the table is "a pitiful thing . . . she's worshiping her idea of God in her personal church" (70). But the same can be said of the other characters who faithfully invoke the sacred in *Small Craft*. Violet reaps what she sows, fittingly enough. Rescued by Monk, she equates God's love with human love—a fundamental tenet of Holy Scripture. "God love you, Monk, like me"—her words at the end of the play—are redolent of a faith that is at once simple and sensual but also one that brings her a resurrection (sustenance and love) upstairs in Monk's apartment. Violet's faith—needing and wanting other people—merits rewards in *Small Craft Warnings*.

But Leona and Monk, though in different ways, show the greatest devotion to and comfort in God. Ironically, Leona is the most worldly character in *Small Craft Warnings* yet the one always in tune with acknowledging the divine, the sacred made flesh. Unlike the spiritually bankrupt Quentin, Leona can fully celebrate epiphanies. ". . . Life! Life! I've never just said, 'Oh well.' I've always said 'Life!' to life, like a song to God, too . . . " (55). Not without ironic humor, she is often likened to a bull, a sacrificial but also hallowed animal (18). God, religious beliefs, and rituals provide the glue that holds her life together. For Leona, God is most endurably present in beauty. Not unintentionally, she is a beautician who generously makes others feel better about themselves; she can form a community of friends in two weeks (55). Like a disciple at the Ascension, Leona criticizes the earth-bound Bill for not looking to the sky, the place from which God will come again on earth. In the process, she articulates her theology of beauty: "You never looked up. Just grunted. In your life you've had no . . . experience! 'Appreciation . . . of the beauty of God in the sky' . . . " (32). In Leona's ecology, she can hear and celebrate the sky and the sound of the ocean—the Book of Nature in which the works of God are writ large.

Her belief in God is also physicalized through her brother Haley, whose "death-day" she boisterously honors at Monk's. Apotheosizing Haley, she invokes the imagery of Christian worship, Easter, and heaven. Haley was "so full of love he had to give it to someone like his music"; his "eyes were two pieces of heaven in the human face," and when he played at church on Easter, "he looked like an angel, standing under the light through the stained glass window." His hair "look[ed] like an angel's halo touched with heavenly light." But her angelic brother, an erased gay man like Allan Grey, Skipper, or Sebastian Venable, "faded fast, just faded out of the world." He was "too beautiful to live and so he died" (33–34). Juxtaposing imagery of metamorphosized young lovers such as Dionysus, Adonis, and Romeo with her Christian beliefs, Leona creates a shrine to God through her brother's beauty, thus making his (and her) creation redeemable. "Without one beautiful thing in the course of a lifetime, it's all a death-time" (34). In Leona's theology, then, God chooses a special person to manifest His love for the greater community and thereby makes life sacred.

Leona's belief in God synergizes her behavior in *Small Craft Warnings*. Not a simple portrait, Leona "got two natures in her" (39). She is both (un)repentant sinner and charitable saint, bully and mother; she is a maternal voice and a gruff masculine presence. Her name reflects both natures—Leo, the lion, and Leona, the woman-mother. John Timpane rightly claims that women like Leona in Williams's plays have a "surplus of possibility which makes them more productive and less exhaustive as characters." Like an avenging barroom Jeremiah, Leona attacks the corruption she sees at Monk's—sexual (Bill and Violet), medical (Doc), communal (the Night Watchman)—and delivers blistering denunciations of false pride and betrayal. Yet she possesses an innate goodness expressed through Scriptural/sacramental imagery Williams associates with her. She brings an infirm Violet meals. Acting like a Madonna, a blessed mother, Leona tries to befriend Bobby, offering to take him to her trailer for protection and a meal. Even caring for the reprobate Bill satisfies her "mother complex" (32). And when she makes plans to leave Monk's, she again envisions herself in a maternal role bringing comfort and hope. What "I think I'll do is a turn back to a faggot's moll . . . You always find one in the gay bars that needs a big sister . . . to camp with and to laugh and cry with . . ." (71). In her pugnacious maternity is mercy.

Sacramentally, Leona is often linked with food. To honor Bill, she wanted to give a "memorial dinner" so she "set up a banquet table [with her] grandmother's silver and Irish lace tablecloth . . . crystal candlesticks with the vine leaves filigreed on 'em in silver . . . and set the candles on either side of my single talisman rose just opened . . . " (17). She also made plans to serve from a "cut-glass decanter of Burgandy" (18), her chalice of love. The imagery here—candles, wine, vines, the rose—suggests Leona's version of the Mass, a ritual, a celebration. But by jilting her Bill leaves only a broken banquet, consistent, as we shall see, with the role of Judas that the script inscribes in him. Leona's failed (last) supper joins other sacrificial meals in the Williams's canon—the tragic dinner with the candelabrum from the Church of the Heavenly Rest in *Glass Menagerie;* Blanche's ominous birthday party in *Streetcar;* the betrayal supper of pot liquor in *Baby Doll*. In all these, vestigia from the sacrament of the Eucharist surface in the preparation and arrangement of the dinner table yet simultaneously show how far from grace such meals are.

Of all the characters in *Small Craft Warnings*, Monk most often puts Christianity into practice, though he may rarely invoke the name of God. If Leona is the play's oracle, shaman, prophetess, Monk is its presiding priest. (A belligerent Leona even puns on his priestly title, calling him "a *monk*ey-faced mother" [23].) True to his eponymous name, he exhibits the chief virtue of such monastic communities as the Benedictines or the Franciscans—hospitality to wayfarers. Williams describes Monk's as a "place of refuge for vulnerable human vessels." He offers these "vessels" a sanctuary. Williams may have had the quintessential monk Thomas Merton in mind when he named and fashioned the bar owner. A few years before Williams wrote *Small Craft Warnings,* when he was received and baptized into the Roman Catholic Church, Father Joseph LeRoy, S.J., gave the playwright a copy of Merton's *No Man Is an Island.* Fr. LeRoy exclaimed: "What better spriritual foundation for Tennessee than this compendium . . . written by a holy monk who knew and lived the principles proposed by Jesus Christ to direct your life and soul" ("Draft") and then continued, "Tennessee agreed that perhaps in the Providence of God, Thomas Merton could do more good . . . He would read the book, he said, and I left him in the hands of a holy man who had once strayed, then saw the light and followed Christ" ("Draft Statement"). Merton the ascetic and Williams the pleasure-seeker merge into Monk, the compassionate innkeeper, the amalgam of Christianity as Williams envisioned it.

Like Thomas Merton, Monk offers the characters in *Small Craft* Christian acceptance, mercy, hope, "principles proposed by Jesus Christ. . . ." In his secularly sacerdotal capacity, Monk hears stories, tales, and confessions, the later "make [him] feel not so lonesome" (52). He becomes so close to his customers/penitents that one who moved away five years ago "willed" Monk "all he owned in the world" (51). Other beloved customers "send [him] postcards from wherever they go and tell me what's new in their lives and I am interested in it" (51). They "take the place of a family" in his life, solidifying his role as patron, father, counselor, confessor. No man (or woman) is an island for Monk. Not without irony, but with a great deal of truth, Monk inadvertently shouts: "I'm running a tavern that's licensed to dispense spirits" (12). Monk's hospitality, compassion, and example are in essence deeply spiritual, the paradigm for grace and redemption in the sordid world of human odors, selfishness, and doubt. As priest, Monk offers his congregation empathy and protection. A peacemaker, he tries to calm Leona and prevent further harm to Violet. Yet he can be strict and forceful, refusing to serve Leona and being less than sanguine with Bill, the selfish stud: "I'm having no violence here" (19). Monk admits he has had some "heart attacks" (52), which symbolically characterize his tenderheartedness. The fact that he lives "upstairs" and befriends, bathes, and feeds Violet further equates Monk with a Godly, kindly presence.

Besides the continuing colloquy of faith shattering or sharing by various characters, another key Christian dimension of *Small Craft* is the number of rituals—sacraments—and other Biblical analogues incorporated in the script. These rituals are conveyed through both verbal allusion and physical representation. The themes of the play are sacramentally constant. Yet if any theme is prevalent in *Small Craft* it is, eschatologically speaking, the ultimate end of life. Almost all the characters are concerned about birth and death, the future of promise or pain.

Leona expresses the topic sentence of *Small Craft Warnings:* "My time has run out in this place" (65). But the play coterminously couples the end of life to its start. Birth and death—and the sacraments of baptism and extreme unction—are linked as "holy miracles" (35). Life and death are precariously balanced on the same plane. For example, Doc recounts what happened on his sick call to Treasure Isle: "The birth of the baby was at least three months premature, so it was born dead. . . ." As an unwitting agent of baptism (as well as an unhoused sexton tolling a death knell), Doc "put this fetus in a shoe box . . . right by the beach . . . where the tide would take it" (65–66). The water, the healing sounds of the ocean, dignifies the death of the baby into a new life, the traditional sense of baptism. The disbarred Doc may not have had the legal right to sign a death certificate, but he appropriates a spiritual one to convey the infant's soul to water. The Christian paradoxical idea of the ocean as spiritual font and grave recurs, but more ominously, when Doc reveals that the mother, who also died, "was a small woman but not small enough to fit in a shoe box" (66), denying her the salvific immersion in the ocean because of his ineptitude. Earlier, in *Streetcar,* Blanche DuBois fantasizes about dying on the water (410), and Williams himself wished to be buried at sea as his beloved poetic mentor Hart Crane was. For Williams, water baptized as well as sanctified the end of life.

The sacrament of confession is overridingly valorized in *Small Craft Warnings* through the spotlight appearances of the many characters who soliloquize on their lives and losses. "Frame freezing . . . the actors" (Sommer), the spotlight falls on each character as he/she details the crimes of the heart that have wounded the speaker and others. As we saw, Leona's moving tribute to her dead angelic brother, Haley, reveals that "he was too beautiful to live" (34), the earth too inhospitable for him (27–28). Quentin confesses the loss of surprise in his life and the "seizures" that preceded his malady. Wanting to escape Bobby, Quentin gives him some money, which Leona aptly (and theologically) likens to "doing penance" for the pickup. Pitifully, Steve bemoans his sad state "my miserable cheap life"—and self-mockingly, even penitently, characterizes his relationship to Violet as being "like a bone thrown to a dog! I'm the dog; she's the bone" (28). Monk confesses the happy extremes of the heart—charity, compassion, the legacy of friendship, Williams's equivalent, perhaps, of the gifts of the Holy Spirit. Prominently, a selfish character like Bill never avails himself of soul-searching confession but instead plots a sexual conquest of a lonely, retired state worker who will support and indulge him because of the power of "Junior." John MacNicholas keenly observed: "In Williams's church, confession is the admission of human frailty which, being uttered, claimed, becomes a community strength" (603). No wonder Quentin and Bill leave impenitently alone but Leona and Bobby go to new communities, new vistas.

Besides references to the sacraments, two key Biblical events infuse Leona's furor and faith, additionally illuminating the Christian ethos of the play. Angry with Bill for leaving her trailer without warning and for dumping her for Violet, Leona knows she can no longer trust him and orders "get your stuff out of my trailer." She then shouts: "I got a suggestion for you . . . take this cab fare . . . *[She throws a handful of silver on the table]*." The episode is palpably realistic, quite like something that might happen in a bar like Monk's. But the stage business resonates with deeper Christian symbolism. Leona throws money (silver) at the deceitful betrayer, Jim, just as Judas might have received his payment in silver for betraying the Christ. The cab fare is allegorized to cover more than transportation; it brands Bill as the betrayer in strong Christian terms.

Leona's anger is once again expressed through Biblical analogues when she encounters the Night Watchman on the beach outside Monk's. In three and one half pages of stage directions bristling with embedded dialogue, diatribe, invective (59–62), Leona battles this "holy Willie," defending herself against his charges of "raising hell" and consorting with young men, "taking [them] over to [her] trailer and making studs of them" (61). Leona retaliates in the tradition of "cast the first stone" by accusing the Watchman of "sneaking around the trailer court . . . in the dark looking in windows" (62). Denying the charge, he asserts, "I go to church. I'm a good Christian man" (61). Assailing his pharisaical pride, Leona retorts: "I've seen your likes in church before. I wouldn't trust you with a . . . " (61). "Does your wife know about the girls you go out with," she probes (62). Leona here suggests John the Baptist crying out against sin and soiled pride in the wilderness of the beach. In her attack, the Watchman is metamorphosed into the "brood of vipers," the Pharisees and Sadducees of John's assault recorded in Matthew 3:12. Leona may even suggest in Williams's script the indignant Christ who deplored those who wrapped their arrogance and hypocrisy in phylacteries of pride and tradition as in Luke 20:45–48 and Mark 11:15–19. Just as the chief priests and scribes tried to find some way to do away with Christ, the Watchman demands Leona's name in order to arrest her and take her off. In these two encounters—with Bill and with the Watchman—Leona speaks against the most fiercely castigated sins in Holy Writ—betrayal and hypocrisy.

Perhaps the most profound religious ritual embedded in the script of *Small Craft* though occurs in the very last piece of stage business. Monk *"sniffs the ratty slipper"* (72) that Violet has just taken off before going upstairs to the security of his apartment. His description of the slipper concentrates on "the human odors" discussed earlier: "Dirty, worn-out slipper still being worn, sour-smelling with sweat from being worn too long, but still set by the bed to be worn again the next day—[on] errands till the sole's worn through, and even then not thrown away, just padded . . . " (72–73). The pun on *sole/soul* is not as outrageous as it may appear. The slipper is a metonymy for Violet herself and, more particularly, for her postlapsarian condition. Monk accepts but tries to mediate Violet's fallen state with his care and compassion. All the while he sniffs the slipper, Monk lavishes mercy on her; and when he urges Violet "don't forget your shower" (72), an act that John MacNicholas labels "the cleansing renewal of human contact" (603), the Christian signification dominates. Monk's action can be seen as the equivalent of the religious practice of washing the feet of the faithful on Holy Thursday night as Christ did to his disciples in John 13:1–16, a ritualistic act of charity and humility, displaying a strong sense of love and fidelity, virtues inculcated through a book like Merton's *No Man Is an Island*.

Two of Christ's injunctions to Peter also help to gloss Monk's behavior. "If I do not wash your feet you can have nothing in common with me" (John 3:18), alluding to the possibility of a bond between Violet and Monk only if she heeds his request to wash. Secondly, Monk's kindness toward the homeless Violet ideally will be transferred to others. Again, Christ tells Peter, "I have give you an example so that you may copy what I have done to you" (John 13:15). Similarly, recall Mary Magdelene washing Christ's feet with perfume and drying them with her hair. Williams inverts the gender of the characters in the parable here but not its intent. Both verbally and physically the script calls to mind the act of feet washing in preparation for Easter resurrection. The water that Monk supplies—plus his commentary on Violet's slippers—further allegorizes him as a disciple, a man of faith in the sordid, secular world, ready to give in the service of another, one of Christianity's, and Williams's, highest goals.

Having *Small Craft Warnings* premiere on Easter Sunday night may have been just a business necessity. But the date surely is appropriate for a play that intensely deals with sin and salvation, loneliness and God, death and resurrection. As I have argued, *Small Craft Warnings* is far more ambitious and cohesive than reviewers have been willing to concede. What they find as a major flaw—the so-called lack of dramatic activity—is neither a fault nor an accurate description. Like the fog that envelops the beach and Monk's bar, the action in the play fittingly stresses the liminal world in which the characters search for spiritual meaning in their lives. On vastly different spiritual levels, the characters at Monk's grope for salvation through their individual responses to God and others. Despite her intemperate outbursts, Leona incorporates many Christian virtues and graces. But the ideal is Monk, whose charity and remembrance mark him—and his cathedral-bar—as the priest, the confessor, and the Christian model in a society needing more, not less, devotion to others and to God.

Works Cited

Bell, Arthur. "Tennessee Williams: 'I've never faked it.'" *Village Voice* 24 Feb. 1972: 58, 60.
Bigsby, C.W.E. *A Critical Introduction to Twentieth-Century Drama: Williams, Miller, Albee.* Cambridge: Cambridge UP, 1982.
Binelli, Mark. "'Warnings' of Williams at His Stormiest." *Atlanta Constitution* 14 Nov. 1997: 12.
Brunkenfeld, Dick. "Buoyed up on a Sea of Troubles." *Village Voice* 10 Aug. 1972: 46.
Brustein, Robert. "Portrait of a Warning." *Observer* [London] 4 Feb. 1973: 35.
Clurman, Harold. "Theatre." *The Nation* 24 April 1972: 540–41.
Devlin, Albert. *Conversations with Tennessee Williams.* Jackson: UP of Mississippi, 1986.
Falk, Signi. *Tennessee Williams.* Rev. ed. New York: Twayne, 1977.
Frank, Leah. "Off-Off-Broadway Reviews." WYNC/830 Radio, 12 Jan. 1976. Copy available at Billy Rose Theatre Library, New York Public Library.

Fedder, Norman J. "Tennessee Williams's Dramatic Techniques." *Tennessee Williams: A Tribute.* Ed. Jac Tharpe. Jackson: UP of Mississippi, 1977.

Free, William J. "Williams in the Seventies: Directions and Discontents." *Tennessee Williams: A Tribute.* Ed. Jac Tharpe. Jackson: UP of Mississippi, 1977. 815–28.

Gutman, Les. "A CurtainUp Review: *Small Craft Warnings.*" *Curtain Up: The Internet Theatre Magazine.* http:www.curtainup.com/smallcraftwarnings.html (29June 1999).

Holman, Curt. "Craft Work: Labyrinth at 7 Stage Back Space." *Atlanta Consitution* 15 Nov. 1997.

Howell, Chauncy. "Sideshows." *Women's Wear Daily* 14 July 1972: 9.

Kolin, Philip C. "Compañero Tenn: The Hispanic Presence in the Plays of Tennessee Williams." *Tennessee Williams Annual Review* 2 (1999): 35–52.

———. "'Night, Mistuh Charlie': The Porter in Tennessee Williams's 'The Last of My Solid Gold Watches' and the Kairos of Negritude." *Mississippi Quarterly* 47 (Spring 1994): 215–20.

Lahr, John. "On Stage." *Village Voice* 6 April 1972: 60.

LeRoy, Joseph, S.J. "Draft Statement." Press release. Bureau of Information of United States Catholic Conference. Washington, DC, 1969.

Leverich, Lyle. *Tom: The Unknown Tennessee Williams.* New York: Crown, 1995.

Lux, Mary. "Tenn Among the Lotus Eaters: Drugs in the Life and Fiction of Tennessee Williams." *Southern Quarterly* 38 (Fall 1999): 117–23.

MacNicholas, John. "Williams' Power of the Keys." *Tennessee Williams: A Tribute.* Ed. Jac Tharpe. Jackson: UP of Mississippi, 1997. 581–606.

Merin, Jennifer. "A Teddy Bear for Tennessee Williams." *Soho Weekly News* 29 Jan. 1976:13.

Nightingale, Benedict. "Down at Monk's Place." *New Statesman* 9 Feb. 1973: 209.

O'Haire, Patricia. "An Old Williams Play Surfaces and So Does He." *Sunday News* [New York] 2 April 1972: sec. 2:35.

Oppenheimer, George. "Williams Founders with 'Small Craft.'" *Newsday,* 16 April 1972: II9.

Pagan, Nicholas. *Rewriting Literary Biography: A Postmodern Approach to Tennessee Williams.* Madison, NJ: Fairleigh Dickinson UP, 1994.

Phillips, Gene, S.J. "Tennessee Williams and the Jesuits." *America* 25 June 1977: 564–65.

Rader, Dotson. "Tennessee Williams: A Friendship." *Paris Review* 81 (Fall 1981): 186–96.

Shattuck, Scott. "Night of the Dreaded Fog People." Program note. Jean Cocteau Repertory Theatre, 25 August 2001–20 September 2001.

Simon, John. Review of *Small Craft Warnings. New York* 17 Apr. 1972: 84.

Smith, Michael. "Theatre Journal." *Village Voice* 6 April 1972: 61.

Sommer, Elyse. "A CurtainUp Review: *Small Craft Warnings:* A Most Welcomed Second Revival." *Curtain Up: The Internet Theatre Magazine. http://www.curtainup.com/smallcraftwarnings2* html5 (5 May 2000).

Sommers, Michael. "Small Craft Warnings." *Star-Ledger* 31 Aug. 2001.

Stasio, Marilyn. "Theatre: *Small Craft Warnings.*" *Cue* Sept. 16, 1972: 9.

"Tennessee Williams Acting in 'Warnings.'" *Variety* 7 June 1972: 1, 60.

Timpane, John. "'Weak and Divided People': Tennessee Williams and the Written Woman." *Feminist Rereadings of Modern American Drama.* Ed. June Schlueter. Rutherford, NJ: Associated UP, 1989. 171–80.

Trenkle, Tom. "Dear Critic." Gifford/Wallace News release. 16 Aug. 1972.

Walker, John. "Theatre in London: The Myth and the Playwright—Tennessee and Shepard." *International Herald Tribune* [Paris] 20 Mar. 1973.

Williams, Tennessee. *Fugitive Kind.* New York: New Directions, 2001.

———. *Memoirs*. Garden City, NY: Doubleday, 1976.

———. *A Streetcar Named Desire: The Theatre of Tennessee Williams*. Vol 1. New York: New Directions, 1971.

———. "Too Personal." *Small Craft Warnings*. New York: New Directions, 1972. 3–6.

———. *Village Voice*, Feb. 24, 1972.

Robert F. Gross

THE GNOSTIC POLITICS OF
THE RED DEVIL BATTERY SIGN

It took *The Red Devil Battery Sign* a long time to make its New York premiere. Closing in Boston in June 1975 after a pre-Broadway tryout, it appeared in a substantially rewritten version in Vienna the following year,
but this long-winded, amateurish production did little to command attention
(Kruntorad 11). After more revision, a 1977 production in London won greater
praise for the performances of its lead actors, Keith Baxter and Estelle Kohler, than
for the script (Marowitz 26–27). The play had to wait until after its playwright's
death for publication in an edited version of the London script. When it finally arrived at the WPA Theater in November 1996, in a re-edited version that both cut
major scenes from the London script and re-introduced material from Vienna, the
response was no better. Williams veteran Elizabeth Ashley was praised for her
bold, smoldering performance, but the play was generally dismissed as an example
of Williams at his "most incoherent" (Brantley) and drew little notice.

It may be in part the lack of a substantial production history that accounts for
the play's critical neglect. Roger Boxill's book-length study of Williams contains
less than two full sentences on *The Red Devil Battery Sign* (157, 170); Ruby Cohn's
overview of the late plays makes only the most fleeting of references to it (233).
Even Jacqueline O'Connor's more thematically focused book-length study of
madness in Williams's plays dismisses it as having nothing significant to bear on
her investigation (17).

On the rare occasions where critics have paid attention to the play, they have
tended to stress its political dimension. In a thoughtful interpretation of *The Red
Devil Battery Sign,* James Schlatter has described the play as "mytho-political" and
assessed it as an attempt by Williams to address the "public imagination" (94), just
as Colby H. Kullman has described it as "socio-political" (656). In a thought-
provoking essay, the late Linda Dorff discussed the play in the context of political
apocalyptic literature and placed it in a tradition going back to the "New Man"

dramas of German expressionism. Bolstered by the rediscovery and successful production of an extremely topical early play, *Not About Nightingales,* and given a sophisticated theoretical framework for a political analysis of the late plays in David Savran's influential *Communists, Cowboys, and Queers,* the 90s saw a praiseworthy correction to the earlier tendency to view Williams as completely apolitical.

Certainly *The Red Devil Battery Sign* invites a political interpretation. Not since *Not About Nightingales* in 1938 had Williams written a play with so much material drawn from the headlines. The New York production foregrounded this material, placing Woman Downtown's dilemma clearly at the center, while moving King to a secondary position. It excised the La Niña subplot (Grosch 120), reintroduced clearer references to the Kennedy assassination from the Vienna version (Brantley), and added documentary video footage of the assassination. If the play were focused on the topical material, it stands to reason that these choices would have clarified and strengthened the play. But Ben Brantley still judged *The Red Devil Battery Sign* as one of the playwright's weakest efforts, pointing out that the conspiracy material was unfocused, and Robert J. Grosch agreed, observing that this material is not central to the play (123).

Overall, this interest in the play's political dimension has not been sufficient to bring about a higher critical evaluation of the work. Productions remain rare, and critical attention, infrequent. James Schlatter's careful analysis leads him to wonder if the play may not merely be a haphazard patchwork of earlier motifs (99). I would like to suggest that, while *The Red Devil Battery Sign* is a text that reveals important insights into the political orientation of Tennessee Williams, those insights are not to be found by immediately addressing the play's topicality. Instead, I would like to save the consideration of the topical material for the conclusion of this essay, and investigate how the play constructs a highly conflicted context in which the political material is situated. The presumption of incoherence, so common in the critical response to Williams's late work, must be resisted. I will approach this dramatic context through Williams's construction of space in the play, which is strongly coded in terms of gender and sexual desire.

The Red Devil Battery Sign is constructed around an opposition between public and private space, one that is rooted in assumptions stemming from the Enlightenment. As recent essays by Frank Bradley and Stephanie B. Hammer have persuasively argued, much of Williams's orientation toward dramatic form ultimately derives (as does most American drama) from the tradition of bourgeois drama, which arose in the late eighteenth century, as articulated in the theories of Denis Diderot (Bradley) and the tragedies of Friedrich Schiller (Hammer). The bourgeois drama expresses its social conflicts spatially, usually as a clash between a vulnerable world of private, middle-class domesticity (hence, the related term "domestic drama") and a threatening, powerful, public world of aristocratic privilege. So, for example, in one of the seminal works of the genre, Gotthold Ephraim Lessing's *Emilia Galotti* (1772), the sheltered heroine is kidnapped on her way to be married and carried off to the prince's villa, from which death becomes her only means of restoring a sense of safety to her beleaguered self. In Schiller's *Intrigue and Love* (1783), the town musician is unable to keep his daughter secure from the desires and machinations of the nearby court, leading to her ill-fated love for the son of the local despot and her death by poison. These and many other eighteenth century bourgeois dramas are generated out of a fundamental opposition between the public and private, an opposition that continues with incredible tenacity through the following two centuries.

This eighteenth century opposition of private and public spaces articulated in the bourgeois drama is an expression of liberal ideology. Moral philosopher Paul Seabright has reflected on the problematics of private space in relationship to liberalism. Private space, he argues, was imagined as the space that was supposed to stand outside the political, and a liberal politics was meant to ensure the autonomy of private space. As a result, liberalism has found it difficult to articulate any goals or norms for the privacy, since to articulate them would be to violate the space's defining autonomy. A liberal politics, Seabright argues, defines and protects the private sphere, but hesitates at defining any content for the protected space (149).

Dealing with these spaces as a philosopher rather than a literary historian, Seabright may underestimate the strong positive values given to characteristics identified with private space in literature arising from liberalism and its founding Enlightenment values (Gray 150). The strong ideological identifications of private space with domesticity, heterosexual monogamy, femininity, maternity, and childhood innocence shape the plotting, thematic material, and imagery of bourgeois drama from *Emilia Galotti* to John Patrick Shanley's *Dinner with Friends*.

In the way it defines space, Tennessee Williams's *The Chalky White Substance,* a posthumously published one-act play, most likely written in the late 70s (Kolin, "Existential" 8), shows Seabright's liberal imagination at work. Set centuries after the Earth has been devastated by a thermonuclear war, it is less interested in presenting the political implications of the political state that has arisen than using this bleak world as a vehicle for an existentialist imagining of a world after the Death of God, or as Philip C. Kolin has aptly described it, "an anti-gospel, a Williams anti-parable" in which Christian imagery is drained of its meaning ("Existential" 9). For our purposes here, it is interesting to observe how Williams delineates the savagery of this world after a nuclear holocaust through the collapse of the private realm. The play shows the final tryst between an attractive and sensitive young man, Luke, and his older and more brutal "protector," Mark (469). In this brutal environment, in which the winds blow unceasingly through a wasteland, spreading the chalky white substance of the title, women have become rare, and men have increasingly turned to homosexual activity to satisfy their lusts. Male bands often set upon younger men and brutally rape them (468–469). Luke has so far been protected from this fate by Mark, and he has gone to unusual and illegal lengths to keep himself sexually attractive to the older man. Although water is strictly rationed, Luke bathes in a secret, subterranean stream to help keep his skin soft for his lover. When Mark discovers this, he hauls Luke off to the authorities, partly in fear that he will be punished as an accomplice but also eager to earn the bounty given to informers. Luke, we are told, will be enjoyed brutally and at large during his incarceration.

In *Chalky White Substance,* the private realm is presented in nostalgic, even sentimental terms. Luke's dwelling contains an old picture of the Madonna, which he fantasizes as his own mother. The world before the war, vaguely but fondly evoked by the men, was one of mothers, wives, and heterosexual domestic units. Luke's access to the hidden spring, where he defies the authorities by responding to his desire to please his lover, was designed by Luke's first "protector" (470). It is a private realm of cleanliness, pleasure, and refined erotic ritual hidden in a world of dustiness, brutality, and savage lust. The moment Luke shares the existence of that private realm with another person, even his own lover, the full force of the debased public realm, which allows no such secrets, immediately descends upon him, and he not only loses the private space but also loses all autonomy and is reduced to an object to be brutally shared in common.

Chalky White Substance is unusual in Williams's work for the degree to which it presents the private realm in idealized terms and takes a far more reactionary view of sex and gender than most of Williams's later plays. Evoking domesticity through a nostalgia for a femininity that is configured primarily in women, it both essentializes them as "the weaker sex," incapable of surviving the rigors of a world permeated by the chalky white substance and presents male/male desire as a fundamentally brutalized and degenerate falling away from a heterosexual ideal (as does *Something Cloudy, Something Clear*). Usually, however, Williams's view of the private/public dichotomy will be more complex.

For Williams is not merely the inheritor of Enlightenment values; he also inherits the questioning of domestic values that entered the Western theatre with modernism. Continuing the private/public dichotomy of the earlier drama, Henrik Ibsen and his successors questioned the unthinking idealization of the domestic realm. With Ibsen's *A Doll's House* (1879) and *Ghosts* (1881), domesticity becomes viewed with increasing suspicion as a realm that is not unblemished by ideological constraints and is at least as much about the exercise of power as the free exchange of love. As a result, modernist comedies and dramas often rebel against domestic idealizations, exalt self-realization as the highest goal, chart a plot of increasing disillusionment with domesticity, and frequently end with the protagonist's departing from that realm. George Bernard Shaw's *Candida* (1897), Noel Coward's *Easy Virtue* (1925), Sidney Howard's *The Silver Cord* (1926), Philip Barry's *Holiday* (1928), W. Somerset Maugham's *The Breadwinner* (1930) are only a few examples of plays that chart the liberation of individual desire from the confinement of domestic tyranny. This genre, of course, not only provides the model for Williams's first stage success, *The Glass Menagerie,* but articulates a negative view of domesticity as incarceration that continues through much of Williams's subsequent work, with *Cat on a Hot Tin Roof, Orpheus Descending,* and *The Two-Character Play* standing out as only a few of the more obvious examples. This view of domesticity is part of a broader thematic tension between captivity and the desire for freedom that runs throughout Williams's work (Gross 91–93). In a number of late plays, including *Lifeboat Drill, This Is the Peaceable Kingdom, Clothes for a Summer Hotel, Kingdom of Earth,* and *The Two-Character Play,* characters suffer from confinement while also being threatened by forces from the outside. The alternatives often seem to be confinement or catastrophe.

These alternatives are clearly demonstrated in *The Demolition Downtown*. Ending with an "avalanche of powdery plaster" (357) — another burst of chalky white substance — covering the stage set as destruction moves ever closer to home, the play reiterates the oppositions of *Chalky White Substance* in a markedly different register. The catastrophe here is not nuclear war as in *Chalky White Substance* but an urban guerrilla action that evokes the unrest in American cities during the 1960s. Set in the living room of a thoroughly conventional, middle-class, heterosexual couple, the Lanes, *The Demolition Downtown* shows them increasingly under pressure as they feel the effects of a revolutionary movement that has seized control of their city, its progress marked by the sounds of explosions outside. Their daughters come home, explaining that their school has been closed, the nuns arrested, and that they themselves have been sexually molested. Along with another couple, the Kanes (no more different from the Lanes than the Smiths and the Martins of Eugene Ionesco's *The Bald Soprano*), the four plan to escape to the country, a pastoral realm of nature and domestic security reminiscent of Luke's subterranean spring in *Chalky White Substance*. When the wives are momentarily left alone, however, Mrs. Kane suggests an alternate strategy. Naked beneath her overcoat, she plans to visit the revolutionary headquarters, where, shedding her coat, she will brazenly offer herself to the sexually starved guerrilla leader, leaving herself vulnerable to the terrifying fate of Luke at the end of *Chalky White Substance*. Mrs. Lane quickly agrees to her friend's plan, and the two exit, singing the revolutionary anthem, while white plaster falls from the ceiling as the demolition strikes closer to home.

The Demolition Downtown contrasts a once-secure private realm with a perilous public one, monogamy with sexual license, and pastoral to urban devastation. But the play is a comedy, and the point of view toward these oppositions is very different from *Chalky White Substance*. Indeed, the two plays relate to each other as photographic print and negative, reproducing the same concerns but with contrasting points of view. In *The Demolition Downtown,* middle-class domesticity has become a form of incarceration. As the play begins, Mrs. Lane returns from spending time outdoors, trying to find temporary respite from her cabin fever, only to find her husband worried and angry at her. "Has the house turned into a jail and are you the warden of it?" she challenges (331). Left with a bar whose stock has dwindled to a single, nearly empty, bottle of gin and a husband rendered impotent by stress, Mrs. Lane finds little pleasure in her home. When her daughters return from school, they report their molestation in casual terms, then run upstairs, where they gleefully sing the anthem of the revolutionary movement. Mrs. Kane envies the girls their remarkable adaptability in chaotic circumstances, and her plan to offer herself to the guerrilla leader seems as much motivated by the desire for sexual pleasure as desperation to survive. She informs Mrs. Lane that the leader has a handsome brother called "The Panther" (357) — a sobriquet that communicates strength and danger as well as elegant sleekness. The phallic peril that was portrayed as lethally menacing in *Chalky White Substance* here becomes aphrodisiac. When the wives leave, singing the revolutionary anthem, leaving the set covered in a shower of plaster dust which seems to suggest ejaculatory abundance rather than the Death of God, the wives seem less desperate Lukes than sexually overstimulated Noras, leaving their doll's houses in search of satisfaction.

It is instructive to read *Chalky White Substance* and *The Demolition Downtown* together. What is refuge in one play becomes prison in the other; what is savage sexual exploitation in one becomes the opportunity for pleasure in the other. The former play looks back in nostalgia for structure; the latter looks forward in hope of energy. Taken together, they demonstrate a deep-seated ambivalence toward private space that is manifested throughout Williams's work. Private space provides safety, but safety can easily turn into incarceration and stultifying inanity. The violent rupture of that space offers the prospect of intense sexual pleasure, but also of destruction. In this respect, the rape of Blanche in *A Streetcar Named Desire* is paradigmatic of Williams's ambivalence toward intense sexual experience. On one level, every Mrs. Lane *is* a Luke, and vice versa.

As relatively short one-act plays, both *Chalky White Substance* and *The Demolition Downtown* present fairly simple models of the private/public distinction. In longer plays, as in real life, the model becomes more complex. As Judith A. Garber points out, cities contain spaces that show gradations between these two extremes (27), such as malls, cafes, libraries, and restaurants—and, as regards Williams's own queer experience, the bar, the beach, the bathouse, and the cruising ground. Even the last, often considered the least ambiguous site of public sex, has been redefined by David Bell as a place where the public and private are in ongoing negotiation (308). In Williams's work, the most significant of these hybrid spaces is the rented room, whether the Moon Lake Casino in *Summer and Smoke* and *Eccentricities of a Nightingale*, or the hotels and boarding houses in the early *Fugitive Kind* as well as *The Night of the Iguana*, *Sweet Bird of Youth*, *Vieux Carré*, and *The Red Devil Battery Sign*. These spaces are private but not impregnable. They are owned by neither party and create a zone of intimacy that lasts only as long as the liaison. They provide a degree of protection from the hostility and inquisitiveness of the public realm and freedom from the long-term captivity of domestic life.

In *The Red Devil Battery Sign*, King flees his home for downtown to gain respite from the suspicions and belittling ministrations of his wife, Perla. This revulsed and desperate flight of a terminally ill man from a domestic realm that relegates him to the status of an invalid hearkens back to the premise of 1923 Luigi Pirandello's one-act play *The Man with the Flower in His Mouth*. There, the "flower" of the title refers to the protagonist's cancer of the mouth, while Williams adopts the same image to describe King's brain tumor (363). Domestic confinement in both plays is presented as a threat to masculine autonomy, which can only be preserved, however briefly, in the face of death by a movement into public space. Both Woman Downtown and King are threatened by confinement in closed spaces and find a temporary solace with each other by creating a common zone of intimacy in the hybrid space of the hotel room.

The treatment of the private/public opposition reaches a crisis in the last moments of the play, with the death of King and the appearance of the Wasteland Boys. Schlatter rightly notes the critical challenge posed by this ending and questions if it is structurally justified by what precedes it (99). I would like to suggest that not only is it *not* justified by what has gone before but that Williams has created an ending that breaks with what has gone before so radically and conflates the play's fundamental oppositions so thoroughly, that it explodes in a gaudy jumble of chaotic impulses that boldly challenge confident interpretation while provoking speculation. It is as if Williams is not only introducing demolition workers into the final moments of his play but is himself acting as a demolition artist, forcing a violent break with a causally structured and realistic dramaturgy. The vacuum left by King's death elicits a catastrophe of dramatic form. While Williams's earlier dramatic works often included violent, catastrophic actions (*Auto-da-Fé, A Streetcar Named Desire, Orpheus Descending*), they did so while still keeping the dramaturgy fundamentally realistic and causally coherent. In the late work, Williams often chooses to be much bolder by doing violence to form as well as content—ripping, fragmenting, leaping across transitions, and violating expectations. These experiments in violated form can be seen as similar to the painting experiments of J. M. W. Turner and Francis Bacon, which, Gilles Deleuze argued, showed a breakthrough from figuration to chaotic intensity (J. Williams, 233–246). Williams's experiments in this vein include *The Milk Train Doesn't Stop Here Anymore, The Two-Character Play, Clothes for a Summer Hotel,* and *Something Cloudy, Something Clear*. The end of *The Red Devil Battery Sign* is one of the boldest of these experiments in catastrophic form.

By this point in *The Red Devil Battery Sign,* the political conspiracy, along with Woman Downtown's plan to expose it, has long ceased to be an important element of the plot. Rather, it is King's resolve to save Woman Downtown from captivity and sexual menace, and Woman Downtown's complementary resolve to save King's life that has provided the impetus for their final scene together. For this hounded, flawed, and middle-aged couple, a modern Antony and Cleopatra (Kolin, "Compañero" 49), political concerns melt away in the light of their common mortal passion. When King shoots the Drummer, who has been pursuing and harassing Woman Downtown, he proves his ability to protect her just as he had earlier asserted his ability to protect his daughter. But when he falls dead an instant later, his victory is put in question. For, as the Wasteland Boys from the Hollow enter and "*seem to explode from a dream,*" forcing the play to make "*its final break with realism*" (376), the audience is confronted with a sequence of highly theatricalized actions that resist any stable meaning within the context developed by Williams up to that moment.

The Boys are urban nomads who live outside the domestic captivity that King has resisted as well as outside the more impersonal, corporate captivity imposed on Woman Downtown. Like the revolutionaries of *The Demolition Downtown,* they set off explosives repeatedly, partly out of self-defense (we are told that they resisted the attempts of the National Guard to round them up by blowing up two police cars with nitroglycerin [289]) but also for reasons that remain unknown. In this respect, they appear as agents of anarchy, opposed to structure and enclosure, and they carry the sexually explosive charge that characterizes so many of Williams's Fugitive Kind.

Gilles Deleuze and Félix Guattari explore the implications of nomadic movement in *A Thousand Plateaus,* and conceptualize it as a traversing and undoing of the segmented or, as they refer to it, "striated" space of the state (474–500). The definition of spaces as either private or public is a segmentation that attempts to control and define movement. The movements of nomads deterritorialize these spaces as they pass through them, rendering them "smooth," only to provoke attempts on the part of state powers to reterritorialize the spaces and segment them all over again. Williams names the territory occupied by the Boys the "Hollow," which connotes a geographical depression but also evokes a smooth space of emptiness, free of the divisions of striated space. Their demolitions, no matter how vaguely defined by the script, erase structures that might otherwise serve to define or mark their space. When the Boys burst on to the stage shortly before the play's conclusion, they seem to erase the realistic setting of the last scene, the pharmacy, and replace it with a space completely defined by their own presence. With their leader, Wolf, they evoke a feral pack, opposed to the closed spaces used by the Red Devil Battery Company—the guarded estate of their president, the mental hospital, and the Yellow Rose Hotel—and their elaborate schemes of containment and control, to which the Hollow Boys respond with straightforward acts of demolition.

The Wasteland Boys and the nomadic redefinition of stage space they bring with them is clearly opposed to the confinement schemes of the Red Devil Battery Company and the anxiety-ridden domestic confinement that Perla tries to maintain over her ailing husband. Less obviously, it is opposed to the ostensibly benign attempts of King to confine Woman Downtown. King is not interested in blasting, Wolf-like, into nomadic space but in redrawing and reinforcing the boundaries of privacy to create a safe space in which his relationship with his paramour can unfold. Although he does not approve of his mistress's confinement, it nevertheless provides him the conditions of privacy and masculine control that he requires for his liaison. At the same time, Woman Downtown's captors do not seem to see her sexual involvement with King as any threat to their plans: sex, it seems, is no different from alcohol, drugs, or electroshock in this regard.

King looks with disgust at his lover's passionate, feral, and nomadic impulses. He reprimands her for her coarse, unladylike language and the way she fiercely mauls his body during their passionate encounters (316). He worries that her sexual voracity will lead her to become a sexual nomad, "The kind that's picked up by any stranger and banged in alleys and the back of trucks" (343). King imagines Woman Downtown pursuing the private activity of sex in public spaces, corresponding to the discursive category of the pervert, who, as David Bell demonstrates, causes panic by threatening to collapse the boundaries that serve to define the private/public distinction (312–313). Even in the violent and debased world of the Yellow Rose Hotel, containment of female sexuality remains a priority. The play begins with a prostitute being told by the bartender that women are not allowed in the bar unescorted (285), and King's values are at one with the bartender's in this respect. Although King bridles at the domestic containment that Perla tries to assert over him, he envisions a closed space, under his control, as the best situation for his lover. In this respect, King's climactic shooting of Drummer may be less an attempt to free Woman Downtown from containment than to prove that he is still "man enough" to protect *his* woman. Colby H. Kullman is right to observe the sinister presence of patriarchal power in the Red Devil Battery Company (675) but overlooks how patriarchy also functions through King.

Yet it is not altogether clear that Woman Downtown's feral strength and energy are to be condemned. She has survived with incredible tenacity and moral fervor, despite abandonment, exploitation, incarceration, and electroshock. The clawing nails that King finds fault with are precisely the instruments she needs to free herself from the Yellow Rose Hotel; when applied to the face of Drummer, they are more than a match for his brute strength and sexual aggressiveness (371).

Even her psychological fragmentation is presented as a kind of poetic eloquence. She is a polyglot, knowing English, French, Apache, Spanish, and the cries of wolves. Her thoughts move from language to language, freely crossing the boundaries of linguistic systems. "Everything translates to something when your head's full of tongues," she explains (292). Traumatized since her abandonment at an early age and repeatedly violated since, her mind roams freely from vulgarity to wistfulness, camp posturing to raw pain. Her life story confers on her agony, fragmentation, and insight similar to what King is experiencing because of his brain tumor. What might be viewed as a pathology by the diagnosticians becomes, for Williams, the circumstances for heightened vision.

Schlatter usefully identifies *The Red Devil Battery Sign* as yet another variation on the classic myth used most often by Williams, that of Orpheus (95). Orpheus is the artist as nomad, cutting across the striated spaces of life and death and temporarily rendering them smooth. He is also the artist and hero as sexual nonconformist, identified in Ovid's *Metamorphoses* as the man who brought male/male sex to the classical world, thus repudiating "the repressive order of procreative sexuality" (Marcuse 155). A story of attempted liberation from captivity through art and love, the Orpheus myth easily carries Williams's preoccupation with themes of incarceration, eros, art, and escape. Trapped in an infernal downtown, which is presided over by the luminous figure of the Red Devil and inhabited by a swarm of Red Devil "monsters" (309), Woman Downtown meets the salvific figure of the singer, King, who not only protects her but opposes her tendencies toward savagery and sexual debasement. In an Orphic utterance of liberation, he carries her to her hotel bed, exclaiming "You are out of that prison" (310). In typical Williams fashion, sexual pleasure confers a moment of emancipation even within incarceration. And yet, the myth of Orpheus does not in most tellings end happily. Eurydice is made to return to the Underworld, and Orpheus is torn to pieces by Thracian maenads, who throw his still-singing head into the river. Mutilation and death ultimately mark Orphic artistry.

The Orpheus myth permeates Williams's work. From the early *Battle of Angels*, through *The Rose Tattoo, Sweet Bird of Youth, Orpheus Descending, The Milk Train Doesn't Stop Here Anymore*, down to *The Red Devil Battery Sign*, Williams repeatedly shows men of erotic or artistic power who move into hostile and alien realms to encounter women who are captive within social or psychological constraints. This reveals an imagination that is fundamentally gnostic. Indeed, the story of Orpheus' descent into the underworld is one that easily lends itself to gnostic speculation (Strauss 1–2). Gnosticism, the term used to describe a group of widely syncretistic religious sects in the first two centuries A.D., holds that the soul is held in the grip of a malevolent material order and can only be liberated through the acquisition of *gnosis* or transcendent knowledge (Jonas 31–37). Gnostic writings envision the cosmos as a vast prison, of which the earth is the deepest dungeon, in which humans are imprisoned (Jonas 43). In this literature, "coming from outside" and "getting out" appear frequently as images (Jonas 55). Repeatedly, the world of the living takes on all the attributes of the underworld, of dread, numbness, oblivion, and, of particular relevance to Williams, drunkenness (Jonas 68). Only in its aversion to sexuality does gnosticism diverge significantly from Williams's vision of the world, for he saw sexual activity as a means of emancipation and awakening in a world of confinement and oblivion (Jonas 72).

Despite all these affinities, I am not about to suggest that Tennessee Williams was a scholar of early Christian and Jewish heterodoxies. Gnostic thought has had a long, largely subterranean history since its inception but has re-emerged strikingly since the Romantic era. Walter A. Strauss has traced its subtle transformations, along with the Orpheus myth, in European poetry from Novalis to Rilke; Hans Jonas has found an affinity between gnostic thought and modern nihilism and existentialism, especially in the work of philosopher Martin Heidegger (320–340); Jane Goodall has devoted an entire volume to the development of gnostic thought in the work of theatrical visionary Antonin Artaud; and (perhaps most important for our purposes here) Harold Bloom has argued that American literature and religion are fundamentally gnostic in their insistence on the rebirth of the fallen soul in this world through self-knowledge (*Omens* 181–184). For Bloom, a uniquely American belief in gnosis can be found in canonical texts of American literature, including works by Emerson, Whitman, Wallace Stevens, and Williams's favorite poet, Hart Crane (*Agon* 145–269), to whom Williams turned to not only for the epigraph to *The Red Devil Battery Sign* but for *A Streetcar Named Desire* as well. The question is not how Williams could have known about gnostic thought but how he could have avoided an awareness of it, especially given that its vision of captive souls caught in an alien world seems to have formed the basis for his understanding of human life. Tennessee Williams was probably a gnostic long before he ever heard the word and would have remained a gnostic even if he had never read Rilke, Crane, or Wallace Stevens.

Woman Downtown is a quintessential gnostic figure. Not is she merely a prisoner at the Yellow Rose Hotel; she has been a prisoner since birth. Blamed by her father for the death of her mother in childbirth, she was raised on a ranch as "isolated as madness" (334) by her father's Native American mistress, who hated her. Growing up with the cries of wild dogs and wolves, the sexual moanings of her guardian (336), and the Apache language (Williams seems to equate this language with wildness and savagery, not civilization), Woman Downtown comes to embody the wildness of her environment. Ignorant of her own body, she believed that the coming of menstruation was the sign of a shameful disease, which led her to lock herself in her room in fear and shame. This behavior met with incomprehension from those around her and led her to be sent to a school for emotionally disturbed children (335). Throughout her life, periods of imprisonment within social roles—as debutante, as trophy wife—have alternated with stays in mental hospitals. While Blanche's commitment to a mental hospital at the end of *A Streetcar Named Desire* seemed to represent her final silencing and disappearance, Williams's portrait of Woman Downtown is one of a savage, tormented, and indomitable vitality. Rather than being broken for once and all, she is a survivor, a Eurydice who can emerge from descent after descent into hell, still alive and howling.

A similar impulse to sequester women is seen in King's relationship to his daughter, La Niña, in a manner that evokes the positive associations of private space found in *Chalky White Substance*. Once a popular singer with her father's band, she seems to have become a Woman Downtown herself. Having fled to Chicago for obscure reasons, she now sings at an actual Chicago nightspot with the sexually suggestive name of "Pump Room." Perla suspects that her daughter has become a prostitute, just as she suspects her husband of frequenting prostitutes. Indeed, a woman's alternative to a private existence in *The Red Devil Battery Sign* always seems to run the risk of prostitution and sexual nomadism. Her father worries that both his daughter and his mistress share the same wildness (317), but La Niña's story turns out to parallel her father's as much as Woman Downtown's. Just as her father became involved with a woman he met in a bar, La Niña meets McCabe in the Pump Room. McCabe is a man who describes his life as nothing but "Emptiness filled with violence" (360) and turns to her to find meaning. They sit at the table in silence until he begins to cry, and she recognizes her father in his suffering (361). Her attempts to console him lead to a sexual relationship, pregnancy, and commitment.

The relationship of King and his daughter has been ambiguous, and Perla is troubled by what she perceives as intimations of incest, complaining that there is something unnatural about the two of them singing love songs together with the band (322). Blind to the powers of idealization and sublimation in artistic activity, she can see only trouble. King certainly is fiercely protective of his daughter, insulting, striking and even threatening to castrate McCabe, until he recognizes the young man's devotion to her and accepts him. When King goes off for his final rendezvous with Woman Downtown, McCabe keeps La Niña from following him, keeping her behind the fence that marks the boundary of the home and reminding her to stay there, remembering the unborn child inside her (366). La Niña is returned from Downtown and is last seen as mother and wife inside the protected domestic space. King does not, however, want her to disappear from the outside world altogether. He makes McCabe promise to return her to her art, one that can stand higher than the demonic image of the Red Devil Battery sign (363). This image, reminiscent of Luke's imaginary mother, the Madonna, in *Chalky White Substance*, fuses art with idealized maternity, but it also transforms La Niña from a figure of Eurydice to a female Orpheus, singing to draw men out of emptiness, violence and materialism, and toward life.

While La Niña can be transformed into a public icon of beauty and purity, masculinity has a more problematic relationship to spectatorship. Once again wishing to contain sexuality within a private space, King is disgusted by the lewd public phallic display performed by Drummer who has been hired without his approval to perform in his mariachi band. This relegation of male sexual display to the private realm is, coming from Williams, both revealing and a tad curious. More than any other playwright, Williams was instrumental in moving the double bed to the center of American drama (both literally and figuratively), and none of his contemporaries more thoroughly exploited the sexual *frisson* of the male actor as beefcake, whether Stanley in *A Streetcar Named Desire*, Brick in *Cat on a Hot Tin Roof*, or Chance in *Sweet Bird of Youth*. Even *The Red Devil Battery Sign* puts the double bed front and center in the development of the play's principal relationship, and the script implies a state of undress for King in I.iii, and explicitly directs Woman Downtown to begin undressing him in II.iii. In the tension created between the condemnation of the Drummer's sexual display and the centrality of King's sexual power and attractiveness, the play exhibits a conflicted attitude toward male sexual display. It is both condemned as threateningly decadent and positioned as absolutely central to the drama.

In the world of bourgeois drama, sexual intercourse is the most private of private acts. It is the unseen event towards which all the presented actions tend and from which they derive their ultimate significance. From the attempted seductions of Lessing's *Emilia Galotti* and Schiller's *Intrigue and Love*, all the way down to recent Off-Broadway hits like *Dinner with Friends*, A. R. Gurney's *Far East*, and Paula Vogel's *How I Learned to Drive*, bourgeois dramas derive their dominant energies as they spin in vortices around unseen sexual acts, usually bathing them in "the eternal glamor of the illicit" (Behrman 233). For a more demystifying treatment of sexuality that strips it of much of its illicit glamor by presenting it onstage, one must turn to the more confrontational and aggressive work of Wallace Shawn (*Aunt Dan and Lemon, A Thought in Three Parts*), Howard Brenton (*The Romans in Britain, The Genius*), Howard Barker (*Victory*), and Mark Ravenhill (*Shopping and Fucking, Some Explicit Polaroids*). Williams paves the way for these later playwrights in his relative frankness about sexual matters for a dramatist of his era, but he nevertheless structures his plays around significant sexual climaxes that are confined to offstage spaces or intervals between scenes.

The death of King and the appearance of the Wasteland Boys could be seen as the demise of striated space and the triumph of the nomadic and smooth. Woman Downtown, no longer constrained by King's project to limit her fierceness, howls like a wolf, testifying her identity with the Wolf's pack, and reverting to her childhood in the wild. The rural waste in which she was raised returns in the urban waste of the Hollow. From this point of view, the ending shows the triumph of smooth space, the nomadic and feral. But this reading is too simple, for Woman Downtown's childhood was a desolate, open space within a segmentation defined by her father, who exiled her because he held her responsible for her mother's death. In what could be seen as a Freudian repetition, the death of King, who has protected and tried to teach Woman Downtown how to control her animal-like, id impulses, repeats her initial paternal abandonment and returns her to her initial wildness and desolation. But even that reading is inadequate, since Wolf surprisingly reinscribes the domestic structure in the waste land. Wolf explains to his followers that Woman Downtown is their mother—"the Mother of all"(377) and "Sister of Wolf" (378). Woman Downtown, both sister and mother to Wolf, with the incestuous overtones that such conflations of familial roles inevitably produce, becomes the marker of essentialized womanhood in this all-male society, a feral La Niña. If before, Woman Downtown was kept from freedom by the machinations of the Red Devil Battery Company and the machismo of King, she is now reintroduced by Wolf as the key figure in a new domestic scenario . A most improbable figure of maternity, Woman Downtown's new position nonetheless seems to be meant to mirror La Niña's pregnancy. This interpretation is the most conservative of the three, suggesting that all female desire must ultimately be contained within maternity, even if that creates a domesticity that men like King feel constrained to flee to assert their freedom.

So, the ending presents, in a highly concentrated form, three actions, each of them contradicting the others: (1) King's death liberating Woman Downtown into a nomadic counterculture; (2) King's death exiling Woman Downtown into an inhuman desolation; and (3) King's death initiating Woman Downtown into a domestic structure. While the La Niña subplot is able to integrate its tensions into the figure of Madonna-as-Orpheus, suggesting a continuation of the Orpheus action beyond King's death, the contradictory impulses of the Woman Downtown plot shatter in a catastrophic explosion, in which the death of the male protagonist leads to a collapse of stable meaning.

So what has this to do with the topicality of *The Red Devil Battery Sign* and its political implications? I would like to suggest that Williams's Orphic politics manifest a strongly apolitical impulse. The gnostic impulse is not to involve oneself in a malevolent realm in which one finds oneself an imprisoned alien; the impulse is to run away. If politics entails purposeful action within the state, as its derivation from the Greek, *polis,* or state, implies, the gnostic flees from such involvement. The papers that put Woman Downtown in captivity and peril command little time and attention, they exist dramatically, more as a justification for her beleaguered situation than anything else. It is important to note in this regard that Williams seemed to put little stock in the specificity of these papers. In a 1975 interview, he described the action of the play as set in the different period, with Woman Downtown being involved with the McCarthy hearings (Devlin 292).

Even when the period was set in the 1960s, Williams dismissed the importance of historical particulars, explaining that "Conspiracies have been going on since the beginning of time. Big money is behind it" (Devlin 253). The gnostic Williams was relatively uninterested in political involvement. He said he found all political movements boring, and admitted that he had never belonged to a political party (Devlin 249). When speaking about America's involvement in Vietnam, his pronouncement betrays his gnostic orientation: "I'm a revolutionary only in the sense that I want to see us escape from this trap" (Devlin 292). In a revealing move, Williams equates being a revolutionary with a gnostic impulse to flee from imprisonment, as if the United States were a Woman Downtown trapped in the Yellow Rose Hotel or a Tom Wingfield captive in a shoe factory. Although Williams seizes upon topical material to create *The Red Devil Battery Sign,* it quickly becomes subordinated to the mythic concerns that had shaped his *oeuvre* from the start.

In this regard, Williams suggests an affinity with a contemporary of his who also freely utilized topical materials toward his own mythic ends—film director Alfred Hitchcock, who not only admitted that the topical material that often fueled his suspense films was arbitrary, but reveled in its arbitrariness. It made, no difference, he explained to François Truffaut, whether Ingrid Bergman and Cary Grant in *Notorious* found uranium in the wine cellar or industrial diamonds—either way it was a "MacGuffin," an device to get the plot underway (Truffaut and Scott 121). For Hitchcock, the device needed to be absolutely important to the characters, but was of no interest to him (Truffaut and Scott 99). The more insubstantial the MacGuffin, the better. His favorite MacGuffin of all was the one invented for *North by Northwest,* because, as he explained, it was ultimately meaningless (Truffaut 100). The photocopied papers of *The Red Devil Battery Sign* function similarly. They account for Woman Downtown's captivity and motivate her desire to escape, but they are conveniently forgotten once they have done the work of establishing a premise for the action. While *A Streetcar Named Desire* abounds in texts that construct the play in its myriad aspects (Kolin, "Paper" 454), this late play reduces textuality to a single copy of questionable import, that seems to be forgotten by the play's end. By the conclusion, Williams is far more interested in his heroine running off to the Hollow with Wasteland Boys than flying off to Washington, D.C., to testify before a Congressional committee. Rather, Williams is presenting us with a vision of the aging artist, torn apart by chaotic passions, trauma, social concerns, suffocating domesticity, illness, drugs (Schlatter notes that "red devil" is the slang term for a powerful sedative [94]), and, most important, impending death. This material might be dismissed as merely autobiographical, but it goes far beyond that. Like Wordsworth and Coleridge, like Browning, Yeats, Rilke, Crane, and Robert Penn Warren, Williams is subjecting the power of art and imagination to everything that threatens to silence it. The topical material is only one of the elements in the mix and not the dominant one.

This is not to say that Williams did not care about the Kennedy assassination, the Vietnam War, and the corruption of American life through corporate interests, but while writing, his mythic imagination quickly won out over his political concerns as a citizen. For Williams the artist, the world is so fundamentally cruel and hostile to the desiring individual that the desperate impulse to escape becomes an immediate response, even though death will inevitably triumph over each desiring individual. The result is a radical individualism that resists incorporation into a civil dimension. Williams's vision is born of a fear and alienation so extreme that the trust needed to sustain the *polis* is absolutely lacking. For *The Red Devil Battery Sign,* this means that proof of international capitalist conspiracies can be little more than Williams's MacGuffin. This fear and alienation may be the result of a deeply instilled, pre-Stonewall vision of male homosexuality as being beyond the pale of representation within the *polis* and incapable of the acts of identification required for political action.

Yet Williams's vision may not be merely the regrettable relic of a period of homophobic persecution. In *Homos,* Leo Bersani has eloquently reacted against the communitarian impulses of many contemporary gay and lesbian critics. Examining works by André Gide, Marcel Proust, and Jean Genet, he argues that there may be a "revolutionary inaptitude for heteroized sociality" in homosexual relations, a dimension that remains salutarily disruptive of heterosexual norms (7). It may be that the much-feared fierceness of Woman Downtown and her transgressions of linguistic, gender, and sexual boundaries, which survive both the deaths of King and Drummer, may contain a revolutionary potential *beyond* Orpheus. A creature with sharp nails for both pleasure and self-defense, as idealistic as Luke, as voracious as Mrs. Kane, a mother to demolition experts, she is as much a sign of the Great Refusal of the corrupt and stunted status quo as Orpheus (Marcuse 155–156). Furthermore, she refuses to be contained as an eternal girl-child like La Niña, married, pregnant and headed for Madonnahood. She is a figure who can easily translate from one language to another but is alien to them all.

In an elegantly compressed formulation, David Savran has situated Williams's dramas at "the impossible intersection of two incompatible and contradictory forms: the one linear, liberal, and realist, and the other episodic, protosocialist, and hallucinatory" (92). Leaving aside the "protosocialist" for a moment (and perhaps considering "anarchistic" as an apt substitute in this particular context), Savran's opposition may be applied to the two protagonists of *The Red Devil Battery Sign.* King, as the liberal realist, struggles to hold on to traditional bourgeois, masculine virtues of autonomy, mastery, sexual difference and striated space, while the play charts his heroic, inevitable demise. At the same time, Woman Downtown continues in her desperation and fragmentation, her resistance to containment and domination, and the play shows her bizarre, improbable, and (in the case of the Wasteland Boys) ultimately incomprehensible survival. Perhaps this contrast provides the most important political dimension of *The Red Devil Battery Sign.* And perhaps it is these qualities which must be emphasized in theatrical production, rather than Williams's MacGuffin.

Works Cited

Adler, Thomas P. "Culture, Power and the (En)gendering of Community: Tennessee Williams and Politics." *Mississippi Quarterly* 48.4 (Fall 1995): 649–665.
Behrman, S. N. *Brief Moment*. New York: Farrar & Rinehart, 1931.
Bell, David. "Perverse Dynamics, Sexual Citizenship and the Transformation of Intimacy." In *Mapping Desire: Geographies of Sexualities*. Edited by David Bell and Gill Valentine. New York: Routledge, 1995: 304–317.
Bersani, Leo. *Homos*. Cambridge: Harvard UP, 1995.
Bloom, Harold. *Agon: Towards a Theory of Revisionism*. Oxford: Oxford UP, 1982.
——. *Omens of Millennium: The Gnosis of Angels, Dreams, and Resurrection*. New York: Riverhead Books, 1996.
Boxill, Roger. *Tennessee Williams*. New York: St. Martin's Press, 1987.
Bradley, Frank. "Two Transient Plays: *A Streetcar Named Desire* and *Camino Real*." In *Tennessee Williams: A Casebook*. Edited by Robert F. Gross. New York: Routledge, 2001: 51–62.
Brantley, Ben. "Up and Down the Grassy Knoll: The Plot Is Thick." *The New York Times* November 14, 1996: C18.
Cohn, Ruby. "Tennessee Williams: The Last Two Decades." *The Cambridge Companion to Tennessee Williams*. Edited by Matthew C. Roudané. Cambridge: Cambridge UP, 1997: 232–243.
Deleuze, Gilles and Félix Guattari. *A Thousand Plateaus: Capitalism and Schizophrenia*. Translated and Foreword by Brian Massumi. Minneapolis: U of Minnesota P, 1987.
Devlin, Albert, ed. *Conversations with Tennessee Williams*. Jackson: UP of Mississippi, 1986.
Dorff, Linda. "Babylon Now: Tennessee Williams's Apocalypses." *Theater* 29.1 (1999): 115–119.
Garber, Judith A. " 'Not Named or Identified': Politics and the Search for Anonymity in the City." In *Gendering the City: Women, Boundaries and Visions of Urban Life*. Edited by Kristine B. Miranne and Alma H. Young. New York: Rowman & Littlefield, 2000: 19–39.
Goodall, Jane. *Artaud and the Gnostic Drama*. Oxford: Oxford UP, 1994.
Gray, John. *Enlightenment's Wake: Politics and Culture at the Close of the Modern Age*. London: Routledge, 1995.
Grosch, Robert J. "Memory as Theme and Production Value in Tennessee Williams: *The Red Devil Battery Sign*." *Tennessee Williams Annual Review* 1 (1998): 119–124.
Gross, Robert F. "Tracing Lines of Flight in *Summer and Smoke* and *The Milk Train Doesn't Stop Here Anymore*." In *Tennessee Williams: A Casebook*. Edited by Robert F. Gross. New York: Routledge, 2001: 91–106.
Hammer, Stephanie B. " 'That Quiet Little Play': Bourgeois Tragedy, Female Impersonation, and a Portrait of the Artist in *The Glass Menagerie*." In *Tennessee Williams: A Casebook*. Edited by Robert F. Gross. New York: Routledge, 2001: 33–50.
Jonas, Hans. *The Gnostic Religion. The Message of the Alien God and the Beginnings of Christianity*. 2nd edition. Boston: Beacon Press, 1963.
Kolin, Philip C. "Compañero Tenn—The Hispanic Presence in the Plays of Tennessee Williams." *Tennessee Williams Annual Review* 2 (1999): 35–52.
——. "The Existential Nightmare in Tennessee Williams's *The Chalky White Substance*." *Notes on Contemporary Literature* 23.1 (1993): 8–11.
——. " 'It's only a paper moon' The Paper Ontology in Tennessee Williams's *A Streetcar Named Desire*." *Modern Drama* 40.4 (Winter 1997): 454–467.
Kruntorad, Paul. "Elend mit Perspektive: Tennessee Williams' 'neues Stück' uraufgeführt." *Theater Heute* 17.2 (February 1976): 10–11.

Kullman, Colby H. "Rule by Power: 'Big Daddyism in The World of Tennessee Williams's Plays." *Mississippi Quarterly* 48.4 (Fall 1995): 667–676.

Marcuse, Herbert. *Eros and Civilization: A Philosophical Inquiry into Freud.* New York: Vintage Press, 1962.

Marowitz, Charles. "Tennessee Revisited." *Plays and Players* 24.12 (Sept. 1977): 26–27.

O'Connor, Jacqueline. *Dramatizing Dementia: Madness in the Plays of Tennessee Williams.* Bowling Green: Bowling Green U Popular P, 1997.

Savran, David. *Communists, Cowboys and Queers: The Politics of Masculinity in the Work of Arthur Miller and Tennessee Williams.* Minneapolis: U of Minnesota P, 1992.

Schlatter, James. "*Red Devil Battery Sign:* An Approach to a Mytho-Political Theatre." *Tennessee Williams Annual Review* 1 (1998): 93–102.

Seabright, Paul. "The Aloofness of Liberal Politics: Can Imaginative Literature Furnish a Private Space?" *Literature and the Poltical Imagination.* Edited by John Horton and Andrea T. Baumeister. New York: Routledge, 1996. 145–169.

Strauss, Walter A. *Descent and Return: The Orphic Theme in Modern Literature.* Cambridge: Harvard UP, 1971.

Truffaut, François and Helen G. Scott. *Hitchcock.* New York: Simon and Schuster, 1967.

Williams, J. "Deleuze on J. M. W. Turner: Catastrophism in Philosophy?" *Deleuze and Philosophy: The Difference Engineer.* Edited by Keith Ansell Pearson. New York: Routledge, 1997: 223–246.

Williams, Tennessee. *The Chalky White Substance.* In *Plays in One Act.* Edited by Daniel Halpern. New York: Ecco Press, 1991: 467–473.

_____. *The Demolition Downtown.* In *The Theatre of Tennessee Williams.* Volume 6. New York: New Directions, 1990: 331–358.

_____. *The Red Devil Battery Sign.* In *The Theatre of Tennessee Williams.* Volume 8. New York: New Directions, 1992: 281–378.

Robert Bray

VIEUX CARRÉ: TRANSFERRING "A STORY OF MOOD"

> *"My end is in my beginning."*
>
> T. S. *Eliot,* "Burnt Norton"

Whereas some playwrights might feign an attitude of oblivious detachment in the face of hostile reviews, Tennessee Williams was especially willing to confront the critics' vitriol during his late years. In a 1975 interview he stated, "I'm quite through with the kind of play that established my early and popular reputation. I am doing a different thing, which is altogether my own, not influenced at all by other playwrights at home or abroad, or by other schools of theatre" (*Conversations* 284–5). Of course, Williams's late work was not quite the revolutionarily independent writing he might have us believe. He deeply admired Beckett, Albee, Pinter, and other playwrights who had experimented with language and structure during the 1950s and 1960s, and he may also have returned to his well-annotated volume of Pirandello when drafting radical, still unpublished versions of *Vieux Carré.* On the other hand, perhaps this observation obscures Williams's true genius for experimentation, for we should not forget that for its time (1944) many techniques used in *The Glass Menagerie* were considered to be radically innovative. In fact, even his apprentice work in the late 1930s such as *Not About Nightingales* or *Stairs to the Roof* demonstrates a bold young playwright unafraid of befuddling his audiences with experimental theatrics such as using screen projections or fusing realism with fantasy. With *Vieux Carré,* however, his innovative techniques seem to have been compromised in an effort to accommodate the dynamics shaping these particular productions and perhaps to appease the recurring cries for plays similar to those from Williams's glory years.

Anyone who studies the developmental stemmata or variants of Tennessee Williams's manuscripts learns that his writing and rewriting processes form an almost bewildering matrix of different forms and shapes. Not only do full-length

722 Toulouse Street, New Orleans. Courtesy The Historic New Orleans Collection, Museum / Research Center.

plays often evolve from poems, short stories, or one-acts, but oftentimes a single play can reveal as many as dozens of different rewrites. "If a play grips me," Williams wrote in 1981, "I'll continue to work on it until I reach a point where I can no longer decide what to do with it. Then I'll discontinue work on it" (*Conversations* 343). Although some plays, such as *Orpheus Descending*, resulted in myriad revisions spanning decades, none occupied his artistic vision longer than *Vieux Carré*. Judging by the remarkable length of time Williams spent both expanding and then contracting *Vieux Carré*, it would seem that only death's grip could pry him away from tinkering with his beloved French Quarter opus.

Williams reworked this play on and off for almost forty years, finally getting it shaped up for production throughout the 1970s, most notably from 1973 to 1977. Although *Vieux Carré* was actually begun in 1939 just weeks after Williams initially arrived in New Orleans, the first published traces of the play are to be found in *The Lady of Larkspur Lotion* (1941) and in "The Angel in the Alcove" (written in 1943; published in 1948). Sometime during the 1960s Williams drafted *Broken Glass in the Morning, or Skylight,* and in 1970 he wrote *I Never Get Dressed Till after Dark on Sundays* (neither was ever published). Williams wove elements of these works into the "Double Bill" *Vieux Carré* in 1973, changed these plays to "A pair of one acts" in 1975, then staged the completely rewritten Broadway version in 1977, in which he fused the two one-acts and eliminated the framing devices as well as the play within a play (Dorff 2). The London version went through extensive revisions that will be discussed later in this essay. According to one of the few friends who spoke with Williams just before his death, Williams was again rewriting *Vieux Carré* as he oversaw a semiprofessional production on the West Side of Manhattan the week of February 24, 1983—the very week he died (Rader 338). Perhaps this is the one play that Williams could never decide "what to do with." In considering the long evolution of *Vieux Carré*, one can better appreciate Williams's dogged determination to see this play successfully produced and more fully understand the critical juggernaut launched against Williams toward the end of his career.

With this memory play Williams recreates an assortment of characters whom he actually knew during his initial residence in the French Quarter, and in many respects *Vieux Carré* merits attention as the quintessential Tennessee Williams New Orleans set piece, as it both adumbrates (in its earliest form) and reflects back upon so many other plays set in the Quarter. *Vieux Carré* thus stands as the beginning and end of Williams's New Orleans cycle. For example, so many of Williams's vulnerable, haunted females, from Blanche to Alma to Hannah, may be traced back to Jane, the psychologically and physically ailing boarder who bears her soul to the Writer. Again, Williams says that he actually knew her (perhaps making her acquaintance during his second residency in New Orleans in 1941), and the impressions that she made upon him would become the ingredients for his creating a host of unforgettable female characters.

However, during the 1977 premiere many of the New York critics focused on the notion of Williams's recycling himself—what they perceived as his stitching bits and pieces of former fully drawn characters such as Blanche and Stanley into relatively minor players such as Jane and Tye. According to Clive Barnes, these latter two characters "are like semblances of Blanche DuBois and Stanley Kowalski, just as the play itself is filled with echoes of other times and places in other Williams's works" (244). "Pale shades of Blanche DuBois and Stanley Kowalski," wrote T. E. Kalem of the New York production (108). The flaw in these comparisons is that these critics have everything exactly backwards, because Williams knew Jane and Tye, whatever their real names were, and had crystallized these characters in his memory long before he ever created Blanche and Stanley. And there are many more differences than similarities with these particular characters. Jane, suffering from leukemia, comes to the Vieux Carré not from a dissipated plantation but from the town of New Rochelle, New York. The gigolo Tye certainly lacks Stanley's vitality and domination. In short, the comparisons really don't hold up under scrutiny. Thus instead of regarding Jane and Tye as pale incarnations of more fully developed characters found in *Streetcar,* they should instead be viewed independently as long-lost Williams acquaintances summoned by memory or, as Williams writes, people who "remain with you only as ghosts; their voices are echoes, fading but remembered" (116). Although the play's situations and thematic underpinnings—destitution, loneliness, the impingement of the past upon the present, loss, aborted communication, desire and death, and the alienation of the artist—work so effectively in other Williams drama, for many reviewers, there seems to be something fundamentally missing from this play. One recurring objection is that the Writer seems too aloof from the action—if he is relatively unconcerned with the pathos surrounding him, why should we, the audience, want to become involved? However, a substantial portion of the Writer's "education" involves his learning to steel himself against others' suffering—in other words, instead of becoming deeply and more sympathetically involved, the Writer learns to store this suffering and channel it into his art. In addition, if a play depends upon atmosphere almost as much as upon character and plot as does *Vieux Carré,* the challenge to directors and producers lies in effectively and faithfully executing the setting and mood. Regrettably, several productions ranging over twenty years appear to have done the play a profound disservice in this respect.

Vieux Carré premiered in May of 1977 at the St. James Theatre. Walter Kerr praised Williams's "most distinctively poetic" voice and asked audiences to "disregard totally the monstrously shabby physical design that is supposed to represent a rooming house in New Orleans . . ."(5). Brendan Gill lamented that "in spite of the title, it could just as easily have been laid in Key West, or even on Fire Island, as in New Orleans" (83). Barnes noted that the play "might be taking place in the Gorbals district of Glasgow" (244). The failure to convey effectively or even adequately the atmosphere in the Broadway production proved a major reason why the play flopped. As T. E Kalem noted, "What was potentially strongest in this chamber-music play of time, place, and memory has been botched by inept direction, wretched lighting and dissonance of mood" (108). Similarly, Leonard Probst lamented, "Williams needed good staging more than ever before, and in this case the director was not able to supply it" (247). Kerr, long a champion of giving Williams the benefit of the doubt, lambasted the "disgracefully served" acting and said, "The physical staging is, if anything, worse; the moment there are more than two people on stage, the performers seem to be making certain that they are standing exactly where they have been told to stand without having any notion whatsoever of which colleague they should be listening to" (5). Recognizing the importance of mood and atmosphere, Kerr reserved his harshest criticism for the "serious disservice done the play by designer James Tilton's setting." (5). Kerr noted that "If a 'memory' play wants anything, it wants atmosphere." Instead, Kerr concludes that because of being distracted by the "setting's oddities," he was unable to follow the dialogue. "I should have been concentrating on searching out the nuances of language and portraiture that were being so ruthlessly masked by an irresponsible production" (5). Reviews of this production also stressed the apparently disjointed and episodic structure of the play. Brendan Gill panned the Broadway production for its "languidly discursive style," (83) and *Variety* said that "Much of the action here is undefined, unclear, and uninteresting" (124).

When the play moved to London, Williams found himself dealing with problems posed by the demands of actors, as had been the case in New York. After "insisting on two cuts that hadn't been his choice in the first place" (Hack 274), Shelia Gish, who played Jane, quit the production. Williams often ordered line changes or would send in rewrites while rehearsals were underway or even during the early part of a play's run (perhaps the most chaotic of these eleventh-hour changes occurred during the tryouts for *The Night of the Iguana*). While these London alterations resulted in a more tightly unified play, they also became a source of great tension during the production and may have affected the overall quality of the acting.

Only more recently has *Vieux Carré* received the kind of appreciation that Williams hoped for in 1977. Of the 1983 WPA Theater production, Mel Gussow wrote, ". . . the work speaks in the lyrical voice of its author" and that the play "is resonant with emotional echoes" (13). The atmosphere was also conveyed much more effectively, as set director James Fenhagen "turned the many rooms and several levels of the boarding house into an imaginative environment" (C13). The 1997 New Heights production in Houston, Texas, garnered perhaps the best reviews of any staging. Critic Everett Evans called it "the strongest and most confident of Williams's later plays . . . *Vieux Carré* deserves a place in the repertoire alongside Williams's much-loved classics" (1). In one of the rare lines to hit the right note, Evans wrote, "*Vieux Carré* frequently represents the playwright at his brilliant best, distinguished by poetic dialogue and deep understanding of the human heart" (1). In Robert Brustein's review of one of the most recent productions, held at Moscow's Tabakov Theatre in October of 2000, he faults the play's direction but contends that *Vieux Carré* "finds its authenticity as a memory play" ("Moscow Nights").

Since much of the play is written from the temporal distance of several decades, one might wonder just how much of this "poetic dialogue" actually took place. As Lyle Leverich had reminded us, Williams did not simply try to recreate the past but rather wrote of "the *impressions* of things past" (447). Thus one should not regard this play as merely a retelling of Williams's first experiences in New Orleans. Talking with William S. Burroughs in 1977, Williams said, "You can't do creative work and adhere to facts. For instance, in my new play [*Vieux Carré*] there is a boy who is living in a house that I lived in, and undergoing some of the experiences that I underwent as a young writer. But his personality is totally different from mine. He talks quite differently from the way that I talk, so I say the play is not autobiographical. And yet the events in the house did actually take place"(*Conversations* 300). Because of the framing via the Writer's memory, the play exudes nostalgia perhaps more than any other Williams play except for *Menagerie*, as it again echoes Williams's recurring theme of the impingement of the past upon the present and the lingering pain of loss. This effect was not lost on Burroughs, who said to Williams that "the recreation of the past—nostalgia . . . came through more there than it does in a film with all the devices of Hollywood" (300). It would appear, however, that Williams sensed the shortcomings of a play based on nostalgia. Acknowledging the play's relationship to the short story "The Angel in the Alcove," Williams said, "At first I thought it was a big mistake to transfer a story of mood— you know, mostly mood and nostalgia—to the stage; that it would seem insubstantial. But now we are running the two plays together . . . " (301). For one not familiar with the long evolution of *Vieux Carré*, the question arises as to *which* "two plays" Williams refers.

In an article tracing the long evolution of *Vieux Carré*, Linda Dorff not only set the record straight on the play's origins, but she also raised some interesting points about Williams's artistic vision during his late years. As mentioned earlier, still unpublished versions of the play contain a play within a play and actor/character relationships that echo Pirandello's *Six Characters in Search of an Author*. In fact, these unpublished versions are really two separate, rather long one-acts fused together under the title *Vieux Carré*, the "two plays" that Williams refers to in his interview with Burroughs. This is but one of the more radical scripts that Williams was contemplating as the play went into production in 1977 (Dorff 1–23). Although additional versions may exist, there are at least seven different variations of this "Double Bill." The manuscripts are located at the Harry Ransom Humanities Research Center of the University of Texas at Austin, New Directions Publishing Company in New York, the Williams collection at Columbia University, Harvard's Pusey Library, at The Historic New Orleans Collection, and the New York Public Library. Whatever unpublished version one studies, the same point is driven home time and time again; what began as a radical experiment evolved into a more "acceptable" memory play that would eventually be compared unfavorably to his first success, *The Glass Menagerie*.

Although one immediately connects New Orleans with *A Streetcar Named Desire*, that signature play is just the most famous of dozens of his works set in the Vieux Carré. None, however, is more atmospherically charged with French Quarter charm and decadence than the play that bears its name. Staging the proper atmosphere and setting in any production of *Vieux Carré* may be the foremost challenge to directors; in fact, the rooming house itself becomes one of the principal characters, taking on a life of its own as the walls become the membranes of shared experiences. As Jacqueline O'Connor notes, in several of Williams's plays "the lower-class boarding or rooming houses . . . serve as the apt encapsulation of his characters' vagabond lives" (101). In *Vieux Carré*, the boarding house atmosphere, one of its fascinating strengths, becomes a debilitating weakness if not handled properly. As a consequence, the process of creating the ambiance of the house and providing just the right touch of the French Quarter beyond the rooming-house walls is at least as important as casting the proper actors or effectively pacing the play's action. Additionally, as Bruce Mann notes, the boarding house "is a mental landscape, the place in the playwright's mind where he stores his creative powers . . ." (143). In short, the significance of the setting is so paramount that it's almost as though 722 Toulouse should be listed among the dramatis personae.

With the possible exception of Montreal, New Orleans is North America's most European city, and the French Quarter as Williams knew it in the 1930s was as exotic as any of the places he had visited in Europe with his grandfather in 1928. As described in the WPA *New Orleans City Guide,* published in 1938 (the year of Williams's first New Orleans visit):

> Many [buildings] are decrepit and dingy, with doors sagging and ironwork rust-eaten; many have been turned into night clubs, apartments, and rooming-houses; others have been invaded by petty tradesmen and shopkeepers; and still others are standing vacant and in ruins, gaunt specters of a charm and culture that are gone. A few are in the possession of the descendants of the original owners, or of others who appreciate their worth and have been kept in good repair. The visitor will find in the French Quarter a strange and fascinating jumble of antique shops, flop houses, tea-rooms, wealthy homes, bars, art studios, night clubs, grocery stores, beautifully furnished apartments, and dilapidated flats. And he will meet debutantes, artists, gamblers, drunks, street walkers, icemen, sailors, bank presidents, and beggars. (56)

Despite recent attempts at gentrifying the cityscape for the never-ending tourist trade, the French Quarter was and is a place where aristocracy mingles with destitution, where despite the odds against the individual, there is always room for laughter amid the despair. It is also a place where carnal desires are not only tolerated but also celebrated and where the seedy underworld and organized crime prosper in courtyard gardens fit for the arrival of European royalty.

All of these elements provided Williams an entirely new sense of "local color," and the rooming house of 722 Toulouse serves as his palette for all the chaotic incongruities of the Vieux Carré. Since the very essence of the play depends so heavily on effectively representing atmosphere and mood, two immediate problems come to mind. First, if the reader or theatergoer has never visited the French Quarter, many of the play's unique elements might seem somewhat inaccessible. For readers of the text and for those audiences seeing a production, having previously experienced the sights, sounds, and aromas of the French Quarter, particularly the food, makes these details all the more interesting and identifiable. (This advantage of familiarity is also helpful in reading a book such as John Kennedy Toole's New Orleans-saturated novel, *A Confederacy of Dunces*. One doesn't necessarily have to have eaten a "Lucky Dog" in order to experience Ignatius's gastric distress, but it certainly helps.) In *Vieux Carré* the atmospheric touches that would be so familiar to New Orleanians must be accentuated just the proper way in order to prove effective to a wider audience.

In fact, Williams was so concerned with conveying a proper **sense** of atmosphere that he went to unusual lengths in order to ensure authenticity. Shortly before the New York City premiere, Williams brought director Arthur Allan Seidelman to New Orleans to tour the French Quarter first hand. Seidelman had worked in movies, but this was to be his first attempt at directing a stage play. Seidelman, Williams, *People* magazine photographer Christopher Harris, and others walked around the Vieux Carré for the better part of a day. Williams also wanted Seidelman to see 722 Rue Toulouse, and the touring party took the stairs up to where Williams had stayed so many years before. Harris, a lifelong resident of New Orleans, said, "Tennessee tried to show Mr. Seidelman the authentic side of the Quarter as well as the tourist stuff. In spite of Tennessee's best intentions, Mr. Seidelman didn't seem to absorb much of the Vieux Carré's ambiance. He just didn't get it"(phone conversation with Harris). In any case, when it came to writing set directions for the play, Williams might be held partially accountable for some of the disastrous staging. Williams often eschewed specific, realistic set directions, and with *Vieux Carré* he especially did not provide a great deal of help: "The stage seems bare. Various playing areas may be distinguished by sketchy partitions and doorframes. In the barrenness there should be a poetic evocation of all the cheap rooming houses of the world. . . . [but] a realistic setting is impossible, and the solution lies mainly in very skillful lighting and minimal furnishings" (4). Ironically, the lighting was one of the many shortcomings critics complained about in various productions.

Williams's characters in the play are also convincingly representative of French Quarter residents and habitués, and Williams achieves authenticity through descriptions of their various occupations. Tye's job as a barker on Bourbon Street evokes the lurid excesses of this strip, which, of course, represent his character as well. The banter between Nursie and Mrs. Wire underscores their ability to live alongside each other, however tenuous their relationship, with what Williams in *Streetcar* called "the easy mingling of the races in the old part of town"(243). The Nightingale's occupation as a quick-sketch artist in a nearby tourist restaurant aligns him with the other parasites who prey on tourists in that area of the Quarter. In addition, the Vieux Carré was and still is full of "bag people." Williams's two beloved crones, Mary Maude and Miss Carrie, forage for food in trash bins as they discuss turning down a fantasy invitation to dinner at the opulent Garden District home of one of Miss Carrie's supposed relatives. With this panoply of misfits, at once comic and pathetic, Williams again demonstrates a masterful balancing act of tone. One New Orleans resident who recognized Williams's genius for his grasp of French Quarter eccentricities summed up the play as follows (in local dialect): "It's like the other Williams plays set in the Quarter. Da chicory's on da stove, da cockroaches are on da walls, and all da characters are on da de-cline."

In considering the radical transformation that culminated in the New Directions text, one cannot help but wonder why the extensive revisions, which resulted in a single, long play, took the place of the double bill. It is important to reiterate that to some extent Williams always regarded his working scripts as blue prints, documents subject to modification not only by the playwright but by actors, producers, and directors as well. When Williams wrote *The Glass Menagerie*, for example, he added Tom's "drunk scene" at the insistence of financial backers George Nathan and Eddie Dowling (Dowling played Tom in the original stage production). In the case of *Vieux Carré*, Sylvia Sidney, who played the landlady Mrs. Wire in the Broadway production, didn't even consider the script to be a play when she first read it—she viewed it as a series of rather unrelated scenes. Williams was usually amenable to working with the requests of his actors, especially when he had settled on one person to play the part. Sidney said, "When I first read the play I was very enthusiastic but disappointed. I said I'd love to do it if it were a *play*, but as it was there were terrific problems. That was late in 1976. Several months later, Seidelman [the director] called me and said, 'Now it's a play, we're ready to go'"(Spoto 324). Williams was attentive to Sidney's demands. As the playwright has acknowledged, "Performers can be enormously valuable in suggesting line changes in a play, I mean if they're intelligent performers" (*Conversations* 326). But Sidney's demands had as much to do with unifying the play's structure as with line changes, and with Sidney's objections and other pressures, Williams returned to the memory play format of earlier versions, fusing the two one-acts in the process. As previously mentioned, the inevitable critical reaction was to compare this late memory play unfavorably to *The Glass Menagerie*, once again measuring Williams against his own past accomplishments and chastising him for failing to live up to his standards set some thirty years before. Williams therefore found himself in a no-win situation. If he broke the mold with boldly experimental works such as *Out Cry* or with the postmodern structure of a play such as *Something Cloudy, Something Clear* (see Kolin), he was vilified for abandoning his roots of poetic realism. But when he obligingly returned to those same roots, his work was immediately (and always unfavorably) compared with *Menagerie*, *Streetcar*, and *Cat*. Although in reality these comparisons were as apples to oranges, in the eyes of the critics, Williams's filet mignon had degenerated into grade "D" hamburger.

The forces that lie behind the production of any successful play necessarily require negotiations and compromises that sometimes test a playwright's autonomy, if not his or her artistic integrity. Consider, for example, the two very different endings of *Cat on a Hot Tin Roof*, one written expressly for Kazin's Broadway production in order to ensure a more receptive audience. An examination of *Vieux Carré*, however, reveals a more troubling interference at work, because in rewriting this play Williams seems to be making major alterations based not necessarily upon his own aesthetics but rather upon three dominant forces: the objections to the script by actors, the cajoling of persuasive directors, and by his anticipation of an audience unprepared to endorse the experimental direction in which his work was heading at this time.

During the 1977 production at the St. James Theatre on Broadway, Williams must have become increasingly frustrated at the reactions his experiment was receiving. Even after dozens of previously "completed" versions, the play was still a work in progress, and neither the script nor its author was fit to meet the public. During rehearsals actors kept dropping lines. Last-minute rewrites kept everyone off balance. The set was grotesquely inappropriate, and Williams was in a deeply despondent mood. According to Diane Kagan, who played Jane in this production, the play was a disaster waiting to happen. "For one thing, there were no tryouts in other cities, as was usually the case. We just kept rehearsing over and over. And there were terrific problems with the set. It was fixed on a revolving turntable, and it didn't work. It became almost laughable to see it happen" (phone conversation with Kagan). Just days before the opening Williams wrote to Maria St. Just, "They had to delay the opening of *Vieux Carré* till May 5th because of the set which is too complicated for any theatre I've ever seen. The Broadway Theatre is finished, in my opinion. I believe I have given them one last play which is lovely, but after that, I want to produce only in England" (*Five O'Clock Angel* 357). Perhaps Williams's comments were simply remarks made in anticipation of yet another disappointing box-office failure. But these words also reflect his frustration with critics and audiences who took perverse glee in denouncing his experimental work and with those influential reviewers who had been writing his artistic obituary ever since his last critical and commercial success in 1961, *The Night of the Iguana*. As John S. McCann notes, "Within the same decade ['70s], Williams's reputation would necessarily suffer from the negative criticism which that decade's weak plays received—and more than likely deserved. But the castigation of Williams in this decade would reach a pitch of verbal abuse that rivaled the most scabrous criticism of the past thirty years as a whole" (xxviii).

When New Directions prepared the text for publication in 1977, the editors chose the London script over the earlier, Broadway version. Such a decision was entirely understandable given the problems associated with the longer New York version. According to Ms. Peggy Fox, who worked on the printed version, "We published the text of the London production because that was what Tennessee wanted. He was very involved in the production itself and felt that his rewrites clarified and focused the play much beyond what it had been in New York. I picked up a copy of the 'director's script' at the London offices of ICM. From that the play was transcribed, then set, and Tennessee read and corrected the proofs" (Fox to Bray).

Problems with atmospheric authenticity also extended to the 1979 paperback edition of the play which featured a photo of a dwelling totally incongruous to the setting. It was that of a shotgun frame house that might have been photographed somewhere *outside* of the Vieux Carré in New Orleans but probably could have been taken in almost any city. To their credit, New Directions was convinced that the most logical photograph would be one of 722 Rue Toulouse, and The Historic New Orleans Collection provided the present cover photo, taken around the time of Williams's actual residence there.

In the New Directions text, which is the only one that has been published, Williams's rewrites resulted in a final version that, as previously mentioned, returned to the framing/dissolving technique of one of his greatest commercial and critical successes, *The Glass Menagerie*. Yet the play has proved to be somewhat disappointing in terms of its sales and number of productions. Despite Williams's extensive final revisions of the printed text, the play still strikes many as being disjointed. Since Williams pared down the two separate one-acts and returned to the more traditional framing/memory format, one questions the legitimacy of its being called loose and episodic and wonders why it cannot simply be accepted as dramatically picaresque. Furthermore, although the framing/memory similarities between *Vieux Carré* and *The Glass Menagerie* have been pointed out, in many ways *Vieux Carré* may be more profitably seen as a well-unified artistic and autobiographical sequel to *The Glass Menagerie*.

When an interviewer asked Tennessee Williams what brought him to New Orleans, he replied, "St. Louis." When Tom/Tennessee finally flees from the Wingfield/Williams household, he is no longer a member of the St. Louis community. His initial journey to New Orleans in 1938 involves a rite of passage into independence and an attempt to break ties with home. (We might also remember that at this very time Williams changed his first name). As the writer tells Mrs. Wire, "I didn't escape from one mother to look for another" (77). But just as Tom in *The Glass Menagerie* cannot escape the haunting, guilt-evoking memory of leaving behind Laura/Rose, the writer in *Vieux Carré* cannot escape the memory of the "fading but remembered" tenants of 722 Rue Toulouse (116). The writer's transient relationships in the boarding house are, of course, much more detached than Tom's interminable incarceration in the Wingfield household, and perhaps this is one reason that the play has not been so well received. The Wingfields' triangle of despair is much more gripping than, say, the Nightingale's respiratory problems, and successful theatre thrives on the ties that bind. However, the Writer's objectivity and his refusal (or inability) to enter into any relationships on a permanent basis actually make him a much more effective and reliable narrator than Tom in *The Glass Menagerie,* whose subjective point of view renders him virtually incapable of any objective recollection and may, in fact, call into question the accuracy or reliability of his memory (see Adler).

The Writer's passage from America's heartland into its most European city involves an artistic baptism that results in nothing less than a complete ontological recalibration. His relocation away from family affords him an emancipation that allows him to become a "shameless spy," one who can enter and exit rooms without necessarily forging any emotional commitment. As the Writer shuffles about the rooming house as a partial participant and recorder of the action, his movement unifies the disparate tableaux into an organic whole. *Vieux Carré* is the story of an artist's maturation, and the play's axis is the atmosphere of the house, along with its transient inhabitants; of much lesser importance is whether or not the characters are all in one room at one time participating in rituals of dialogue that bind them together.

In addition to the Writer's narrative framing, Mrs. Wire also provides continuity as the ruler of this zany roost, and although her jaundiced eye is less reliable than the Writer's cataract-obscured one, her relationship to the boarders, which vacillates between cruelty and tenderness, helps to form both tension as well as unity throughout the play. If one insists on viewing the play as disjointed, it is perhaps because the story of Jane and Tye seems, for some, a distraction. (Indeed, we will recall that in earlier drafts, theirs *was* a separate play). But I maintain that the critical observations of the play's being "episodic" and "disjointed" are more the functions of the perceiver than the object. Criticism based on this particular objection seems to represent the determination of those who were intent on seeing Williams fail in his waning years as a playwright.

As Annette Saddick points out in her book about the final plays, "In his later years, Williams was defeated before he ever began. Reviewers tended to exhibit hostility toward experimental drama in general, and Williams never had a chance to be taken seriously in the first place by critics. His later reputation, therefore, tells us more about the critical biases in the popular and academic press in this country than about Williams's work per se" (150). With *Vieux Carré*, one hopes that future productions will adhere more faithfully to the atmosphere Williams attempts to create and take liberties beyond Williams's scant stage directions to ensure that the ambiance of the French Quarter is at least adequately represented. In addition, perhaps the earlier, more radically innovative versions might eventually be staged and published in order for Williams's true experimental genius to be further recognized. As Keith Hack noted, *Vieux Carré* is "certainly the most interesting play I know about the coming of age of an artist, about what it takes to grow up and be a writer. I think it's actually a better play than *Glass Menagerie* because it's more complex—more ambitious" (268). No one ever dismissed Williams's ambition as a young writer, and one imagines that the day will come when his later accomplishments will be critically appraised in a more temperate and judicious light than now illuminates the *oeuvre* of his post-*Iguana* years.

Works Cited

Adler, Thomas P. "The (Un)reliability of the Narrator in *The Glass Menagerie* and *Vieux Carré*." *The Tennessee Williams Review* (Spring 1981): 6–9.

Barnes, Clive. "*Vieux Carré* by Williams is Haunting." *New York Times* 12 May 1977: C22. Rpt. in *New York Theatre Critics' Reviews* 38 (1977): 244–47.

Brustein, Robert. "Moscow Nights." *The New Republic Online.* 16 October 2000 <http://www.thenewrepublic.com/101600/Brustein101600.html>.

Clinton, Craig. "The Reprise of Tennessee Williams's *Vieux Carré* : An Interview with Director Keith Hack." *Studies in American Drama, 1945–Present* 7.2 (1992): 265–75.

Devlin, Albert J., ed. *Conversations with Tennessee Williams.* Jackson: UP of Mississippi, 1986.

Dorff, Linda. "All very [not!] Pirandello": Radical Theatrics in the Evolution of *Vieux Carré*." *Tennessee Williams Annual Review* 3 (2000): 13–33.

Evans, Everett. "*Vieux Carré* is Williams at His Best." *Houston Chronicle* 15 Mar 1977.

Federal Writer's Project of the WPA for the City of New Orleans. *New Orleans City Guide*. Boston: Houghton Mifflin, 1938.

Fox, Peggy. Email to the Author. 5 August, 2001.

Gill, Brendan. "Consolations of Memory." *The New Yorker* 23 May 1977: 83.

Gussow, Mel. "*Vieux Carré* by Tennessee Williams is Revisited." *New York Times* 5 April 1983, Sec. 3:13.

Harris, Christopher. Telephone Interview. 5 September, 2001.

Kagan, Diane. Telephone Interview. 21 January, 2002.

Kalem, T. E. "Down and Out in N. O." *Time* 23 May:108.

Kerr, Walter. "A Touch of the Poet Isn't Enough to Sustain Williams's Latest Play." *New York Times* 22 May 1977, sec. 2:5.

Kolin, Philip. "*Something Cloudy, Something Clear*: Tennessee Williams's Post-modern Memory Play." *Journal of Dramatic Theory and Criticism* 12 (Spring 1988):35–55.

Leverich, Lyle. *Tom: The Unknown Tennessee Williams*. New York: Crown,1995.

Madd. "*Vieux Carré*." *Variety* 18 May, 1977:124.

McCann, John S. *The Critical Reputation of Tennessee Williams: A Reference Guide*. Boston: G. K. Hall, 1983.

O'Connor, Jacqueline. "'Living in this little hotel': Boarders on Borders in Tennessee Williams's Early Short Plays." *Tennessee Williams Annual* Review 3 (2000): 101–115.

Probst, Leonard. "*Vieux Carré* " *New York Theatre Critics' Review* 38 (1977): 246–247.

Rader, Dotson. *Tennessee: Cry of the Heart: An Intimate Memoir of Tennessee* Williams. Garden City, NY: Doubleday, 1985.

Saddik, Annette J. *The Politics of Reputation: The Critical Reception of* Tennessee Williams's Late Plays. Madison, NJ: Assoc. UP, 1999.

Spoto, Donald. *The Kindness of Strangers: The Life of Tennessee Williams*. Boston: Little, Brown, 1985.

Williams, Tennessee. *Five O'Clock Angel: Letters of Tennessee Williams to Maria St. Just, 1948–1982*. New York: Knopf, 1990.

———. *A Streetcar Named Desire. The Theatre of Tennessee Williams*. Vol. 1. New York: New Directions, 1971.

———. *Vieux Carré*. With introd. by Robert Bray. New York: New Directions, 2000.

Verna Foster

WAITING FOR BUDDY, OR JUST GOING ON IN *A LOVELY SUNDAY FOR CREVE COEUR*

A Lovely Sunday for Creve Coeur is a wry farce (in the Chekhovian sense) in two scenes about four women. The play was written in about 1975 as a long one-act and first performed as *Creve Coeur* at the Spoleto Festival in Charleston, South Carolina, in 1978. Revised as a full-length play and retitled, *A Lovely Sunday for Creve Coeur* had its New York premiere in 1979 at the Hudson Guild Theatre, whose relatively intimate space proved more congenial than the large theatre in Charleston for this "chamber" play (Devlin 313–314). Apart from its London premiere at the Old Red Lion in Islington in 1986, for the next twenty years *A Lovely Sunday for Creve Coeur* was rarely staged. Recently, however, productions have been more frequent, and they have met with some success.[1]

Though the play has received some praise from reviewers and occasionally from critics, it has also often been compared unfavorably with Williams's earlier plays or dismissed as a half-hearted return to his earlier realistic style and familiar themes.[2] Consequently critics have spent more time in rehashing those themes than in examining the play's dramaturgy and have ignored Williams's own suggestion that the play is "almost a different genre" from his other work (Devlin 314). *A Lovely Sunday for Creve Coeur,* in fact, blends the psychological realism of the earlier plays with the grotesque style Williams developed later in his career.

Any given production, of course, can emphasize either a realistic or a grotesque style. However, productions that deemphasize the play's grotesque elements seem to have been less successful than those that allow the grotesque its full force. Williams himself praised Charlotte Moore's Helena in the first two productions for being unrealistic and preferred the "rough, massive, craggy, gothic quality" that Jan Miner brought to the role of Bodey in the earlier Charleston production to Peg Murray's more realistic performance in New York (Devlin 314). The New

York production, in turn, seems to have been more satisfying than the London premiere, which was but "a shadow of its New York self. What is missing is Williams's flair for grotesque comedy" (Billington, *Guardian* 3 July 1986). Directors of recent successful productions of *A Lovely Sunday for Creve Coeur* have sought to balance psychological realism and grotesque comedy. In fact, in directing Northlight Theatre's 1998 production in Skokie (Chicago), Cecilie D. Keenan felt that the challenge lay in making the characters "full-bodied and not just slapstick" (Smith, *Chicago Tribune* 11 Feb. 1998), while in the Alliance Theatre Company's "outrageously comic" production, the women were played as "caricatures" of "outsize dimensions" (Brock, *Atlanta Journal-Constitution* 19 Oct. 2001).

Greater understanding of the grotesque elements in Williams's work has aided in the critical re-evaluation of several of his late plays in recent years. The grotesque, present even in Williams's earlier, more realistic drama, overtly informs later plays such as *The Mutilated, The Gnädiges Fräulein, The Two-Character Play*, and *In the Bar of a Tokyo Hotel*, works in which Williams invents a dramatic style that draws on the dramaturgy of the theatre of the absurd (as well as on his own earlier experiments in dramatic form). The importance of the grotesque in *A Lovely Sunday for Creve Coeur* has yet to be fully appreciated. It does not have the "cartoonish" quality that Linda Dorff identifies in several of Williams's other late plays (16, 24). Rather in *A Lovely Sunday for Creve Coeur* Williams blends the Chekhovian poetic realism of his earlier, more popular plays with some of the comically outlandish or monstrously bizarre elements of the absurdist style he developed especially in plays of the 1960s.[3]

Bodey (Sonja Lanzener, right) joins Dottie (Genevieve Elam, left) in exercising in the Alliance Theatre Company's *A Lovely Sunday for Creve Coeur*. Photo by Michelle Hollberg.

Through his depiction of the lives of four women who are all waiting for something on one ordinary Sunday, Williams works out existential themes of loneliness, anxiety, limitation, and confinement. His portrayal of the women's lives is sociologically and psychologically precise, but through his incorporation of techniques akin to those of Ionesco, in particular, Williams shocks his audience into glimpsing the frightening emptiness behind the women's everyday routines so that we come to view the seriocomic ordinariness of such lives with less complacence and more understanding.

The four women in *A Lovely Sunday for Creve Coeur* spend their Sunday seeking or preparing or simply waiting for something that they hope will happen. Dorothea (Dotty), a high school civics teacher in her late youth, awaits a gentleman's phone call, that of Ralph Ellis, the principal of Blewett High School (Williams's own *alma mater*). On the basis of a few dates and a sexual encounter in his ("Flying Cloud") car, Dotty has deluded herself that Ralph will marry her. While waiting, Dotty does her exercises, takes Mebaral tablets for her nerves, and drinks sherry. Bodey, Dotty's eccentric German-American roommate, hoping that Dotty will marry her twin brother, Buddy, prepares a picnic that she intends to share with both of them at Creve Coeur amusement park. Helena, a sharp-tongued fellow teacher at Blewett High School, tries to persuade Dotty to make a financial commitment to a more upmarket apartment she plans to share with her. Sophie Gluck, Dotty and Bodey's hysterical upstairs neighbor, whose mother has recently died, simply seeks company in Bodey's apartment. At the end of the play, incited by Helena, Dotty demands the Sunday newspaper carefully hidden by Bodey and finds an announcement of Ralph's engagement to a girl in his own country club set. Dotty decides to join Bodey and Buddy at Creve Coeur.

A Lovely Sunday for Creve Coeur, like *Waiting for Godot*, focuses on what the characters do while waiting rather than on what they are waiting for (neither Ralph nor Buddy appears in the play). Nor is there any surprise, since it is apparent from the beginning that Ralph is not going to phone or marry Dotty. The play's mild suspense inheres in the way that Dotty chooses to deal with her disappointment. Early in the play she asserts, "Without romance in my life, I could no more live than I could without breath" [133]. But her quick recovery from a literal loss of breath while exercising negates this idealistic position and anticipates instead her final acknowledgment that she can after all live or at least "just go on" (199) without romance, even at the risk of "being asphyxiated gradually by [Buddy's] cheap cigars" (133). The impossibility yet necessity of going on is a theme as characteristic of Williams as it is of Beckett.

If the play centers on Dotty's choice, its conflict lies in Bodey's and Helena's competing desires for Dotty's future, worked out as a farcical struggle for her allegiance. Bodey, a warm-hearted "Earth-Mother" (according to Clive Barnes in the *New York Post*) or "heifer" (in Helena's deliberate distortion of her surname, Bodenhafer), and Helena, described by Bodey as a "well-dressed snake" (173), despite their differences, both fear loneliness. Bodey wants Dotty to marry her fat, beer-drinking, cigar-smoking, blue-collar twin brother, Buddy (who, though unromantic, is apparently decent and good-natured), so that Dotty will be taken care of and have a family, Buddy will have an attractive wife of whom Bodey is fond, and Bodey herself will have little nieces and nephews to care for. Bodey's design for Dotty's future, however self-serving, is essentially life affirming. Helena, resigned to spinsterhood, aims to remove Dotty to a more elegant apartment and a polite female lifestyle (bridge parties and so forth), not only because she needs someone to share the expenses but also because she, too, fears being alone ("There's nothing lonelier than a woman dining alone" [161]). For a woman like Dotty who, like so many of Williams's no longer youthful heroines, must have a man to feel fulfilled ("I've got to find a partner in life, or my life will have no meaning" [133]), the life offered by Helena can only be a kind of death. Williams makes this contrast explicit when Bodey says that she wants "a *life*" for Dotty and Helena sarcastically responds, "You mean as opposed to a death?" (173). The fourth woman, Sophie Gluck, hysterically fearful of being alone in the *gespukt* (162) apartment upstairs in which her mother died and constantly seeking comfort from Bodey, represents the most terrifying possible future for Dotty: a life without either male or female companionship as bulwark against the imaginary horrors generated by one's own mind. Sophie grotesquely underscores and symbolizes the loneliness that all of the women in the play have experienced or fear.

Loneliness, Williams emphasised, is "the main theme" of *A Lovely Sunday for Creve Coeur* (Devlin 315). The loneliness that, according to Williams, "haunts every individual" (Leverich 347) is the natural condition of many, perhaps most, of Williams's major characters throughout his plays and is usually the driving force behind their sexual desire. More than a simple lack of companionship, the loneliness of Williams's characters is a metaphysical as much as a social condition, an existential sense of isolation that borders on the absurd. In his earlier plays Williams represents anxiety and loneliness through psychological realism. But even in these plays he extends the limits of realism through his use of heightened poetic language and expressionism to convey the peculiar emotional experience of characters such as Laura in *The Glass Menagerie*, Blanche in *A Streetcar Named Desire*, or Serafina in *The Rose Tatoo*. In his later plays an absurdist view of life, often implicit in Williams's representations, becomes more overt as his dramaturgy evolves from its basis in realism.

A comparison of *A Lovely Sunday for Creve Coeur* with an earlier version of the play highlights the distinctive ways in which Williams's dramaturgy and characterization developed in the two decades between them. *A Lovely Sunday for Creve Coeur* clearly has its origin in *All Gaul Is Divided*, an unsolicited and unfilmed screenplay Williams wrote in the 1950s, even though he said that he had forgotten the screenplay when he wrote the stage play. (Jenny, Dotty's counterpart in the screenplay, is a Latin rather than a civics teacher—hence the title's allusion to Caesar.) In a note written in 1979 Williams describes the style of *All Gaul Is Divided* as belonging to the period "critics refer to as 'the early Williams'" (*All Gaul Is Divided* 3). Some differences between "the early Williams" of the screenplay and the "different genre" of the stage play are attributable to the media for which Williams was writing. Other changes point to Williams's more complex goals in the later work.

Williams presents his four female characters in *A Lovely Sunday for Creve Coeur* in more intimate detail than their counterparts in the screenplay and renders their motives more credible; at the same time, by their absence, the men take on representative and symbolic qualities, becoming whatever the women in the play, and the audience, think they are. Williams also articulates more precisely the play's themes of loneliness and limitation by setting it in the depressed 1930s (rather than the 1920s of the screenplay), by condensing and confining its action (including preserving the unities), and by exaggerating the salient traits of three of the characters to the point of caricature. The exception (or at least partial exception) is Dotty, who is more normal, more believable, and also more likeable than Jenny so that the audience has greater emotional investment in the choice she finally makes.

Having spent two years in a sanatorium, Jenny truly is an "emotionally fragile" person, as Helena mistakenly supposes Dotty to be (146), but her self-involved hysteria, even in front of her students, makes it difficult to sympathize with her. Her roommate, Beulah Bodenhafer, a less bizarre incarnation of the later Bodey, similarly wants her friend to marry her brother, Buddy, a widower with one child in this version. But given Jenny's mental instability, Buddy's impatience with her on the one occasion that he appears, and her dislike of Buddy's daughter (an already-existing niece for Beulah to love), such a union seems a much less likely objective for any of the characters than it becomes in *A Lovely Sunday for Creve Coeur*. Jenny herself dreams of marrying Harry Steed, the gym teacher at her school and a former country club golf pro, who is obviously, like the later Ralph, an opportunist. The news of his engagement finally induces Jenny to settle for Buddy.[4]

Williams mistakenly believed that *All Gaul Is Divided* sustains dramatic tension better than *A Lovely Sunday for Creve Coeur* because the audience does not learn of Steed's engagement until the end of the screenplay (*All Gaul Is Divided* 3). In fact, the audience is no more likely to expect that Jenny will marry Steed than that Dotty will marry Ralph. And, in any case, this kind of plot-based suspense is not the point. In *A Lovely Sunday for Creve Coeur* Williams builds on the limitations already implicit in *All Gaul Is Divided* to create a different kind of (explosive) tension by overtly restricting and confining his heroine's options in every possible way-through the play's structure and through his characterization and deployment of the other three women. The farcical conflict between the domestic roommate and the socially aspiring friend, for example, more sharply delimits Dotty's choices in *A Lovely Sunday for Creve Coeur*. Lucinda, the friend in the screenplay, has not opted for an all-female lifestyle (in fact, she tries to obtain Steed for herself), and, though more devious, she is less entertainingly sarcastic in her sparring with the roommate than is the later Helena.

The fourth character in *A Lovely Sunday for Creve Coeur,* Sophie Gluck, has no counterpart in *All Gaul Is Divided*. There is a brief appearance by an Upstairs Neighbor, but Sophie is basically a new character, though Williams has transposed on to her Jenny's mental breakdown, hysteria, and inability to cope with life. (Sophie perhaps takes the place, too, of Rosie, the ungainly bulldog cared for by Beulah and despised by Lucinda.) Since, in general, Williams condenses characters and action in *A Lovely Sunday for Creve Coeur,* the addition of Sophie Gluck, who is in no way necessary to the development of such plot as there is, draws attention to her importance as a keynote character who underscores the play's themes of loneliness, limitation, and fear of confinement. Ironically misnamed "Gluck" (luck-like Beckett's Lucky perhaps) and, as her first name implies, standing for some kind of wisdom, Sophie is "the specter that confronts" (186) all of the women.

Sophie, in particular, exemplifies Williams's dramatic strategy in *A Lovely Sunday for Creve Coeur*. Though grounded in mundane reality as a bereaved German neighbor who has spent time in a mental institution, Sophie seems at first inexplicable. "An unknown creature of demented appearance" (152), as Helena describes her, Sophie communicates through moans, wails, and a ludicrous, shrill hybrid of German and English; she rolls her eyes *"like a religieuse in a state of sorrowful vision"* (154), shuffles (154), dribbles (160), and at the end of the first scene is afflicted with a sudden onset of diarrhea (brought on by hot coffee), after which she floods the bathroom. The incident is meant to be funny, certainly, though Williams cautions against *excessive scatology* (163). But more than being merely funny, Williams's depiction of Sophie points to a dramaturgy akin to that advocated and practised by Ionesco.

While expressing admiration for dramatists such as Beckett, Pinter, and Albee, Williams said that he was "not crazy about Ionesco" (Devlin 99). Nonetheless, Ionesco's definition of what theatre should be provides helpful insight into Williams's practice in *A Lovely Sunday for Creve Coeur*. In his essay "Experience of the Theatre" (1958), Ionesco argues for a theatre that exaggerates its effects, "through caricature and the grotesque," to the point of becoming "unendurable," to "paroxysm"; for drama "lies in extreme exaggeration of the feelings, an exaggeration that dislocates flat everyday reality. Dislocation, disarticulation of language too." Such a theatre is necessary because "We need to be virtually bludgeoned into detachment from our daily lives, our habits and mental laziness, which conceal from us the strangeness of the world" (24–25). Though more domesticated, Sophie bears some of the same marks of affliction as the title character in *The Gnädiges Fräulein,* Williams's 1960s "slapstick tragedy" that most strongly evokes the Ionescan absurd.[5] Sophie speaks in a disarticulated language (as, in a different way, does Bodey). She exhibits behavior that is *"grotesquely tragic"* (160) or comically grotesque to the point of becoming "unbearable." By her very presence Sophie dislocates everyday reality so that the audience is "bludgeoned" into seeing afresh the "strangeness of the world," represented in this play as the confined world of women who are not rich and who are no longer young. Helena comments on this strangeness; Bodey's apartment and everything that happens in it, especially Sophie, seem to her "fantastic" (158). But Helena, too, is fantastic.

Like Ionesco's oddly upsetting bourgeois rooms and the caricatures of middle-class people who inhabit them, the set and characters in *A Lovely Sunday for Creve Coeur* are obviously distorted versions of a familiar reality. The dreary apartment buildings seen through Bodey's peculiarly large windows evoke, Williams suggests, *"the dried-blood horror"* of urban neighborhoods in Ben Shahn's paintings (119). The light coming in through the huge windows is unnaturally bright—a *"fiercely yellow glare"* (119) that heightens the "nightmare of clashing colors" in which the apartment has been decorated: purple carpet, orange drapes, "violent yellow daisies" on the lampshades, "exploding" roses on the wallpaper (172). The decor is naturalized to the extent that it reflects Bodey's enthusiastic but disastrous attempt to make the apartment cheerful and allows Helena an opportunity to express her distaste for the lower-middle-class vulgarity of clashing colors and numerous decorative objects such as a green china frog and a stuffed canary. But the exaggeration of the glaring lighting and violent colors goes beyond either naturalism or even the expressionism of Williams's earlier plays. In *A Lovely Sunday for Creve Coeur,* the garish decor directly assaults the audience's senses. It is not only Dotty who is trapped in Bodey's overwhelming milieu; the audience's nerves are jarred as well. Rick Paul, designer of Northlight's production, commented on the "hallucinatory feeling" of the apartment (Smith, *Chicago Tribune* 11 Feb. 1998), and Maeve Walsh, reviewing Graeae's production in England, described the apartment as a "Technicolor headache" (*The Independent* 24 March 1999).

The Artaudian assault on our eyes is augmented by an assault on our ears. Early in the play Dotty has to shout at Bodey to make herself heard since Bodey is not wearing her hearing aid. A stage direction indicates that *"The shouting is congruent with the fiercely bright colors of the interior"* (124). The play, in fact, is full of unnaturally cacophonous noises. At the start of the play Dotty's combined counting and panting *"assails our senses"* (119) as she does her exercises; subsequently, the audience hears Buddy's voice "barking" from the unattended phone (141), Bodey slamming drawers (143), Bodey's screeching hearing aid (166), and so on. The play is punctuated too by Helena's unpleasant laughter (*"like a cawing crow"* [189]) and Sophie's choric wailing and moaning. Ruby Cohn observes that in his plays of the 1960s and 1970s Williams "expanded both his visual and sonic repertory" (242). The harsh and repetitive sounds Williams uses particularly in his later plays (for example, the startling piano chords in *The Two-Character Play* or the horrid noises made by the cocaloony birds in *The Gnädiges Fräulein*) are disturbing in a manner similar to the unsettling aural effects in some of Ionesco's plays or even Sam Shepard's later *Fool for Love*. The loud and peculiar noises heard throughout *A Lovely Sunday for Creve Coeur,* together with its violently clashing colors, construct a physical space almost palpably oppressive in its effect on the audience.

This space, the apartment in which Dotty feels suffocated (she literally faints) but survives, is Bodey's natural environment. Bodey is just as outlandish, as "fantastic" (125, 158), as the apartment itself. Her heifer-like attributes, her deafness to anything she does not want to hear, the extraordinary quasi-Germanic—"dislocated"—syntax of her sentences ("I'm not too dumb like which you regard me to know why you're struck so funny by 'hoof it'" [153–154]), as well as the huge artificial flowers—chrysanthemum, poppy, or tiger lily—with which she attempts to cover her hearing aid (and which perhaps make her look like a prize cow) make Bodey as much caricature as character. Displaying the same "tenacity to existence" as little Hilda, the stuffed canary that lived "more than ten years in such confine-ment" (142), Bodey thrives in the apartment that is, in effect, an extension of her personality, a haven for Sophie, and a kind of hell for Helena.

The glare and clutter of the apartment offend Helena's eyes and taste from the moment that she enters it. Even more alarming, as if taking on a life of their own, objects in the apartment seem farcically complicit with its owner in inflicting phys-ical humiliations upon the sophisticated Helena. Baking soda gets sprinkled on Helena's clothes (142); a box falls out of a closet that she opens (143); coffee splashes (150). While Helena's criticisms of the apartment may at first seem nor-mative, Williams emphasizes her status as intruder by characterizing her, in con-trast to the warm, nurturing, heifer-like Bodey, as a predator. Helena stares and moves like a *"predatory bird"* (136, 138); her resemblance to a bird is accentuated by the *"round, white-rimmed"* sunglasses (139) she puts on against the glare. Bodey compares her to a hawk or a buzzard or "a well-dressed snake," adding that she talks "with a kind of a hiss" (173). Certainly what Helena says is insidious and sar-castic, though also often very funny, and many of her lines might well be hissed: "The syntax of that sentence was rather confusing" (165).

Williams's grotesque characterization of Bodey as heifer and, especially, of Hel-ena as snake invites a mythic reading of the farcical conflict between the two women for Dotty's future (or Dotty's soul). In such a reading Helena Brookmire (whose name, like the other names in the play, evokes a moral and psychological caricature, in her case something evil and slimy) is the threatening intruder who has come to tempt Dotty away from Bodey's eden and disrupt her plans to take Dotty to Buddy and Creve Coeur. Though Creve Coeur may signify heartbreak for Dotty, for Bodey it is a romantic paradise: "nice and cool . . . through green country . . . flowers . . . fireflies . . . the lake shore," where Buddy will ask Dotty to marry him (173–74). Bodey wins, since Dotty chooses to follow her to Creve Coeur, and Helena is cast out.

The inevitability of Buddy and Creve Coeur is kept in the forefront of the audience's attention throughout the play by Bodey's single-minded preparation of the picnic. Bodey thus acts as the comic agent of Dotty's fate or, in a metatheatrical reading of the play, as the director of its action (Rocha 191–92). Bodey's prepara-tion of the picnic while Dotty's hopes are dashed also evokes one of the principles of Chekhovian dramaturgy: "Let the things that happen on the stage be as com-plex and yet just as simple as they are in life. For instance, people are having a meal at the table, just having a meal, but at the same time their happiness is being created, or their lives are being smashed up" (Chekhov 19). *A Lovely Sunday for Creve Coeur* does not "drift" as Chekhov's plays seem to, its action being, if any-thing, overdetermined. But the Chekhovian ordinariness of the Sunday routine (the cooking, eating, and drinking) in Bodey's apartment grounds the play's gro-tesque elements in a realistic context that helps the audience to sympathize with the disappointments and limited opportunities of all the women.

One limitation that Williams renders both painfully realistic and comically gro-tesque is the women's uneasy relationship with food. Dotty is plump, despite strenuous exercising, and drinks too much sherry. Helena is obliged to pay for her slim figure and her social style by turning up her nose at Bodey's crullers ("Pastries are not included in my diet" [150]) and often dining alone. Even Bodey, who gets the most enjoyment out of everything she does, is spattered repeatedly with hot fat in the course of preparing food for others. And hot coffee gives Sophie, graphically, diarrhea. The women's enslavement, in one form or another, to food (its preparation, its social implications, its effect on their bodies) reinforces the audience's sense of the restrictions (habitual as well as social) placed on them and that they also impose on themselves, specifically as women.[6]

Only Dotty has any choice at all. Dotty is like the pigeon that Helena notices outside the window at the end of the first scene—"Capable of flight but perched for a moment in this absolute desolation . . ." (167). The direction in which Dotty will fly, the choice she will make, inevitable though it seems, structures the play and gives it its meaning. In a mythic or allegorical reading of the play Dotty is everywoman, choosing life, however diminished, over death. In a realistic reading she "will settle" (174) for Buddy. In a symbolic reading she is waiting and, like Vladimir and Estragon, finds ways to pass the time while waiting, for a savior— Ralph, she thinks—who turns out to be Buddy (a substitution that is actually not as bad as Vladimir and Estagon's apprehension that their Godot might be Pozzo).

The gentleman caller who disappoints is a familiar figure in Williams's earlier plays. In *The Glass Menagerie* Jim symbolizes "the long-delayed but always expected something that we live for" (145) but is unavailable for Laura; Blanche's millionaire, Shep Huntley, becomes the Doctor who takes her to an asylum. Buddy, however, seems more promising, if only because he does not appear in the play; and Dotty is not Laura, though she might be considered a workaday version of Blanche Dubois, without her brilliance and psychological complexity but with a much greater instinct for survival. The meaning of *A Lovely Sunday for Creve Coeur,* Williams emphasized, is that Dotty (like Stanley and Stella and unlike Blanche) goes on: "She goes right on to Creve Coeur" (Devlin 316).

Dotty's trajectory in *A Lovely Sunday for Creve Coeur* may be read as a comic, in places even parodic, revision of Blanche's journey in *A Streetcar Named Desire* as several critics have noted (Thompson 196, Saddik 129–130). But the later work is by no means merely a rewriting of Williams's most famous play to please fans of "the early Williams," nor is it simply a parody to titillate more jaded cognoscenti. *A Lovely Sunday for Creve Coeur* is an independent and different kind of play, in which Williams's mix of realistic and absurdist techniques underscores what is comically grotesque, and thus absurd, rather than what is painful in his heroine's experience of love, loss, loneliness, and disappointment.

Both Dotty and Blanche journey from "belle reve" to "creve coeur," but while Blanche's streetcar takes her via "Cemeteries" to "Elysian Fields," the one Dotty is about to take goes only to an amusement park. Blanche constructs a romantic persona for herself that corresponds to her name ("white woods"); not quite a Southern belle, Dotty has "a Southern belle complex" (186) and goes by a familiar diminutive. Insisting on their dissimilarity, Williams described Dotty as "amusingly foolish," while Blanche is "really rather bright and witty" (Devlin 316). This distinction is not quite just to Dotty (or to Williams's own lines). Though lacking Blanche's self-knowledge, her intellectual irony, and her poetry, Dotty, too, can be "bright and witty" in small ways. When Bodey says that Buddy is shaping up for her, Dotty sarcastically inquires, "Does he regard me as an athletic event, the high jump or pole vault?" (121). Unlike Blanche, however, Dotty cannot be witty at her own expense and so appears foolish in her romantic hopes of Ralph Ellis.

Both Blanche and Dotty have been hurt by disastrous romantic relationships with men who could not satisfy them sexually. Blanche married a sensitive young poet whom she drove to suicide when she discovered his homosexuality; in guilt and despair she tried to make up for the emptiness in her life through "intimacies with strangers" (386); when she decides to settle for dull but decent Mitch, her past catches up with her and she is destroyed. Dotty, too, was in love with a brilliant young artist—in her case, a musician, who suffered from premature ejaculation. She finally abandoned this lover in an act of self-preservation for which she feels no guilt: "Best years of my youth thrown away, wasted on poor Hathaway James" (169). Dotty's account of this unfortunate romance and its simultaneous symbolic re-enactment in particular emphasize how in *A Lovely Sunday for Creve Coeur* Williams presents unhappiness as more ludicrous than tragic. As Dotty describes Hathaway's "affliction" (the "embarrassing evenings," the "plunging," the "wet stain"), the unlucky Sophie is suffering from her own "affliction" of diarrhea in Dotty's bathroom, which she floods with water (165, 169).

Even though Dotty continues to cling for a while to her dream of a romantic marriage, her resilience in leaving Hathaway tells us that she is a survivor. Her "heartbreak" over Ralph's engagement to another girl, instead of devastating her, makes her quickly change her mind about settling for Buddy. After a brief gesture, raised fist and nodding head, acknowledging the way of the world and *"discharg[ing] her sense of defeat,"* Dotty *"springs up determinedly,"* prepared to move on to Creve Coeur (199). Where Blanche finally succumbs to her own desire for illusion or "magic" (385), Dotty is granted a wryly comic (if pyrrhic) victory over delusion.

The solution to Dotty's problem, marriage at any cost, may sit uncomfortably with some contemporary audience members, even though the play is set in the 1930s when women had fewer opportunities than they do today. Certainly Williams was under no illusion about marriage as a panacea, as he makes clear in other plays and through his brief caricature in this play of a married couple in the off-stage (and well-named) warring Schloggers. But marriage does provide one obvious solution for loneliness—not just for Dotty, for whom marriage is the only acceptable way of life but, vicariously, for Bodey and also for Buddy (whose needs critics ignore). And though Helena regards Dotty's need for a man as a "lingering symptom" of her "Southern belle complex" (186), it is not clear that Helena herself has remained single by choice. While it is tempting to read Helena's singleness and interest in Dotty as "quasi-lesbian," Williams insisted emphatically that "There is no lesbianism involved" (Devlin 315). Williams's denial notwithstanding, lesbian desire remains a possible reading for both Helena's and Bodey's investment in

Dotty, though in Bodey's case quasi–incestuous desire for her twin brother (in whose "wonderful side" [174] she hopes to interest Dotty) is no less likely an explanation of her latent motives. In wooing Dotty, Bodey stands in for Buddy (perhaps grotesquely invoking Shakespeare's twins in *Twelfth Night*).

A Lovely Sunday for Creve Coeur invites speculation about the characters' psychosocial or psychosexual motives because Williams allows the women to reveal themselves in realistic, intimate, and suggestive detail through the topics (Buddy, the phone, food, being alone) to which they recur obsessively throughout the play. But the dramatic methods by which Williams evokes his characters' desires and fears are much more overt and exaggerated than the Chekhovian manipulation of text and subtext that underlies the presentation of character in his earlier plays. Dotty and Helena soliloquize as well as converse; Bodey, Helena, and, especially, Sophie each grotesquely embodies and enacts the view of existence she holds; and the play's visual and aural effects bombard the audience's senses. A psychological or sociological reading of *A Lovely Sunday for Creve Coeur* remains possible but can provide only an inadequate and partial account of the play.

Williams's use of nonrealistic, especially absurdist, techniques emphasizes that the anxiety evidenced by all four women in *A Lovely Sunday for Creve Coeur* is a metaphysical horror of being alone—"*Allein, allein*" (161)—in an environment that is not just a lower-middle-class apartment building in St. Louis on a hot Sunday but is claustrophobic, alarming, "*gespukt.*" The women's several aspirations for marriage, family, companionship, or a better address are all means of covering over the abyss, as Helena makes rather clear when she tells Dotty that only by advancing "in appearances" can they protect themselves "from a future of descent into the Gluck abyss of surrender to the bottom level of squalor" (187).

Helena, Bodey, and Dotty all have different ways of dealing with Sophie and, thus, with their own fears of the possible future she represents. Helena tries to shut her out. Bodey wants to move her into a more cheerful apartment. Dotty at first tries to ignore her; but, being "a girl that understands human afflictions" (165), Dotty finally embraces and comforts Sophie as she finds her own strength (and perhaps optimism) to go on to Creve Coeur. Dotty's last reassuring words to Sophie and to herself and the audience are "We'll be back before dark" (200). The play thus ends on a note of hope. That is, of course, unless we interpret the ending metatheatrically: at this point "THE LIGHTS DIM OUT" (200). Williams's complex dramaturgy allows us to read the play's conclusion either way. But much as we may want Dotty to find consolation with Buddy, an audience attuned to the play's deployment of sensory impressions is more likely to see in the dimming lights that any such hope is illusory and absurd.

Notes

1. For reviews of the New York premiere, directed by Keith Hack and with Shirley Knight as Dotty, see *New York Theatre Critics' Reviews*, 337–340. For reviews of the British

premiere, see *Financial Times*, 2 July 1986; *Guardian*, 3 July 1986; *Sunday Telegraph*, 6 July 1986; *Times*, 2 July 1986. Notable recent productions include those by Northlight Theatre, Skokie in 1998 (see Smith; Christiansen), Chain Lightning at the Connelly Theatre, New York in 1999 (see Russo), and the Alliance Theatre Company in Atlanta in 2001 (see Brock). "Broken Heart," described as "after" Williams's play, was performed by the Yanka Kupala Theatre of the Republic of Belarus in 1999 (http://nac-bibl.org.by/tkupala/en/repertory.html). Graeae Theatre Company, the British disabled people's theatre company, toured the play throughout England in 1999. All of Graeae's performances of the play were simultaneously spoken by the actors and signed by an interpreter integrated into the action as a silent commentator (see Walsh). The role of Bodey, played by a deaf actor, was considered especially pertinent to the company's goals. The play's inclusion as part of the Coventry Women's Festival suggests its relevance for women spectators as well. I am grateful to Graeae Theatre Company for providing me with information about their production.

2. On academic criticism of the play up to the mid-1990s see Rocha. Two recent critics generally sympathetic to the late plays offer contrasting views of *Creve Coeur*. Saddik regards it as "the most strictly realistic" of the later plays (128) and "a weak version of a dramatic style which Williams was no longer committed to" (132–33). Dorff, however, notes the play's "outrageous" exaggeration of "trivial details of everyday life" (24).

3. On Williams and the absurd, see Thompson 11, 189, and Saddik 76–78, 135–50.

4. Williams variously refers to the text of *All Gaul Is Divided* as a "teleplay" or "screenplay" (*All Gaul Is Divided* 3). It is hard to see how a satisfactory film could be made from this script, but it might have made an interesting television drama along the lines of Paddy Chayevsky's *Marty* (1953), in which a stout, lonely butcher settles for a plain history teacher.

5. For example, both Sophie and the Gnädiges Fräulein (also ironically named) are bizarrely dressed and physically indecorous (the Gnädiges Fräulein wears bloodstained bandages over her gouged-out eyes); both make unhappy, inarticulate sounds; Sophie speaks of being alone, and the Gnädiges Fräulein sings *"All Alone"* (244); both women evoke religious images, Sophie appearing like a "religieuse *in state of sorrowful vision*" (154) and the Gnädiges Fräulein like *"a saint under torture"* (245). In addition, like Bodey, the Gnädiges Fräulein has calcified eardrums and has to be shouted at.

6. Like a number of other characters in the late plays, at least three of the women also suffer the limitation of handicaps: Bodey's deafness, Dotty's nervous condition, Sophie's mental breakdown. See Rocha 187.

Works Cited

Barnes, Clive. "Williams' 'Creve Coeur' Is an Exceptional Excursion." *New York Post*, 22 Jan. 1979. *New York Theatre Critics' Reviews* 338.
Billington, Michael. "*A Lovely Sunday* . . ." *Guardian* (England), 3 July 1986.
Brock, Wendell. "Alliance Mounts 'Lovely' Production of Little-Known Williams Work." *Atlanta Journal-Constitution*, 19 Oct. 2001.
Chekhov, Anton. *Plays*. Trans. and introd. Elisaveta Fen. Harmondsworth: Penguin Books, 1954.
Christiansen, Richard. "Kindness of Friends Local Premiere Captures Essence of Tennessee Williams." *Chicago Tribune*, 13 Feb. 1998.

Cohn, Ruby. "Tennessee Williams: The Last Two Decades." Matthew Roudané, ed. *The Cambridge Companion to Tennessee Williams*. Cambridge: Cambridge UP, 1997: 232–43.

Devlin, Albert J. *Conversations with Tennessee Williams*. Jackson: UP of Mississippi, 1986.

Dorff, Linda. "Theatricalist Cartoons: Tennessee Williams's Late,'Outrageous' Plays." *Tennessee Williams Annual Review*, 2 (1999): 13–33.

Ionesco, Eugene. "Experience of the Theatre." *Notes and Counter-notes*. Trans. Donald Watson. London: John Calder, 1964.

Leverich, Lyle. *Tom: The Unknown Tennessee Williams*. New York: Crown Publishers, 1995.

New York Theatre Critics' Reviews 40 (1979): 337–340.

Rocha, Mark W. "*Small Craft Warnings, Vieux Carré*, and *A Lovely Sunday for Creve Coeur*." Philip C. Kolin, ed. *Tennessee Williams: A Guide to Research and Performance*. Westport, CT: Greenwood, 1998: 183–193.

Russo, Francine. "Women's Rites." *Village Voice*, 16 Feb. 1999.

Saddik, Annette J. *The Politics of Reputation: The Critical Reception of Tennessee Williams' Later Plays*. Madison, NJ: Fairleigh Dickinson UP, 1999.

Smith, Sid. "A Different Tennessee Williams Takes Stage at Northlight." *Chicago Tribune*, 11 Feb. 1998.

Thompson, Judith J. *Tennessee Williams' Plays: Memory, Myth, and Symbol*. New York: Peter Lang, 1987.

Walsh, Maeve. "*A Lovely Sunday for Creve Coeur*." *Independent* (England), 24 March 1999.

Williams, Tennessee. *All Gaul Is Divided. Stopped Rocking and Other Screenplays*. New York: New Directions, 1984.

———. *The Glass Menagerie. The Theatre of Tennessee Williams*. Vol. 1. New York: New Directions, 1971.

———. *The Gnädiges Fräulein. The Theatre of Tennessee Williams*. Vol. 7. New York: New Directions, 1994.

———. *A Lovely Sunday for Creve Coeur. The Theatre of Tennessee Williams*. Vol. 8. New York: New Directions, 1992.

———. *A Streetcar Named Desire. The Theatre of Tennessee Williams*. Vol. 1. New York: New Directions, 1971.

George W. Crandell

"I CAN'T IMAGINE TOMORROW": TENNESSEE WILLIAMS AND THE REPRESENTATIONS OF TIME IN *CLOTHES FOR A SUMMER HOTEL*

At the conclusion of Tennessee Williams's *Sweet Bird of Youth,* Chance Wayne steps to the forestage and directly addresses the audience with this appeal: "I don't ask for your pity, but just for your understanding—not even that—no. Just for your recognition of me in you, and the enemy, time, in us all."[1] Time is here personified as the "enemy" against whom Chance is the vanquished opponent. The representation of time as the enemy, or, similarly, as "life's destroyer," highlights a conflict frequently dramatized in the plays of Tennessee Williams as a struggle between "being" and "nonbeing," with time, through the agency of death, triumphing in each of these unequal contests.[2] As Williams writes in "The Timeless World of a Play": "As far as we know, as far as there exists any kind of empiric evidence, there is no way to beat the game of *being* against *nonbeing,* in which nonbeing is the predestined victor on realistic levels" (262). Characters in Williams's plays, Chance Wayne for example, articulate a similar message: "Time—who could beat it, who could defeat it ever? Maybe some saints and heroes, but not Chance Wayne" (*Sweet Bird* 123).

The progress of these unequal struggles may be witnessed by observing Williams's characters, the embodiments of life on stage, as each is progressively ravaged by time. Chance Wayne and the Princess Kosmonopolis in *Sweet Bird of Youth,* Blanche DuBois in *A Streetcar Named Desire,* and F. Scott and Zelda Fitzgerald in *Clothes for a Summer Hotel* are among the many characters whom Williams depicts as victims of time's destructive progress. Although years younger than the middle-aged Princess, Chance nevertheless succumbs to the decaying influence of time. As he explains to Kosmonopolis, "the age of some people can only be calculated by the level of—level of—rot in them. And by that measure I'm ancient" (*Sweet Bird* 122). The Princess herself, long ago "separated from an appearance of youth," thinks of herself as having "retired to the moon," a place she describes as a "withering country, of time coming after time not meant to come after" (*Sweet Bird* 33). *Streetcar*'s Blanche DuBois is comforted by the darkness in which her age is concealed, but in the glare of a naked light bulb stripped of its paper lantern, she speaks of masking the effects of time: "I don't want realism. I want magic! . . . Yes, yes, magic! I try to give that to people. I misrepresent things to them. I don't tell truth, I tell what *ought* to be truth."[3] The victims of time in *Clothes for a Summer Hotel*, among them Scott and Zelda Fitzgerald, have already succumbed to death, but by a different sort of theatrical magic, they are given the semblance of life. Appearing as ghosts in a ghost play, these characters enact the impossible. Scott Fitzgerald, for example, meets Ernest Hemingway, after the latter's suicide, and together they revisit earlier times spent together. Insubstantial shadows thus give substance to an alternative representation of events, challenging both history's record and history as a method of interpreting the truth.

In these uneven struggles against time the destroyer, it is neither saint nor hero who triumphs over time but only the artist, in whose imaginative worlds time is "arrested" and "confined" in order to illuminate the *real* world in which we live ("Timeless World" 261). As Williams explains, the dramatist works a special kind of magic to impart meaning and to give "dimension and dignity" to otherwise ordinary occurrences:

> In a play, time is arrested in the sense of being confined. By a sort of legerdemain, events are made to remain *events*, rather than being reduced so quickly to mere *occurrences*. The audience can sit back in a comforting dusk to watch a world which is flooded with light and in which emotion and action have a dimension and dignity that they would likewise have in real existence, if only the shattering intrusion of time could be locked out. ("Timeless World" 262–263)

Of course, in "real" existence, artists, too, succumb to time's decay, but as Williams implies, if the artist is successful, art can indeed triumph over time, and the successful dramatist imbues his characters with an immortality that can be realized only in the "timeless world of a play."

For Tennessee Williams, the great challenge confronting the playwright is the task of relating these two unrelated places—the dramatic world from which time is *excluded* and the real world in which time is *included*. As Williams writes, "[t]he diminishing influence of life's destroyer, time, must be somehow worked into the context of his play," and "unless he contrives in some way to relate the dimensions of his tragedy to the dimensions of a world in which time is *included*—he will be left among his magnificent debris on a dark stage, muttering to himself: 'Those fools . . .'" ("Timeless World" 263–264).

Williams's dramatic representation of time often departs from expected norms by subverting chronology and by transgressing the limits of realistic drama set in recognizably historical time and space. In early plays, such as *The Glass Menagerie*, *Camino Real*, and *Vieux Carré* (first produced in 1977 but begun as early as 1939), memory, or imagination in the form of dreams, is Williams's dramatic tool of choice for misrepresenting time. In later plays, such as *The Two-Character Play*, *Clothes for a Summer Hotel*, and *Something Cloudy, Something Clear*, Williams substitutes for historical time an *aesthetic space*, a representation of time that permits the exploration of an alternative temporality and a virtual reality that bears no mimetic relationship to the world outside of the plays' dramatic boundaries and yet, paradoxically, illuminates that *real* world. Of these three later plays, *Clothes for a Summer Hotel* is the only one to transcend the limits of death in order to expose the limits of transcendence. An examination of time in these later plays of Tennessee Williams reveals that *Clothes for a Summer Hotel*, more than its later counterparts, dramatizes something unique in the Williams canon: a lack of faith in the future to transform the present. Similar to Keats's "still unravished bride" in "Ode on a Grecian Urn," the characters in Williams's *Clothes for a Summer Hotel* are immortalized in a time "still always present."[4] Similar to the shades that populate Dante's *Inferno*, they "live" forever in a place from which they cannot imagine (a better) tomorrow.

Unlike conventionally realistic dramatic space, Williams's aesthetic space is arranged and furnished not to re-construct a time or a place in the past as it once was. Instead, the aesthetic space affords a view of the past that transforms occurrences into meaningful events, claiming for art what history has typically taken as its exclusive province—the representation of the past and the interpretation of past events. In this aesthetic space, alternatives to a strictly chronological arrangement of events may be presented, just as alternative versions of "history" may be represented, including, as Blanche imagines, "what *ought* to be truth" (*Streetcar* 385). In "Three Players of a Summer Game," a short story that is much more than a preliminary sketch for *Cat on a Hot Tin Roof*, Williams articulates a perspective on time, an aesthetic view, that sheds light on his dramatic technique. Similar to Blanche DuBois, the narrator of this story misrepresents what happens, making no apology for the story's infidelity to fact. The "bits and pieces" that made up the chronology of the past are instead re-arranged and re-presented to illuminate a hidden truth:

> . . . these assorted images, they are like the paraphernalia for a game of croquet, gathered up from the lawn when the game is over and packed carefully into an oblong wooden box which they just exactly fit and fill. There they all are, the bits and pieces, the images, the apparently incongruous paraphernalia of a summer that was the last one of my childhood, and now I take them out of the oblong box and arrange them once more in the formal design on the lawn. It would be absurd to pretend that this is altogether the way it was, and yet it may be closer than a literal history could be to the hidden truth of it.[5]

For Tennessee Williams, the discovery of hidden truth and the exploration in depth of "truth of character" (*Clothes* 202) requires a method different from that of

"[t]he straight realistic play."[6] As an alternative to "the exhausted theatre of realistic conventions" (Williams "Production" 131), Williams imagines a plastic theatre
that, as Anne Fleche explains, "suggests multiple perspectives, a relative space-time
relationship, that breaks the temporal hold on the form as causal, chronological,
continuous."[7] Not surprisingly, when *Clothes for a Summer Hotel* debuted in 1980,
critics who continued to view Williams's drama through the biographical/histori-
cal lens saw only a "blur."[8] From a more distant perspective, it now appears that
Clothes for a Summer Hotel is merely one of the last in a series of plays, including
more celebrated works such as *The Glass Menagerie, A Streetcar Named Desire,* and
Camino Real, that aim to misrepresent reality. Tom Wingfield misrepresents reality
by "remembering" events that he could not have witnessed (e.g., the scene
between Amanda and Laura before Tom arrives home from the warehouse with
Jim O'Connor, the Gentleman Caller). Blanche DuBois and Stanley Kowalski each
misrepresent reality in *A Streetcar Named Desire* in such a way that Stella is forced
to decide between their rival versions of history. Ultimately, Stella chooses to believe that her husband could not have raped her sister: "I couldn't believe her story
and go on living with Stanley" (*Streetcar* 405). Similarly, the dream of Don Quixote in *Camino Real* misrepresents the world we live in by bringing together historical figures from different times to a place called the Camino Real. If *Clothes for a
Summer Hotel* resembles these plays in aim and technique, it differs from them in
measure. In *Clothes for a Summer Hotel,* we see Williams's most radical and most
postmodern manipulation of time to achieve the effect of misrepresentation.
Clothes for a Summer Hotel differs also from these earlier plays in tone, for it is the
only play among this group to suggest that escape from suffering, either through
madness or death, is impossible.

   Clothes for a Summer Hotel was the last Tennessee Williams play to open on
Broadway before the playwright's death in 1983. It debuted at the Cort Theater on
Williams's sixty-ninth birthday, March 26, 1980, but closed after just 15 performances. Among the Williams plays that have appeared on Broadway, it may very
well be the least well known, even though its characters are familiar to most
theater-goers—F. Scott Fitzgerald, his wife Zelda, and Ernest Hemingway. Set in
an asylum on a windy hilltop near Asheville, North Carolina (reminiscent of
Highland Hospital, where Zelda perished in a tragic fire in 1948), the play is ostensibly about the relationship between two literary figures, Scott and Zelda Fitzgerald, about their conflicted lives together and their competing desires. At the same
time, it's a commentary on the past as seen through the lens of a later time, a postmodern critique of realism's and modernism's great faith in the future to remedy
or cure the present.

   Misrepresentation, as a dramatic technique, enables Williams in both *Something
Cloudy, Something Clear* and *Clothes for a Summer Hotel* to reconfigure the past.
Memory is an aid that Williams has often found useful in this process. By means of
remembrance, Tom Wingfield in *The Glass Menagerie* attempts to exorcise the
ghosts of his past. Memory, expressed publicly in the form of a confession, serves
to empty Tom's guilty conscience, to purge repressed feelings, in effect, to destroy

the past before it has a chance to annihilate him. *Vieux Carré* is the "late" play that most nearly resembles *The Glass Menagerie* in its use of memory, but as Linda Dorff has suggested, *Vieux Carré* may actually predate *The Glass Menagerie* in its conception. Introducing the 2000 edition of the play, Robert Bray observes: "In a paper presented at the 1999 Tennessee Williams Scholars' Conference in New Orleans, Williams specialist Linda Dorff exploded conventional notions about the play's evolution by tracing the working script back to January of 1939—the actual time that Williams lived at 722 Rue Toulouse."[9] Similar to Tom Wingfield in *The Glass Menagerie,* the Writer in *Vieux Carré* acts as a narrator whose recollection of the past shapes the vision that the audience observes on stage. By means of asides, the narrator also functions to "illuminate situation and character" (Bray xi). More important, the Writer, like Tom Wingfield, is haunted by his memories. The boarding house in which he once lived is occupied in his recollection by "shadowy occupants like ghosts."[10] In both plays, confession serves to limit the past, by allowing one individual to establish once and for all what happened, to create a unified and unchanging history of events.

But by the time Tennessee Williams comes to write *Clothes for a Summer Hotel,* the playwright no longer represents memory as the product of a single consciousness, a unified and unalterable vision of the past. Memory is presented, instead, as a social construct, the product of multiple and often conflicting points of view, each of which and all of which together function to challenge chronological history and its monocular, time-bound vision. Unlike earlier plays in which a mediating narrator provides a unifying account of events (e.g., Tom Wingfield in *The Glass Menagerie,* Don Quixote in *Camino Real,* or the Writer in *Vieux Carré*), *Clothes for a Summer Hotel* offers a more fragmented and also a more postmodern view of the world. This use of multiple perspectives, characters remembering shared experiences from differing points of view (including perspectives from beyond the grave), calls into question historical accounts that present the past as uniform and unchanging. As Jeanette Malkin writes, postmodern writers "build on the audiences' knowledge of the past (or, rather, of how the past is usually represented), in order to question and disrupt that knowledge through multiple, conflated perspectives."[11] Unlike in earlier plays, memory, as a theatrical device in *Clothes for a Summer Hotel,* foregrounds past events against a different and more contemporary social background. In this respect, Williams's reconstituted view of memory resembles that of Maurice Halbwachs, for whom memory is "not about the retrieval of a possibly repressed but essentially unchanging past, but rather about the shifting 'social frames that allow the past's reconfiguration to emerge in the present'" (qtd. in Malkin 23). Williams similarly experiments with the simultaneous presentation of distinct historical times in *Something Cloudy, Something Clear.* According to Williams, the time of the play is both "September, 1940 and September, 1980."[12] By means of a technique that the character August refers to as "double exposure," past and present are dramatized simultaneously (*Something* 7). Events that took place four decades ago thus may be re-evaluated in light of subsequent history as well as shifting, and presumably more enlightened, social frameworks.

In a critical appraisal of Rainer Maria Rilke, the German poet whom Williams read and greatly admired, C. A. Patrides borrows the phrase "magic contemporaneity" (from Hans E. Holthusen) to describe Rilke's poetic world: "Rilke's universe . . . involves not so much time as space: time-as-sequence is suspended, to be displaced by the timeless subsistence of all art in a continuous spatial present so that, as has been said, 'all things which are real (that is, which can be felt) subsist side by side in a kind of *magic* contemporaneity.'"[13] A similar magic contemporaneity describes the dramatic world of *Clothes for a Summer Hotel* in which events from 1924, 1940, and 1961 appear as contemporaneous with each other. Similarly in *Something Cloudy, Something Clear*, events four decades apart are superimposed upon one another, and all appear within a "continuous spatial present" (Patrides 16).

At the rise of the curtain in *Clothes for a Summer Hotel*, the theatrical space is defined by a facade of the asylum in which Zelda Fitzgerald lived and later perished. In the shadow of the asylum facade, characters then re-define that space as, for example, a little hotel in France, or the home of Mrs. Patrick Campbell, one of the Fitzgeralds' Paris friends. The asylum also functions as a figurative and literal site of confinement, keeping the inhabitants within its guarded gates and excluding all unwelcome guests, including time. In this respect, it resembles the aesthetic stage space of Williams's *The Two-Character Play*, in which Felice and Clare are trapped in a theater from which all other people are barred. In Williams's aesthetic space, from which historical time is also excluded, characters, while physically present to each other, may actually occupy, simultaneously, different "historical" times. To illustrate, a stage direction preceding the first act in *Clothes for a Summer Hotel* notes that Scott Fitzgerald "appears as he did when he died in his mid-forties" (*Clothes* 205). If time could be pinpointed in *Clothes for a Summer Hotel*, this statement would suggest a historical date of 1940, sometime before Scott's death on December 21st. In the same scene, however, Zelda speaks of her reluctance to meet her "former" husband, knowing that he has already died (hence her characterization of the meeting as "impossible") (*Clothes* 210). Unlike Scott, Zelda is aware that she speaks from beyond the grave as when she remarks to an intern at the asylum: "I thought that obligations stopped with death!" (*Clothes* 210). Only by an act of theatrical legerdemain is this fantastic scene possible: characters physically present to each other but each with a different awareness of his or her own time and place. To Scott, Zelda appears very much alive, although not well. To Zelda, Scott appears almost unrecognizable, an apparition of his former "remarkably handsome" self (*Clothes* 212). The disparity in viewpoint enables those "in the know," including the audience, to view the past with ironic detachment, as when Zelda greets Scott for the first time: "Is that really you, Scott? Are you my lawful husband, the celebrated F. Scott Fitzgerald, author of my life?" (*Clothes* 213).

The characters August and Clare in Williams's *Something Cloudy, Something Clear* experience a similar kind of detachment from the other players on stage. Speaking from the vantage point of 1980 in the presence of a character, Kip, living in 1940, August remarks, "I have guts now. But I also had them then," a comment that baffles Kip: "Now? Then?" (*Something* 38). Speaking more to the audience than to Kip, August replies: "Present and past, yes, a sort of double exposure," to which the still-confused Kip replies, "I don't understand" (*Something* 38). As if dismissing a childish inquiry, August explains, "You're not supposed to, Kip" and promptly changes the subject (*Something* 38).

In scenes from both *Something Cloudy, Something Clear* and *Clothes for a Summer Hotel,* the radical misrepresentation of time permits the past to re-emerge in the present, only to be re-interpreted in light of more contemporary social and moral values. The second act of *Clothes for a Summer Hotel,* for example, stages a meeting between Zelda ("in her younger guise") and Edouard, the young, French aviator, with whom, according to the historical record, she had an affair in 1924 (*Clothes* 41). The conversation between the two, however, frustrates attempts to fix the "historical" time of their meeting. When Zelda presumes that Edouard later perished in a tragic airplane crash, he corrects her romantically mistaken notion by noting that he merely grew old, "weighted down with honors" (*Clothes* 48). Although Edouard and Zelda do not know everything that subsequently happens to the other one, each character nevertheless has an awareness of events beyond the time of their "present" meeting and, with this knowledge, they comment on what was once their life together. In this impossible encounter, characterized by its "magic contemporaneity," audiences witness a woman whose "madness" seems to have been precipitated by the men in her life, by Edouard's rejection of her love, and by Scott's stifling of her freedom—sexual, intellectual, and spiritual. In the background of this scene, the image of the asylum stands out, illuminated by the light of contemporary social attitudes toward women, as an emblem of an imprisoning patriarchal society, from which for Zelda (in particular) and for women (in general) there is no escape.

Clothes for a Summer Hotel thus differs from earlier Williams plays in which transcendence is presented as both possible and desirable. In earlier, more realistic plays, including *The Glass Menagerie,* simply to imagine the past is one way to escape the immediate present. In Amanda's case, the past provides a comforting refuge from the more inhospitable present. For her son, Tom, it is the future that offers comfort and hope. In both cases, the desire to transcend the present moment is expressed in spatial terms. For Amanda, simply to imagine another place, Blue Mountain, is sufficient to "depart" from her present reality. Similarly, when Tom is on the verge of committing himself "to a future that doesn't include the warehouse" where he works, the young Wingfield expresses his desire in terms of moving to another place.[14] As he says to Jim O'Connor, "I'm tired of the *movies* and I am *about* to *move!*" (*Glass* 201). Felice and Clare in *The Two-Character Play* actually achieve a kind of transcendence by imagining a warmer place than the theater in which they are playing and literally shed their coats to give credence to their fantasy: "I think the feeling of summer would come more easily to us if we took our coats off."[15]

The privileging of the past and the future in *The Glass Menagerie* and in other plays has the effect of neutralizing the present moment. According to Elizabeth

Ermarth, "living in historical time is to live in a medium still informed by the dialectical habit, which means to live with one's immediate present effectively neutralized by the perpetual fiction of alternative possibility."[16] Even in later works, such as *I Can't Imagine Tomorrow* and *The Two-Character Play*, Williams dramatizes characters trapped within a confining world whose present reality is neutralized by the possibility of change. The characters One and Two in *I Can't Imagine Tomorrow* are so frightened by the prospect of change that they endlessly "repeat the ritual" of their neutralized daily lives.[17] In a moment of hopeful optimism, One imagines a world without change, a world also without time: "If there wasn't a thing called time, the passing of time in the world we live in, we might be able to count on things staying the same, but time lives in the world with us and has a big broom and is sweeping us out of the way, whether we face it or not" (*I Can't Imagine* 141). Thinking always in terms of transcending the present moment, One and Two are ill prepared to deal with the concrete reality of their impending deaths. As Ermarth explains: "Historical thinking entails a perpetual transcendence of, one might even say flight from, the concrete, and because of this, it offers no assistance to those who must deal with material limitation, including the ultimate material limitation of death" (31). Similar to One and Two in *I Can't Imagine Tomorrow*, Felice and Clare in Williams's *Out Cry* (revised and re-titled *The Two-Character Play*) endlessly perform a play-within-the play called *The Two-Character Play*. Fearful of the great unknown beyond their doorstep, they, too, endlessly repeat a ritual performance. Always anticipating the possibility of change but never changing, Felice and Clare lack the courage necessary to bring their performance (and their lives) to an end—by committing suicide. As Clare remarks to Felice about the performance: "It never seems to end but just to stop, and it always seems to stop just short of something important when you suddenly say: 'The p[er]formance is over'" (*Two-Character* 360). Felice defends his faith in the possibility of transcendence by responding: "It's possible for a play to have no ending in the usual sense of an ending, in order to make a point about nothing really ending" (*Two-Character* 360). Despite Clare's protest that "[t]hings do end, they do actually have to" (*Two-Character* 360) Felice reasserts his great faith in the future, deferring until then any decisive action: "We'll face everything tomorrow" (*Two-Character* 361). Ultimately, the prospect of a better tomorrow prevents both Felice and Clare from being able to pull the trigger at the "end" of *The Two-Character Play*. Consequently, they "live" forever, confined, however, in "a state theatre of a state unknown" (*Two-Character* 313).

As if in response to realism's great faith in the future to remedy the ills of the present, *Clothes for a Summer Hotel* goes beyond "the material limitation of death" only to expose as a lie the great promise of transcendence (Ermarth 31). In the final scene of the play, for instance, an intern suggests to Zelda that she be kind to her dead husband by offering "him a sort of last sacrament" (*Clothes* 273). Displaying her lack of spiritual faith, Zelda responds by saying "[t]he Everlasting ticket that doesn't exist" (*Clothes* 273). From her vantage point beyond the grave, Zelda is amazed to see that "the lies of Christ were such beautiful lies" (*Clothes*

273). Depicting a world from which time has been excluded and from which there is no possible transcendence, *Clothes for a Summer Hotel* describes an alternative temporality that, in some of its details, more nearly resembles Dante's *Inferno* than the Kingdom of Heaven. Williams's hellish asylum is guarded by "black iron gates," which admit only an occasional visitor (*Clothes* 204). Within the confines of the asylum, conversation is made difficult by fierce winds that carry voices away (*Clothes* 206). Dante's second circle (the final "resting" place of lustful lovers) is likewise a place buffeted by "warring winds."[18] So, too, Zelda's "lunatic" mind, which is not "retentive of present things" (*Clothes* 212) but has premonitions of future events (*Clothes* 219), resembles the minds of Dante's lost souls, whose "knowledge of the present is not clear" but who "see ahead to what the future holds" (Dante 161). Linda Dorff similarly observes that "[t]he ghosts in *Clothes for a Summer Hotel* linger in a purgatorial state of present-time limbo, frozen in static moments that dissolve any possibility of future redemption.[19]

Similar in another respect to Dante's *Inferno*, Williams's asylum is a place where suffering is seen as the tragic consequence of separation. In this context, the asylum is not a healing institution where therapy serves to remedy and reunite. Therapy, instead, is a painful process that leads to recognition. The lesson that F. Scott Fitzgerald learns, as he explains to Zelda, is "[t]he mistake of our ever having met!—The monumental error of the effort to channel our lives together in an institution called marriage. Tragic for us both" (*Clothes* 73). Although for broken relationships the asylum offers no reconciliation, Zelda consoles herself with the fact that "[s]omething's been accomplished: a recognition—painful, but good therapy's often painful" (*Clothes* 74). In this conclusion, *Clothes for a Summer Hotel* embraces suffering as a sufficient compensation for separation from one another, and so long as suffering is sufficient, there is no reason for remedy or cure, just as there is no need to transcend the present moment and likewise no need to imagine (a better) tomorrow. As Alain Robbe-Grillet observes: "Tragedy, if it consoles us today, forbids any solider conquest tomorrow. . . . There can be no longer any question of seeking some remedy for our misfortune, once tragedy convinces us to love it."[20]

The tragic tone of *Clothes for a Summer Hotel* suggests that even while Tennessee Williams adopts some of the techniques of postmodern narrative in this and other late plays, he nevertheless continues to express himself in what Elizabeth Ermarth terms the discourse of "tragic humanism" (120): "In this discourse, the subject, the 'I,' can exist only in exile: across an abyss from the wholeness, the unity, the oneness that 'I' posit and desire in order to make sure that it is always elsewhere" (121). If it is in *Something Cloudy, Something Clear, The Two-Character Play,* and *Clothes for a Summer Hotel* that we witness characters exiled from wholeness, it is in the Williams's short story, "Desire and the Black Masseur," that we see Williams's most overt statement about humankind's attempt to mask this fundamental lack: "The nature of man is full of . . . makeshift arrangements, devised by himself to cover his incompletion. He feels a part of himself to be like a missing wall or a room left unfurnished and he tries as well as he can to make up for it."[21]

Incomplete by nature, Williams's characters typically live in a state of exile, separated in time and space either from a desired other or a desired other place–the always elusive elsewhere. In *Something Cloudy, Something Clear,* August thinks of his separation in time from Kip in terms of exile: "To live as long as forty years after that ecstacy. . . . It's enough to reconcile you to exile, at last, to the dark side of the moon or the unfathomably dark hole in space" (12). Exile also characterizes the fate of Felice and Clare in *The Two-Character Play,* who are banished to "a state theatre of a state unknown" (*Two-Character* 313). Similar to this state theater, the asylum in Williams's *Clothes for a Summer Hotel* is likewise a site of exile. Separated by death from her husband, from her lover, and from the world in which she once lived, Zelda Fitzgerald must resort, like others (including Felice and Clare in *The Two-Character Play*), to some of the "makeshift arrangements" that Williams says man has devised to cover his fundamental lack of wholeness: "The use of imagination, resorting to dreams or the loftier purpose of art, is a mask he devises to cover his incompletion" (Williams "Desire" 217).

While in the early plays examined here, memory *(The Glass Menagerie),* imagination *(A Streetcar Named Desire),* and dreams *(Camino Real)* serve to hide man's incompletion, in the later plays it is art, and more specifically performance, that mitigates the suffering brought about by the failure of transcendence, the inability to escape an inhospitable place. In *Staging Place: The Geography of Modern Drama,* Una Chaudhuri coins the term "geopathology" to describe "[t]he characterization of place as a problem."[22] For some protagonists, as Chaudhuri argues, place "exerts so powerful and paralyzing an influence . . . that simple *departure* becomes their overriding mission and desire" (56). For others, "[p]erformance succeeds . . . in easing the symptoms of . . . geopathic disorders, the suffering caused by one's location" (Chaudhuri 57–58). Alone, afraid, and suffering the ill effects of a chillingly cold theater, Felice and Clare ease their symptoms by deciding to lose (consciousness of) themselves in another performance of *The Two-Character Play.* August and Clare in *Something Cloudy, Something Clear* are likewise players in a drama who agree to "drop the metaphysics" and "play it straight" (13). Zelda Fitzgerald likewise plays a role. Exiled from the possibility of wholeness, she resorts to performance as therapy, not to cure her ills, but to mitigate the effects of exile from wholeness.

The effect of performance in *Clothes for a Summer Hotel* is to blur the distinction between life and art. The theater in which Zelda performs is an asylum, which Zelda, in turn, likens to the theater of Hollywood, that West coast "world of make-believe" (*Clothes* 16). "Isn't it a sort of a madhouse, too?" she asks Scott (*Clothes* 10). "You occupy one there, and I occupy one here" (*Clothes* 10). Exiles in the timeless world of a play, each of the characters in *Clothes for a Summer Hotel* reminds us that existence is preciously brief, limited even to the duration of a single performance. As Gerald Murphy remarks to an uncomprehending Scott Fitzgerald: "It will all be over in . . . one hour and forty-five minutes" (*Clothes* 3). The implication, too, is that to perform is to live, and to live is to perform, or as Williams concludes: "The great and only possible dignity of man lies in his power deliberately to choose certain moral values by which to live as steadfastly as if he, too, like a character in a play were immured against the corrupting rush of time" (Williams, "Timeless" 262). In life, then, as in drama, performance is the only stay against the "enemy" time.

Notes

1. Tennessee Williams. *Sweet Bird of Youth. The Theatre of Tennessee Williams*. Vol. 4. (New York: New Directions, 1972): 124. Subsequent references refer to this edition.
2. Tennessee Williams. "The Timeless World of the Play." *The Theatre of Tennessee Williams*. Vol. 2. (New York: New Directions, 1971): 262–63. All citations refer to this text.
3. Tennessee Williams. *A Streetcar Named Desire. The Theatre of Tennessee Williams*. Vol. 1. (New York: New Directions, 1971): 385. All references refer to this edition.
4. Tennessee Williams. *Clothes for a Summer Hotel. The Theatre of Tennessee Williams*. Vol. 8. (New York: New Directions, 1992): 280. Subsequent references are cited parenthetically.
5. Tennessee Williams. "Three Players of a Summer Game." *Collected Stories* (New York: New Directions, 1985): 304–305.
6. Tennessee Williams. "Production Notes." *The Theatre of Tennessee Williams*. Vol. 1 (New York: New Directions, 1971): 131. All references refer to this edition.
7. Anne Fleche. *Mimetic Disillusion: Eugene O'Neill, Tennessee Williams, and U.S. Dramatic Realism* (Tuscaloosa: U of Alabama P, 1997): 73.
8. Douglas Watt. "Williams' Ghost Play Shrouds New Insights into Fitzgeralds." *New York Daily News* (27 March 1980). Rpt. *New York Theatre Critics' Reviews*. Eds. Joan Marlowe and Betty Black. Vol. 41. 310.
9. Robert Bray. "Introduction." *Vieux Carré* by Tennessee Williams (New York: New Directions, 2000): viii. Subsequent references are cited parenthetically.
10. Tennessee Williams. *Vieux Carré* (New York: New Directions, 2000): 5.
11. Jeanette R. Malkin. *Memory-Theater and Postmodern Drama* (Ann Arbor: U of Michigan P, 1999): 20. Subsequent references cite this text.
12. Tennessee Williams. *Something Cloudy, Something Clear* (New York: New Directions, 1995): x.
13. C. A. Patrides. "Time past and time present." *Aspects of Time* (Manchester: Manchester UP, 1976): 16. All references refer to this edition.
14. Tennessee Williams. *The Glass Menagerie. The Theatre of Tennessee Williams*. Vol. 1 (New York: New Directions, 1971): 201. Subsequent references are to this edition.
15. Tennessee Williams. *The Two-Character Play. The Theatre of Tennessee Williams*. Vol. 5 (New York: New Directions, 1976): 367. All references refer to this text.
16. Elizabeth Deeds Ermarth. *Sequel to History: Postmodernism and the Crisis of Representational Time* (Princeton: Princeton UP, 1992): 34. Subsequent references refer to this text.
17. Tennessee Williams. *I Can't Imagine Tomorrow. Dragon Country* (New York: New Directions, 1970): 139. All references refer to this edition.
18. Dante Alighieri. *The Divine Comedy. Vol. 1: Inferno*. Trans. Mark Musa (New York: Penguin, 1984): 110. Subsequent references refer to this edition.
19. Linda Dorff, "Collapsing Resurrection Mythologies: Theatricalist Discourses of Fire and Ash in *Clothes for a Summer Hotel*." *Tennessee Williams: A Casebook*. Ed. Robert Gross. (New York: Routledge, 2002): 162.

20. Alain Robbe-Grillet. "Nature, Humanism, Tragedy." *For a New Novel: Essays on Fiction*. Trans. Richard Howard. (1965; Freeport, New York: Books for Libraries P, 1970): 61.
21. Tennessee Williams. "Desire and the Black Masseur." *Collected Stories* (New York: New Directions, 1985): 217.
22. Una Chaudhuri. *Staging Place: The Geography of Modern Drama* (Ann Arbor: U of Michigan P, 1995): 56. Subsequent references refer to this edition.

Works Cited

Alighieri, Dante. *The Divine Comedy. Vol. 1: Inferno*. Trans. Mark Musa. New York: Penguin, 1984.
Bray, Robert. "Introduction." *Vieux Carré* by Tennessee Williams. New York: New Directions, 2000.
Chaudhuri, Una. *Staging Place: The Geography of Modern Drama*. Ann Arbor: U of Michigan P, 1995.
Dorff, Linda. "Collapsing Resurrection Mythologies: Theatricalist Discourses of Fire and Ash in *Clothes for a Summer Hotel*." *Tennessee Williams: A Casebook*. Ed. Robert Gross. (New York: Routledge, 2002). 153–172.
Ermarth, Elizabeth Deeds. *Sequel to History: Postmodernism and the Crisis of Representational Time*. Princeton: Princeton UP, 1992.
Fleche, Anne. *Mimetic Disillusion: Eugene O'Neill, Tennessee Williams, and U.S. Dramatic Realism*. Tuscaloosa: U of Alabama P, 1997.
Malkin, Jeanette R. *Memory-Theater and Postmodern Drama*. Ann Arbor: U of Michigan P, 1999.
Patrides, C. A. "Time Past and Time Present." *Aspects of Time*. Manchester: Manchester UP, 1976. 1–18.
Robbe-Grillet, Alain. "Nature, Humanism, Tragedy." *For a New Novel: Essays on Fiction*. Trans. Richard Howard. 1965. Freeport, NY: Books for Libraries P, 1970. 49–75.
Watt, Douglas. "Williams' Ghost Play Shrouds New Insights into Fitzgeralds." *New York Daily News,* 27 March 1980. Rpt. *New York Theatre Critics' Reviews*. Eds. Joan Marlowe and Betty Blake. Vol. 41. 310.
Williams, Tennessee. *Clothes for a Summer Hotel. The Theatre of Tennessee Williams*. Vol. 8. New York: New Directions, 1992. 201–280.
———. "Desire and the Black Masseur." *Collected Stories*. New York: New Directions, 1985. 205–212.
———. *The Glass Menagerie. The Theatre of Tennessee Williams*. Vol. 1. New York: New Directions, 1971. 143–237.
———. *I Can't Imagine Tomorrow. Dragon Country*. New York: New Directions, 1970. 131–150.
———. "Production Notes." *The Theatre of Tennessee Williams*. Vol. 1. New York: New Directions, 1971. 131–134.
———. *Something Cloudy, Something Clear*. New York: New Directions, 1995.
———. *A Streetcar Named Desire. The Theatre of Tennessee Williams*. Vol. 1. New York: New Directions, 1971. 239–419.
———. *Sweet Bird of Youth. The Theatre of Tennessee Williams*. Vol. 4. New York: New Directions, 1972. 1–124.

———. "Three Players of a Summer Game." *Collected Stories*. New York: New Directions, 1985. 303–325.

———. "The Timeless World of a Play." *The Theatre of Tennessee Williams*. Vol. 2. New York: New Directions, 1971. 259–64.

———. *The Two-Character Play. The Theatre of Tennessee Williams*. Vol. 5. New York: New Directions, 1976. 301–370.

———. *Vieux Carré*. New York: New Directions, 2000.

Norma Jenckes

"LET'S FACE THE MUSIC AND DANCE": RESURGENT ROMANTICISM IN TENNESSEE WILLIAMS'S *CAMINO REAL* AND *CLOTHES FOR A SUMMER HOTEL*

"I believe in Michelangelo, Velasquez and Rembrandt; in the might of design, the mystery of colour, the redemption of all things by beauty everlasting and the message of art that has made these hands blessed. Amen." Quoting this dramatic prayer, Tennessee Williams invokes the blessing and authority of Bernard Shaw. In this appropriation of the dying painter's *apologia pro vita sua* from *The Doctor's Dilemma* he insists in the "Afterword" to *Camino Real* that this is his creed as a playwright (423–424).

In Williams's late work we hear that same cry of the bloodied but unbowed late romantic artist. More particularly, Williams flew the banner of beauty as spiritual revelation, "the redemption of all things by beauty everlasting." Although one can find the vein of romanticism and the gospel of beauty in all Williams's works, the last works, especially *Clothes for a Summer Hotel,* take up most urgently a call that he issued loudly and clearly in his seminal work of fantasy, *Camino Real*. Using legendary and historical figures in a dream play set in an unnamed place, a structure of blocks instead of scenes, and a narrator and commentator who steps straight out of some sordid Berlin late-night cabaret, *Camino Real* dramatizes images of sleep and dreaming to construct a modern version of the Dantean dark wood. Williams does nothing less in *Camino Real* than renovate the dream vision of the Middle Ages into a contemporary, almost postmodernist, nightmare. Strindberg had already given a modernist rendering of this allegory of spiritual questing in his dream plays. Williams's play pays homage to the dream quest tradition from Dante's *The Divine Comedy* to Chaucer's *The Book of the Duchess* to Calderon's *Life is a Dream* to *A Dream Play* and *The Ghost Sonata* of August Strindberg. His best realized invocation of that vision, *Camino Real*, rouses the specters that haunt his last plays and lead to the later experiment that he called "A Ghost Play"—*Clothes for a Summer Hotel*—his last allegory of salvation through love and beauty.

Camino Real invokes a romantic economy of desire, which exploits various options of love and betrayal. This scenario that equates human tenderness with the power of frail violets that can break through rocks insists that the only antidote to betrayal and the death of the heart is to love. This terse summary of the theme of *Camino Real* arouses the sense of the danger of sentimentality inherent in the material. The audacity of *Camino Real* is that it dares to proclaim during the Cold War many of the commonalities that linked the romantic espousal of love and beauty with the revolutionary energy of love of the people and the beauty and power of brotherhood. At one point Gutman asks, on being told that dreamers and romantics are harmless, "what is harmless about the love of the people? Revolution only needs good dreamers" (450). In that same scene a group of people recall and chant the most dangerous word in the world, "hermano" or brother. "It's inflammatory," Gutman warns. "I don't suppose it can be struck out of the language altogether but it must be reserved for strictly private usage in back of soundproof walls" (451).

Here Williams reconnects the romantic with the revolutionary and makes clear that in *Camino Real* he is not merely interested in the aesthetic agenda of a romantic poet like Keats but in the social and political agendas of revolutionaries like Shelley and Byron as well. Of course, in the anti-utopian and cynical turns of the postmodernist moment such phrases as "love of the people" and "brotherhood of man" have been derided and dismissed as part of the grand narrative of human emancipation, which we associate with the Renaissance and the Enlightenment. For some, especially since the collapse of the Soviet Union, the end of the Cold War, and receding of the socialist horizon, these slogans of human possibility have become new embarrassments and are also branded with the damning label of sentimentality.

Williams tried to head off that criticism of sentimentality in *Camino Real* by his internal discussion of self-pity in the play itself. In the last scene, Don Quixote offers to Kilroy some advice—a kind of summation of his long experience: "Don't! Pity! Your! Self!" He explains:

> The wounds of the vanity, the many offenses our egos have toendure, being housed in bodies that age and hearts that grow tired, are better accepted with a tolerant smile—like *this!* (589)

However to anticipate an objection is not the same as to answer it. For those of us who would discover the artistic principles of Williams's late creations the aesthetic status of sentimentality needs to be explored. The accusation cannot be fended off with an exhortation and deserves a longer examination.

To interrogate the subject of sentimentality and its manifestation in the work of

Tennessee Williams requires a more theoretical understanding of the constructions of sentimentality in modernist literature. Suzanne Clark has discussed the connection of the sentimental with the feminine. She notices the way in which the label of "sentimental" is used as an epithet "within criticism to trigger shame, embarrassment, and disgust" (11). One of the reasons that it is important to engage it in the discourse about Williams's work is that it is always used as the term of abuse that cannot be countered. What emerges in the unpacking of the term itself is that it was associated with women writers and is tarred with the brush of the Victorian which modernism sought to banish and substitute with its own rubric of the anti-sentimental. "The word does not just mean an emotional fakery. It marks the limits of critical discourse as if they were natural" (11).

Williams's embrace of the feminine in his own nature is inscribed in his work not only in his creation of notable, sympathetic roles for women but also in the upholding of domains of sensibility and sublimity that are associated with female discourse. In Williams's revolt against the modern banishment of sentiment he draws on the wells of feeling enshrined in romanticism—one of the antecedents of modernism. But he also, in his insistence that beauty is the material reflection of sanctity and is a kind of harbinger of redemption, invokes the long tradition of spiritual writing from the biblical *Song of Songs* to John of the Cross to the Little Flower. Williams's artistic choices are over-determined as he seeks to create a new presentation of the ethos of love and beauty that can overcome the anti-sentiment dogma of modernism.

Williams's creation of characters exhibits the stresses of his neo-romantic agenda. Although *Clothes for a Summer Hotel* is explicitly described as a ghost play, *Camino Real* must also raise the dead to flesh out its *dramatis personae,* which includes such figures as Don Quixote, Casanova, Lord Byron, and the Lady of the Camellias. They are all ghosts, and in that sense their fate is already sealed. The characters in *Camino Real* are the legendary dead and others soon to be dead caught at this last frontier. The central character Kilroy, from "Kilroy Was Here," had been in the public imagination no more than a scrawl on a wall. The turning of a defiant slogan into a powerless character has dramatic consequences. As Bigsby notes," Now Kilroy is here. He has waited too long. He is trapped. From ironic hero he has been changed into eternal clown" (54).

In *Clothes for a Summer Hotel* figures from the more recent past—Scott and Zelda Fitzgerald, Ernest Hemingway, and even the great Shavian actress Mrs. Patrick Campbell—are paraded in a parable that seems to be almost a dramatic illustration of Puccini's anthem for his heroine Tosca, "I lived for love, I lived for Art." What is the nature of their new enactment? Linda Dorff has also noticed connections between the characters of the two plays, but she finds that

> Like the meta-characters Lord Byron, Camille and Casanova from *Camino Real* (1953), the Fitzgeralds function as archetypal masks through whom Williams negotiates his own myths of artistic creation, death and resurrection. (154)

By considering all the characters of both plays as merely masks for various aspects of the playwright's personal mythopoesis, Dorff has stripped them of their humanity and individuality. She has also ignored the fact that beyond the personal myth of the artist, all the figures, fictional and historical, are associated with the period of romanticism and raise large social and political issues that were first articulated in that era. That is the question that both plays raise.

Both plays unfold an imaginary locale. Williams has purposefully located his *Camino Real* in an unnamed port city, "a tropical seaport that bears a confusing, but somehow harmonious, resemblance to such widely scattered ports as Tangiers, Havana, Vera Cruz, Casablanca, Shanghai, New Orleans" (431). In a recent essay Frank Bradley also comments on the setting of *Camino Real,* but he finds a biographical element in the transient nature of the port city that "reflects Williams's own itinerancy, *en route* between various points of reference—the Siete Mares and the Ritz Men Only; the known and the unknown" (57). However, beyond biography, the images that the play presents in its structure of blocks—the square, the fountain, the stealthy meetings, and constant encounters between characters at all levels of class and privilege—could not be imagined in a modern metropolis of the center. It can only be imagined at the margins. As Marshall Berman found in his discussion of the city as setting in Baudelaire's work, so we discover in Williams's city scene of *Camino Real.*

Berman finds something "exotically archaic" in Baudelaire's primal modern scenes. He insists that the life and energy of Paris, like that of the unnamed city of Williams's *Camino Real,* shows the unresolved conflicts of "class and ideological conflicts, emotional conflicts between intimates, conflicts between the individuals and social forces, spiritual conflict within the self"—which "our epoch has found new ways to mask and mystify." Berman traces this obscuring of conflicts to the design of our urban spaces. In fact he locates just such a suppression of public life as one of the motivations in the new modern designs:

> If we picture the newest urban spatial complexes we can think of—all those that have been developed since the end of the Second World War—including all our newer urban neighborhoods and new towns—we should find it hard to imagine Baudelaire's primal encounters happening here. This is no accident; in fact, for most of our century, urban spaces have been systematically designed and organized to ensure that collisions and confrontations will not take place here. The distinctive sign of nineteenth century urbanism was the boulevard, a medium for bringing explosive material and human forces together; the hallmark of twentieth century urbanism has been the highway, a means for putting them asunder. (165–66)

Thus even in his evocation and painstaking delineation of setting Williams insists on a premodern reality in a contemporary world.

That necessity to resort to another time to illustrate the present moment generates the play's cast of characters. What is most striking about the figures that Williams chooses to populate his fable is that so many are drawn from the era of romanticism. Byron, Casanova, Marguerite Gauthier, are shadows from the late eighteenth and nineteenth centuries. They are the remnants of romanticism in a modern world, and they are desperately out of their element and doomed.

In like manner, the British critic Raymond Williams in his essay "The Metropolis and the Emergence of Modernism" has generalized about the persistence of aspects of romanticism within modernism. He has commented on the nineteenth-century antecedents to the theme of urban alienation in twentieth-century modernist works. Williams describes the wealth of images and tropes of urban blight, and he delineates the ways that several themes of modernism have romantic, premodern roots.

> Britain went through the first stages of industrial and metropolitan development very early, and almost at once certain persistent themes were arrived at. Thus the effect of the modern city as a crowd of strangers was identified in a way that was to last, by—Wordsworth. (Timms and Kelly 17)

In these and many other ways, *Camino Real* enlists the tropes of romanticism to dissect the problems of a 1950s world landscape. Some critics have narrowed this usage of the past to detect an anti-McCarthyism relevance in the play. It is possible to accommodate a specific political reading within a larger discussion of the revolutionary legacy of romanticism, which is part of its appeal to the dramatist. Romanticism is a literary period that rises and falls with bourgeois revolutionary energy. Once this energy is perverted into the frozen forms of state capitalism or fascism, romanticism is doomed. Bigsby has cited many instances of Williams's denunciations of growing American corruption and power after World War II and his own psychic suffering as an artist in a country that has become "death merchant to the world" and where he felt isolated with the identity of artist "which must always remain a word most compatible with that of Revolutionary" (37–39).

When a play as complex as *Camino Real* appears, the challenges it makes to the status quo are often strongly felt but not articulated. The theatre critics themselves can be so caught in the currents of the times that all they experience is dismay at the strange new thing that has been set before them. Many commentators have recognized that *Camino Real* marked a departure, a watershed in the work of the artist. Now that we have his complete works we can see that he laid claim in that play to the territory that had been the hidden foundation of all his earlier work and that would be the repeated ground zero of his last plays.

Why is romanticism over now? Perhaps it cannot cohabit with postmodernism and the late capitalism and often state fascism of the current era. However, in some eerie sense Williams in *Camino Real* is prescient about some aspects of our current reality. He offers an early evocation of what we now define as globalization. He establishes a society where constant movement is the norm. There is international access and the population is drawn from many countries, times, and places. There is in the "fugitivo," with its uncertainty and arbitrariness, an image of the postmodern sense of exile, homelessness, dislocation, and imminent departures and disappearances that we associate with the politics of mass manipulation. The geography of diasporas evokes the simultaneous distance and yet connectedness and even interdependence between center and margins, metropolis, and colonies. What Williams proffers in the face of encroaching globalization is a hope of romanticism armed only with love as its ultimate weapon. Both as weapon of choice and of necessity: Williams knew love would not suffice against the forces of violence and death, but it was all he could imagine brandishing.

Perhaps Williams, with his extraordinary artistic sensitivity, like a canary in the mines of the 1950s, was sensing in the accession of the Right Wing led by Joseph McCarthy in the United States a premonition of the eventual international triumph of the forms of late capitalism. Perhaps that is why *Camino Real* talks to us now in tones that are not just relevant but prophetic. Do we see in the person of Gutman the spokesman of the New World Order? Do we see in the unnamed city of unscheduled departures the eradication of the nation state and older forms of loyalty and political connection? Williams can imagine no forms of resistance that could be successful. We watch as those who defy the rule of Gutman meet their fates and are consigned to the street cleaners.

The last statement that is made at the play's end that the "violets have broken through the rocks" is a fact that we must take on faith since we do not see it. It seems to be an insistence that there are natural forces at work that will reassert themselves and break down the imposed constraints of social and political tyrannies. The last note of the play raises the hope of something that will assert itself and that something in human and social relations equates with the power of love and the transformative power of the experience of love.

Williams never retreated from that position; in fact he re-sounded it and echoed it during his last decade of writing. It is the dramatic exploration and expansion of this idea that connects *Camino Real* to his later plays, especially *Clothes for a Summer Hotel*. At the same time that Williams pronounces the power of beauty and love, he never ignores the individual failures and betrayals of loves and lovers and the physical decline and decay of the body. It is part of his realism that he insists that love and beauty are both the supreme goods and that human love and lovers will always disappoint each other and human beauty always fade.

Caught in this paradox of the inadequacy of the human, we perhaps expect Williams to propose the answers found within the mystical tradition. In that line of writing and practice from ancient to modern times, when the love that is human is seen to be lacking, incomplete, or only a partial and transient reflection of another love, the adept moves towards the Divine. This is a move that Williams never makes in his works. They remain forever poised on the threshold between the domains of the worldly and the otherworldly, but they never cross that threshold. That reluctance to move into the consolations of the spiritual is one of the most poignant aspects of Williams's late writings. This recalcitrance to seek a divine remedy for human woe keeps him eternally in the camp of the wretched of the earth—so always—one of us. In the camp of suffering at the heart of its mystery of pain and madness, Williams pitches his final tent.

In *Clothes for a Summer Hotel* Williams has audaciously exposed the objective correlative for his most hidden and private anguish, and it is revealed to be Zelda Fitzgerald in a last windblown rendezvous with her already dead and illustrious husband, Scott. In his often-quoted summary of the essence of every life Schopenhauer reminds us:

> Life is deeply steeped in suffering, and cannot escape from it: our entrance into it takes place amid tears, at bottom the course is always tragic, and its end is even more so. (635–36)

Williams's late plays deserve our attention because they remain true to this vision that he developed at great personal cost. He has staged this drama at the intersection of pain and art, thus embracing "the paradoxical impossibility and simultaneous necessity to represent, to communicate, to speak of suffering" (Schweizer 3). The tragic is not extraordinary but the ordinary lot of men and women. This recognition of the ubiquity of suffering keeps his work dramatically rooted in the experience of everyday life. Even his most fantastic creations exude the stuff of daily routine. Refusing to turn from the human lover to the divine, they persist in their material love even when it falters or perhaps especially when it fails. His plays attest to the divine by the process of elimination — that is all that is left when they are over. Williams's desiring subjects cling to the consolations of the flesh, even the most failed and shamed ones, disdaining more spiritual sustenance.

Lyle Leverich, in his biographical study *Tom*, insists that "the most pervasive influence in his life and career was that of the poet Hart Crane, to the same degree that Shelley influenced Crane. Crane was the true touchstone"(592). So the genealogy of romanticism can be traced back from Crane to Shelley. But surely one hears in Williams always the moral imagination of John Keats. The insistence that beauty is truth and truth beauty sounds the major chord of Williams's work. His morality is a form of aestheticism; he loved the beautiful losers. But they had to be beautiful — that was their redemption and their salvation. We find that salvation by beauty in Brick and Blanche and Alma and Sebastian and, most poignantly, in the blemished beauty of Laura. *Camino Real* is the fullest statement of Williams's romantic credo; it sums up what went before it and prophesies and helps to explain everything that comes after. It is a kind of keystone to the arch of Williams's body of work.

Like Keats, Williams was determined to conjure the thing that had been and to contain it in a literary artifact. His late plays are acts of distillation against the ravages of time and dissolution. *Clothes for a Summer Hotel* is drenched in longing not only for the old flaming torment between Zelda and Scott Fitzgerald but also for the intense masculine communion between Fitzgerald and Hemingway.

In one scene Hemingway and Fitzgerald step forth, and they bring into focus for a brief moment the possibility of a frank exchange between the two dead American writers. Williams seeks in his play to show the dramatic tensions that held them in thrall to each other and that also doomed their friendship. The homoerotic element is held under fine control in this piece, and instead of imagining a moment between such intense male friends as Skipper and Brick from *Cat on a Hot Tin Roof*, we are given a chance to overhear the two writers as they wrestle with their genius and their battling desires to both befriend each other and best each other.

In *Clothes for a Summer Hotel* Williams creates a ghost play in which every character is already dead. He imagines a meeting between Zelda and Scott in which Scott arrives at the asylum in North Carolina under the assumption that Zelda has recovered. The unfolding of the scene displays both the reality of Zelda's decline in her tattered tutu and her unalloyed longing to be a great dancer—to be creative in her own right. Williams adheres to the biography of Zelda's last years and gives us many details of her life after Scott's death. Her life ended in a tragic fire in an asylum with Zelda incinerated in a locked ward where she was recovering from insulin shock therapy (Milford 382–383).

Those facts of Zelda's demise obviously shocked and dismayed Williams, but his play moves well beyond those emotions. In the two acts he created a poignant picture of her longing to find an authentic form of self-expression and the complicity, yes, loving complicity of Scott and society's refusal to take that need seriously. The truth and beauty of their love are allowed to be seen while the total incoherence and incongruity of their life together are both admitted and examined. The strength of Williams's vision is that, by creating a world of ghosts, wherein the voices are often wafted away by a great wind and the heat of the passions cancelled by the heat of the final immolation, he neither denies nor overstates the action of their destructive lives.

Every life is destructive because in the act of living we destroy ourselves. Williams was well aware of the aptness of that Shakespearean phrase—"consumed by that which it was nourished by." This is the central and unflinching knowledge of the play. Each scene recovers scenes of love and often betrayal from the past. We learn that even as Scott is visiting Zelda, he was living with Sheila Graham during the last years of his life in Hollywood.

Zelda forces Scott to confront the truth of both their failed marriage and the myth of the storybook marriage. She insists that

> legends fade. It seems he finally faced that. He just now admitted that despite its ideal, relentlessly public appearance, it had been, I quote him, a monumental error; and that it had been a mistake for us ever to have met. Something's been accomplished: a recognition—painful but good therapy's often painful. (74)

Scott refuses to accept that verdict on his life and their marriage. For him none of that matters; he holds onto the "covenant with the past" that he re-offers in the last line of the play. He presses upon Zelda through the gates of the asylum, closing like the gates of death, the ring, "The ring, please take it—the covenant with the past." She does not take it, but he never stops offering it to her in his last words— "still always present. Zelda!" (77).

What Williams grants Scott is the heroism of his tenacity; he refuses to give up on Zelda, and he refuses to give up his love. Much as she pushes for a kind of release or an admission of the emptiness of their connection, he cannot make that statement. He is like the violets that broke through the rocks in *Camino Real* in his refusal to give up the force of his own attachment to Zelda. We see that attachment as a kind of lodestar that guides them no matter what betrayals each and both have enacted. The attachment and the sanctity of their connection are in his eyes eternal and break through even the adamantine rock of death.

Williams figures Scott and Zelda as emblems of the infinite possibility and longing of human love. For him that part of us most mirrors the divine: that we are capable of immortal longings against all the odds of our corrupting flesh and our demented minds. That curtain image of unending love upholds Williams's covenant as an artist.

What is the postmodern construction of love? Surely it is an historically constructed emotion and state of being that can be and is affected by the material conditions of the society in which it rises and falls. In the era of late capitalism love has become a commodity: for sale to the highest bidder and largely perfomative. Williams the romantic can never endorse this definition, but there is a contradiction in his late work that surfaced in *Camino Real* and propels his last plays. Living in an increasingly postmodern cultural moment, he was tragically caught up in the struggle to make sense of a world that felt senseless.

Since Williams already represented the persistence of romanticism within the modern tradition, his response to the overtaking of modernism by postmodernism is ambivalent. Throughout the controversies of modernism between form and substance, realism and surrealism, he had kept flying one banner: the proclamation of love as the dominant value and beauty as love's sign. The traditional emblems of love have been progressively emptied out in his work from *Camino Real* to *Clothes for a Summer Hotel*. But the idea of love, the hope of love, a nostalgia for love, continue to exert an implacable force on his imagination. Williams cannot abandon the search for love; even though he can no longer imagine what love would look like once human love is exhausted. In his work he approaches derision, and he skates close to sentimentalism, but he refused to jettison the old maps and guidebooks as corrupt and damaged. The intensities, passions, and ecstasies of the romantics Shelley, Keats, and Hart Crane are for him the highest achievements of literary art. They set goals for his own writing that years of dissipation, infidelity and various addictions could not dim but only make more elusive, receding, and desirable.

Throughout his writing career, Williams represented the residue of romanticism that is within modernism—much like the debris of modernism that is within postmodernism that Jameson describes in his essay on "Postmodernism and Consumer Society" (Brooker 177–178). Often Williams hid the struggle of the romantic under the veneer of realism in plays like *Cat on a Hot Tin Roof*, *Streetcar Named Desire*, and *Glass Menagerie*. In *Camino Real* he lifted the veil of realism and exposed the romantic heart of his entire project. In his last plays he went further. He could not stand to mask the pre-occupation of his romantic sensibility; he refused to clothe it in garments of realism. In a play like *Clothes for a Summer Hotel*, he moved toward pure expression of the failure of love within the unregenerate romantic heart. The despair of love's failure is never embraced, and it never causes the lovers to doubt the value of love's enterprise—the unlocking of the cold stone of the human heart, the breaking through of the icy surfaces of human relations to discover the warm pulse of eternal Eros.

The problem of the imagination emerges as a dominant concern in *Camino Real* and continues as the subtext of his later work. In *Clothes for a Summer Hotel* the imagery of his ghost play uses eliding time frames of a fantasy stage present to commingle with recalled moments of past lives. Never understood when they were originally experienced, these moments grow even dimmer in the re-enactment. What was the significance of Zelda's infidelity? What was the motivation of Hemingway's derision of the golden couple? Unresolved questions and ambiguous answers recede and surface, wax and wane in the moments that the ghosts share on that windy hill before the gates of the asylum. These still-missed communications demonstrate the extraordinary dissonance between memory and desire which imagination must attempt to bridge. It generates a fearful asymmetry in which the greater the desire of the past, the weaker or more unsatisfactory the present memory. As Elaine Scarry comments in her meditation on literary imagination, "It is when we are soaked with the longing to imagine that we notice, as John Keats confessed, 'the fancy cannot cheat so well/As she is fam'd to do'" (4).

Drenched in longing, Williams's ghost play substitutes the gauzy, soft focus of a longed-for, remembered thing for the vividness of the ongoing and still-undecided struggles enacted on *Camino Real*. As he advanced his work, Williams's dramaturgy enacts final things. Like Beckett's, his late plays inhabit that brief space just on the edge of certain extinction. The ghosts in *Clothes for a Summer Hotel* meet in a spectral space where they seek yet another chance at confrontation and reconciliation. In the play Williams achieves something bold and new; he enters the ground zero of his suffering. He has approached the mysterious locus of pain, the place of abjection and abandonment. When we meet Zelda fatter and in a bedraggled tutu at the gates of the asylum, we know that we have crossed over into the very site of the wound, like Philoctetes with the bow of Achilles. The wound in Williams has been biographically referred by countless critics to the long history of his sister Rose, and no doubt, it has vital connections there. But I wish to suggest that in the late plays for Williams the gate of the asylum has become the simulacra for the hidden, shameful, and most derided aspect of human suffering: mental anguish. It represents the pain of loving and the mystery of it. How do we stand it? What does it feel like? It is one of the basic touchstones of the tragic artist. Much as Williams inflected his work with laughter, irony, and the saving reality of comedy, beneath it all the plangent sense of tragedy was always breaking through. His core figure, the tiny doll inside all the nesting Russian dolls of his experience, is that waif of love and beauty still attempting to dance at the very gates of the madhouse.

In *Clothes for a Summer Hotel,* there is no focus on plot. The ending is already known; so all of the exigencies of plot are suspended in a pure form of wishful thinking that is the hallmark of profound grief. His stage action encompasses all the gestures of mourning: once more to see the dead beloved, to unsay the harsh words, to hear one's name called aloud, to stretch a hand for the impossible touch. The sense of an ending already endured endows the action of *Clothes for a Summer Hotel* with a terrible peace. As Frank Kermode has observed, "The crucial point is that in much the same way as the end of the Bible transforms all its contents, our sense of, or need for, an ending transforms our lives: between the tick of birth and the tock of death" (196).

In both *Camino Real* and *Clothes for a Summer Hotel* there is a fantasy component. The staged world as it emerges in *Camino Real* appears as an apocalyptic crypto-fascist state where the lost remnant of romantics, lovers, dreamers, fighters, revolutionaries are caught in a last stop before oblivion. The dramatic world comprises elements of fantasy, dystopia, and realism. Certainly, it is in *Camino Real* that we feel the force of Williams's commitment to construct an alternative world, what postmodernists would call a simulacrum. The world as other-world has been alluded to in Blanche's reveries of Belle Reve in *Streetcar Named Desire* or in Amanda's reconstruction of the gentlemen callers and Laura's dream world of perfect crystalline in *Glass Menagerie*. However, in *Camino Real* we have gone through the looking glass of desire; we are in the menagerie. Williams realizes his ambition to present the other-world as primary world most successfully. It makes apparent the hidden agenda of attaining the sanctuary of an alternative reality that lies beneath all Williams's work. That imaginative agenda haunts his last plays and shapes their dreamy scenarios. In *Camino Real* Williams has entered the world of metadiscourse; he is staging a world that has as its salient purpose to comment upon the deficiencies of the world of the everyday that his audiences know from their experience.

To that degree the play does comment on the repression and rising police state tactics of McCarthyism in the United States of 1953 that some critics have discovered as its major theme. However, Williams's presentation of these sociopolitical problems leads to an idiosyncratic diagnosis and solution. To him they are problems that come from a failure of attachment and a poverty of the imagination. They are social formations that elevate the brute facts: the dry well, the disease-ridden courtesan, the predatory street cleaners, the gypsy prostitute, the worn-out prize-fighter, over the romantic aspirations in the heart's core that only imagination can nurture: the flowing of human kindness to end the drought, the healing of sexual contact despite infidelities, the re-virginization of objects of desire, the violets breaking the rocks.

Tennessee Williams's work participates in the movement of successive cultural realities from romanticism to modernism to postmodernism. In describing this movement as reflected in his work, I am concurring with and drawing upon the accounts that Frederic Jameson has provided over the past twenty years of analysis of the phenomenon of postmodern transformation. He has described the movement as a kind of series of "realisms" that are embedded in an unending process of "decoding" and "demystification" of some preceding ideal or illusion, followed historically by "the various moderns" (128–130).

Each of the literary movements can be conceived as operating alongside the one just before it and the one to come after. The rupture is never so total or absolute; strands of past and future braid into the present cultural moment. In some writers' work, the seams show more than in others, or they are dedicated to developing only a few of the strands of the fabric of the imaginative amalgam which is powerful in their historical present. Williams in *Camino Real* declares that, despite his staging of modernist realism in earlier works, his ideological core is romantic, and he pulls from the back of the carpet the older figure of romanticism. Once he has shown us his aesthetic hand in that fashion, we can detect the fugitive Byronic figure in all his work past and future. In the later works Williams discarded the brilliant disguise of modernist realism and dedicated his craft to uncovering the embattled romanticism still raging in his artistic soul where the beautiful losers always reigned supreme.

In so doing Williams took an incredible artistic risk; one that looms large as a crime for both modernists and postmodernists. He risked entering the realm of the sentimental, bearing that label and seeing it affixed to his work. In *A Lover's Discourse,* Roland Barthes took that gamble and explained the low status of the sentimental:

> Discredited by modern opinion, love's sentimentality must be assumed by the amorous subject as a powerful transgression which leaves him alone and exposed; by a reversal of values, then, it is this sentimentality which today constitutes love's obscenity. (175)

This precisely describes the reaction to the last plays of Williams, who was well aware of the accusation and the penalty both modernist and postmodernist critics would exact were he found guilty.

In *Clothes for a Summer Hotel* Williams sought to elude the denigrating label by pre-empting it. He created a play around the two greatest romantic icons in American literary history, Zelda and Scott Fitzgerald. Of course they are excessive; they're maudlin; they're self-dramatizing and narcissistic; that is the nature of their characters. By choosing two people whose love had been already totally romanticized and idealized, Williams cannot be accused of adding the sentiment; it was already there implicit in the choice of subject matter. Actually, in contrast to the chaos, anarchy, and self-destructiveness of their lives, Williams's depiction appears finely controlled, elegant, and elegiac. In his representation of the two infinitely reproduced and reproducible love objects of the Jazz Age, Williams located his profound meditation on both the insufficiency of desire and the absolute necessity for it.

Inevitably, the play refuses us certainty about the subjectivity of the glamorous figures; they and their obsessions inhabit a world of aftermath. That is the primary way the play reads as postmodern—everything is already over. All possibilities, the culturally constructed roles, masks, and personae, have been tried and discarded and can only be tried again and discarded again. It is a POST-ALL world, where everything has already happened. The stage world and the people who populate it are ashes blowing in the fierce cosmic wind that hurtles us through the universe. In that howling void love and beauty enact their eternal *pas de deux:* Scott offers again his ring and his undying love, and yet again Zelda refuses both and turns back to dance to the undying music of the spheres.

Works Cited

Barthes, Roland. *A Lover's Discourse*. Trans. Richard Howard. New York: Hill & Wang, 1978.

Berman, Marshall. *All That Is Solid Melts into Air*. London: Verso, 1983.

Bigsby, C.W.E. *Modern American Drama 1945–1990*. Cambridge: Cambridge UP, 1992.

Bradley, Frank. "Two Transient Plays: *A Streetcar Named Desire* and *Camino Real*." Gross 51–61.

Brooker, Peter, ed. *Modernism/Postmodernism*. London: Longman, 1992.

Clark, Suzanne. *Sentimental Modernism*. Bloomington: Indiana UP, 1991.

Dorff, Linda. "Collapsing Resurrection Mythologies: Theatricalist Discourses of Fire and Ash in *Clothes for a Summer Hotel*." Gross 153–172.

Gross, Robert F., ed. *Tennessee Williams. A Casebook*. New York and London: Routledge, 2002.

Jameson, Fredric. *Postmodernism or the Cultural Logic of Late Capitalism*. London: Verso, 1991.

Kermode, Frank. *The Sense of an Ending*. Oxford: Oxford UP, 2000.

Leverich, Lyle. *Tom: The Unknown Tennessee Williams*. New York: Crown, 1995.

Milford, Nancy. *Zelda*. New York: Harper & Row, 1970.

Scarry, Elaine. *Dreaming by the Book*. New York: Farrar, Straus, Giroux, 1999.

Schopenhauer, Arthur. *The World as Will and Representation*. 1818. Trans. E. F. J. Payne. 2 vols. New York: Dover, 1969.

Schweizer, Harold. *Suffering and the Remedy of Art*. Albany: State U of New York P, 1997.

Timms, Edward, and David Kelley, eds. *Unreal City. Urban Experience in Modern European Literature and Art*. New York: St. Martin's, 1985.

Williams, Tennessee. *The Theatre of Tennessee Williams*. Vol. 2. New York: New Directions, 1990.

———. *Clothes for a Summer Hotel*. New York: New Directions, 1983.

James Fisher

"IN MY LEFTOVER HEART": CONFESSIONAL AUTOBIOGRAPHY IN TENNESSEE WILLIAMS'S *SOMETHING CLOUDY, SOMETHING CLEAR*

Far from the failure many critics labeled it, Tennessee Williams's last play, *Something Cloudy, Something Clear* (1981), is both a triumph of autobiographical confession and a culmination of prevalent themes in Williams's plays. With an astute recognition of the significance of 1940 as the watershed year of his personal and professional lives, Williams allows his dramatic alter-ego, August, to follow his personal autobiographical chronology, moving from his apprenticeship as a writer toward his first important work. *Something Cloudy* captures the time Williams moved out of his protected St. Louis world, connected as it was with his past and his family, and into a brave new world as an artist, a homosexual, and an engaged citizen of a world he would depict in all of its wondrous and, at the same time, corrupting qualities. *Something Cloudy* also demonstrates Williams's continued desire to probe his own persona and to experiment with the tools of the stage at the end of his life, confirming his status as perhaps the most searching American theatrical artist of his generation.

Critics of Williams's late plays tend to march to a familiar drumbeat—for them, Williams was played out after the early 1960s and his late plays were, in their view, slight affairs revisiting themes he had explored with greater artistry in his golden period from the mid-1940s to 1960. However, along with another final Williams work, his free adaptation of Anton Chekhov's *The Sea Gull* retitled *The Notebook of Trigorin* (1981), *Something Cloudy* suggests that although Williams's late plays were less operatic in scope than earlier works, he continued to explore new themes and techniques while also extending recurrent threads in the fabric of his dramatic persona. And, importantly, *Something Cloudy* and *Notebook* serve as the frankest autobiographical confessionals in Williams's canon. In these final dramatic statements, Williams firmly abandons the romanticized hopefulness that made his name as a dramatist while, it must be noted, he clings to a deep romantic longing for it. He boldly moves forward in structure, style, and content, abandoning the underlying thematic foundation of the defining works of his dramatic output; it is, as Philip C. Kolin writes, a new Williams, "untranslated into metaphor" (Kolin 45).

Even when respectful to Williams's prior reputation, the critical response to *Something Cloudy* and *Notebook* was harsh and, it must be said, misunderstands what Williams was attempting to achieve. Michael Feingold spoke for many when he lamented in the *Village Voice* that August, Williams's portrait of himself in *Something Cloudy,* depicted not "the poet pining for doomed love, but the unscrupulous, horny bastard on the make" and added that only the play's secondary characters suggested Williams's capability at "more than alternately wallowing in sentiment and kicking himself for the falseness of his wallow" (Feingold 89). Feingold's sentiments were largely shared by Catharine Hughes, who found employment of the "memory play" device self-indulgent; for Hughes, Williams had become a "prisoner of a form of myopia" and his work was "too personal, too autobiographical to communicate the inner world of its creator" (Hughes 202). Of an October 2001 revival of the play at the New York Art Theatre, *Back Stage* critic Julius Novick wrote that the play is "elliptical, meandering, self-indulgent, with scattered moments of potential beauty and poignancy," that Williams was pursuing his lost talent through "miasmas of drugs and booze" (Novick 43). John Clum, focusing on the homosexual aspects, felt that Williams's writing became "murkier" (Clum 163) as it became more autobiographical. This is certainly not so—if anything, *Something Cloudy,* and those Williams additions to Chekhov in *Notebook* are vividly direct and clear. The autobiographical nature of these plays is their most significant strength and both deal with three central issues: Williams's sexuality, the pressures of the artistic life, and the connections between time and memory.

Notebook underscores the Chekhovian inspiration on Williams; unlike other influences on Williams, Chekhov's impact grew over the years of Williams's playwriting career. Like other late Williams plays which defy generalization, given their uniqueness in structure, character, and theme, *Notebook* and *Something Cloudy* particularly make use of Williams's trademark dramatic ornaments—in many respects inspired by Chekhov—while breaking new ground. In these two last plays, Williams extends his dramatic autobiography toward the most honest depiction of his life's struggles he could manage.

Notebook, the less important of these two works in the sense that it is an adaptation as opposed to a wholly original play, stresses the aesthetic similarities Williams shared with Chekhov (despite, as well, many significant differences), and mostly by key thematic threads in Chekhov's play that remarkably connect it with aspects of Williams's own life, especially in the areas of artistic struggles, family relationships, and homosexuality. These can be located in the two central male characters of *The Sea Gull*, a mature writer and a young one.

That *Notebook* emerges as less an adaptation than a Williams original is not at all surprising—for Williams, the drama was nearly always autobiography. He refashions *The Sea Gull* into another play entirely, one resting on the diverse strengths of the original in the areas of plot, theme, and character but also a unique dramatic creation of its own. *Notebook* does not supersede *The Sea Gull;* it stands beside it, borrowing key elements from Chekhov and refracting them through the vision of a writer of similar poetic sensitivities but with a more liberated sensibility and a penchant for unrestrained emotion and sexuality. The individual styles of these two dramatic masters were on many levels complementary. Both dramatists plumbed the depths of their own lives for dramatic material—certainly most dramatists do, but few with the unflinching honesty both exhibit. Williams and Chekhov share a lyrical bent, and both created characters yearning for a romantic view of life and dignity despite their individual frailties and failings. Both playwrights are disinclined to render judgment of their characters regardless of their transgressions and failings; only those figures with a fundamentally brutal nature are treated harshly. Their most typical characters are caught between two worlds (one dying, one not yet fully born), finding acceptance difficult in a presently unfriendly reality while, at the same time, yearning for a return to a happily remembered past that may or may not have existed.

Williams's lifelong fascination with *The Sea Gull* centered on the personal connections he made with the play's two leading male characters: Constantine Treplev and Boris Trigorin. Constantine's fragility, his struggles as a fledgling writer, and his tragically strained relationship with a domineering mother certainly drew Williams to the play as a young man (and these concerns are evident in August), but as he aged he was increasingly inclined to relate to Trigorin's world-weariness, imagining in Trigorin the sexual questioning and ambivalence about life and the value of art he himself was experiencing—and as August reflects. Williams merges aspects of both, presenting August simultaneously at the beginning of his artistic career and at the end of it. Merging the remembered past with the present, he creates a dual existence for August, surrounding him with a dramatic atmosphere in which the many facets of autobiography may be revealed.

As Williams's frankest plays exploring homosexuality, *Notebook* and *Something Cloudy* oblige Williams to plunge deeply into his own sexual history. And, as Bruce J. Mann writes, in *Something Cloudy* the approach is "expressionistic rather than realistic" (Mann 144). This begins in *Notebook,* in which Williams's changes include the introduction of a bisexual life for Trigorin, a choice controversial to both critics and Chekhov purists. Viewing *Notebook* in tandem with *Something Cloudy* is informative in regard to the winter of Williams's self-dramatizing discontent. Like Williams (and August), Trigorin is insecure about his gifts as an artist, and he blunts his anxieties and boredom through sexual promiscuity (for Williams, alcohol and drugs provided further blunting). Trigorin turns to a seduction of the naïve aspiring actress Nina as a distraction from the emasculating dominance that his mistress, Arkadina, holds over him. Williams shifts this catalytic but decidedly secondary character into the central figure of *Notebook* solely by deciding that Trigorin both revels in and is troubled by his sexual attraction to men. August similarly grapples with his sexual identity, not yet doubting his abilities as an artist (as Trigorin does) but insecure and anxious to realize himself as a dramatist. Trigorin and August conclude Williams's self-dramatizing and, as such, offer the final word on his homosexual life.

Certainly there is little or no bitterness about or condemnation of homosexuality in *Notebook* and *Something Cloudy,* something glimpsed in earlier works, especially *Cat on a Hot Tin Roof* and *Suddenly Last Summer;* by the time Williams writes these final plays, he has become at least ambivalent, if not frankly accepting, of homosexuality in general as well as his own proclivities. *Something Cloudy* presents August, its gay character, as a complex human being—if Williams is offering some final statement on sexuality in this play, the image is one of a gay man with the same struggles and problems as those facing any individual, regardless of gender preference. The homosexual is not an outcast here as he is in *A Streetcar Named Desire* in

Tennessee Williams, Craig Smith, and Eve Adamson (l–r) in rehearsal at Jean Cocteau Repertory. Photo Gerry Goodstein.

the person of Blanche DuBois's dead husband Alan, nor is he a predator, as most vividly depicted in *Suddenly Last Summer's* Sebastian Venable. It is perhaps not surprising that neither of these characters actually appears in either play—both are dead before the action begins. In 1940s/1950s drama—and even for a playwright of Williams's unparalleled courage—a gay man could not survive.

Even by the 1980s, critics largely condemned *Notebook*—as they would *Something Cloudy*—disturbed, in part, by Williams's revelations about his sexual persona through the bisexual Trigorin and the homosexual August. This same problem may explain the rocky critical reception *Something Cloudy* received when it opened on August 24, 1981, in a Jean Cocteau Repertory production at its tiny Bouwerie Theatre.

The autobiographical aspects first emerge in the play's title, *Something Cloudy, Something Clear,* which provides the central autobiographical metaphor. Smaller in scale than many of Williams's earlier works, *Something Cloudy* is no less imbued with their major attributes and no less searching, original, and complex in its themes and exploration of characters. The play is, at various turns, delicate, heartbreaking, and poetic, and its small cadre of characters are rich in complexity and no less memorable than Williams's more famous creations, dating back to *The Glass Menagerie,* an earlier work of autobiographical confession that *Something Cloudy* expands on. At least on its surface, *Something Cloudy* is the logical counterpart of *Menagerie*—a franker, more sophisticated exploration of a major transition point in Williams's life. In *Something Cloudy,* Tom Wingfield of *Menagerie* is transformed into August, a young, aspiring playwright seeking his first theatrical break and, at the same time, is seen at the end of his life reflecting, often critically, on the choices made by his younger self.

In *Menagerie,* Williams focuses on his mother and sister; in *Something Cloudy,* his gaze shifts to Kip Kiernan, the long-ago love of his life, an individual whose memory "lives on in my leftover heart" (Rader 347), as Williams touchingly described it nearly forty years after Kip's death. Kip's memory is the catalyst of *Something Cloudy*—as a figure out of Williams's past who represents many things, not least Williams's conflicted feelings about being a homosexual, Kip is the soul of *Something Cloudy* and August is its flesh. Like Trigorin, August battles for self-acceptance, strives for artistic achievement, and, as importantly, grasps for ways to avoid what he comes to see as the unavoidable corruptions of living in the real world while, paradoxically, contributing to the corruption of Kip, much as Trigorin casually corrupts Nina in *Notebook.*

Something Cloudy unravels Williams's past and present in a tapestry of images on life and death that brush against some fleeting meditations on love and art. Spending the summer of 1940 on Cape Cod, August becomes enamored of the other-worldly Kip, who is spending the summer on the beach with the fragile and ethereal Clare, a delicate being Williams describes as "apparitionally beautiful" (Williams 1). Kip, recovering from unsuccessful surgery for a brain tumor, and Clare, suffering the ravages of diabetes, are both doomed creatures struggling to maintain scraps of human dignity despite their lack of resources, both financial and emotional, and their tragic lack of a future. August finds in himself powerful feelings for both as he becomes somewhat reluctantly entangled in their lives. He cannot save them, of course, nor can they save him from his future; however, they are able to provide some clarity and comfort to each other out of the cloudy mists of existence.

Aside from the presence of Kip, obvious autobiographical elements emerge in all aspects of the play, most obviously in the inclusion of other actual individuals from Williams's past. These include Williams's childhood sweetheart, Hazel Kramer; the legendary mercurial stage actress Tallulah Bankhead; and Frank Merlo, Williams's longtime lover, whose lingering death in 1963 haunted the last twenty years of Williams's life. Other Williams intimates are given fictional names: theatrical producers Lawrence Langner and Armina Marshall are seen in the play as Maurice and Celeste Fiddler, and actress Miriam Hopkins, star of Williams's *Battle of Angels*, is called Caroline Wales. Only Clare is entirely fictional, a delicate heroine reminiscent of Laura Wingfield (and, as such, Williams's sister, Rose) and, in some respects, Alma Winemiller of *Summer and Smoke/Eccentricities of a Nightingale*, Blanche DuBois of *A Streetcar Named Desire*, and other Williams heroines. These fragile beings are sometimes innocents. In *Something Cloudy*, Kip is certainly such a figure, but Clare is as well. She is not a true innocent, of course, but remains one in spirit, in her longing to be pure. Williams frequently equates the loss of virginity with a loss of innocence and sensitivity—the passage into sexuality is frequently a painful transition, something rarely more evident than in *Summer and Smoke/Eccentricities of a Nightingale*. Alma Winemiller fears and rejects sexuality, which she equates with bestiality, and places a higher value on spiritual love described in poetic terms. Williams similarly sees Chekhov's Constantine in this light—in *Notebook*, he shares Alma's spiritual need, and Nina comes to understand it as well following her abandonment by Trigorin. Clare has long since lost her virginity, but not the lyrical desire for purity and grace and a longing for safety from the brutalizing experiences of life Blanche similarly seeks in *A Streetcar Named Desire*.

The connections between *Something Cloudy* and earlier Williams works are apt but should not be overstated. Kolin accurately asserts that "it is egregiously misleading to see *Something* as a botched imitation of *The Glass Menagerie*, an *apologia pro vita sua*, or a wholesale dramatization of the *Memoirs*, a sensational *Portrait of the Artist as a Queer Young Man* for the stage. *Something Cloudy* is not simply an autobiographical hall of mirrors" (Kolin 38). However, as Mann notes, in the play we are seeing "the older Williams watching his younger self" (Mann 146); *Something Cloudy* is unmistakably autobiographical—in the sense of being a confessional of the real and imagined events (the cloudy and the clear) in the playwright's young life viewed from the end of that life, more unsparingly honest than most American dramas probing autobiographical terrain (even if, as Mann asserts, Williams is able to view his actions "in a more forgiving light" [Mann 148]), with only a few exceptions to be found in such overtly autobiographical plays as Eugene O'Neill's *Long Day's Journey into Night* or Larry Kramer's *The Normal Heart* and *The Destiny of Me*. Critics carped about presumed evasions of truth in Williams's autobiographical bent, but the play scrupulously follows the known facts of Williams's life in 1940 and his portrait of August could hardly be described as self-aggrandizing as might be said of another autobiographical dramatic self-portrait, Arthur Miller's depiction of himself as the lawyer Quentin in *After the Fall* (1964), an account of Miller's stormy marriage to Marilyn Monroe.

The "explosions of self" in *Something Cloudy* reveal August both as "writer and redactor, a viewing participant and a speaking subject" (Kolin 40), allowing Williams to debate with, reflect on, and reinvent his memories. Like the chorus of classical drama or the clever servants of Renaissance comedy—or more appropriately the ironic *brillantes* of Pirandello's plays—August has one foot in the play and another outside its semi-realistic frame. As both participant and observer, present in the time of the play as well as in the present (forty years on), August is granted not only omniscience—about his past and his persona—but also a measure of control. He is a puppet master controlling the direction of the action, both what the audience sees and those moments he chooses to revisit in his past—only Clare shares some of his awareness of the future.

The autobiographical elements of *Something Cloudy* extend even into August's physical persona. Clare describes his appearance as unusual, especially due to his cloudy eye, but Kip says, "he looks queerer than queer" (Williams 4). More kindly, Kip also finds that there is "something nice" (Williams 5) in August's clear eye. Clare, too, finds it appealing, leading August to wonder what she sees: "Appealing for what? Sympathy? Forgiveness? [*He looks away.*] She would discover later that there was much to forgive" (Williams 20). Forgiveness can also be found in the appearance of August's childhood sweetheart, Hazel (the dramatic embodiment of Williams's first St. Louis girlfriend), who suddenly appears on the dunes calling to him. She inspires feelings of guilt, reminding him that he betrayed her love by spying on naked young men at the Lorelei swimming pool locker room. August remembers Hazel's loyalty fondly, but is pained by his recollection of this pure spirit—even more so when Clare tells him that while he was drunk he spoke of her, corrupting this memory.

The brutal and brutalizing nature of desire is, of course, the most complex and controversial aspect of Williams's autobiographical confessional. His sometimes cautious, often courageous confession of his own sexuality begins almost immediately following his first success, *The Glass Menagerie*. Williams does not deal overtly with his homosexuality in *Menagerie* or most of his plays prior to 1970, but an awareness of Williams's life makes it possible to locate some hints in *Menagerie* that are played out more fully in *Something Cloudy*. Tom Wingfield, an aspiring artist like August (an artistic or poetic bent is a frequent metaphor for the homosexual in pre–World War II literature and drama) is pushed by his domineering mother, Amanda, to find a potential suitor for his fragile, deeply repressed sister, Laura. Laura gets her gentleman caller, at least briefly, but there is no girl in Tom's life and he flees his suffocating family life for the Merchant Marine. It is no coincidence that August becomes sexually involved with a Merchant seaman in *Something Cloudy;* observing *Menagerie* through Williams's lens of sexuality begs the questions: What is Tom's sexuality? Is he gay, straight, or bisexual? Does it matter? There is certainly nothing obvious in the text to expose a sexual preference, but the absence of any indication of a relationship may be worth noting. More important, *Menagerie* focuses on other aspects of Williams's autobiography—those related to his sadly bitter family dysfunction, to the difficulty of survival for the romantic, artistic, and sensitive nature in a world of harsher realities (eternally a Williams theme), and for the debts an individual owes the past, to those he loves, and to himself. As such, *Menagerie* may be the most Chekhovian of Williams's plays prior to *Notebook,* and also the most autobiographical.

Williams frequently revisits the relationship of love and sex as previously discussed in regard to *Summer and Smoke/Eccentricities of a Nightingale.* In *Something Cloudy,* August and Clare debate the issue, with both agreeing that, as August says, "Being loved is a hard thing to believe . . ." (Williams 24). Williams indicates that August is close to panic in Kip's presence as a sexual encounter seems possible. The 1980 August interrupts his seduction of a similarly fearful Kip to reflect on the possibility that the relationship may have held more than mere sexual desire but accepts that they are engaged in a "negotiation of terms" (Williams 32) that only as a dream could become more than mere sex. Kip's acquiescence to August's demands—and his resultant loss of innocence—are metaphorically rendered by Williams, as Kip, about to enter August's waterside shack for their encounter, observes a meteor falling into the sea. Following their encounter, a deeply ashamed, emotionally bruised Kip stretches out on the floor of the nearby wall-less shack—his innocence permanently lost—while August takes another step down the road of accepting that love may not be a possibility, at least for him.

The faint possibility of love fades and becomes sex in a brutalizing form, and, as such, Kip's loss of innocence seems a true violation. When Clare learns of the encounter, she is furious—she believes August has promised her he would not attempt to seduce Kip. She did not want to imagine him violated as she has been by Bugsy Brodsky, the small-time hood who has been both her protector and brutalizer. Kip exhibits fearfulness that August has allowed Clare to sense his disapproval of her tawdry life with Brodsky. Corrupted in body, she is, in Kip's eyes—and, ultimately, in August's—pure in spirit. In this, Clare ranks among Williams's iconic heroines—Blanche DuBois of *A Streetcar Named Desire,* Alma Winemiller of *Summer and Smoke/Eccentricities of a Nightingale,* Marguerite Gautier of *Camino Real,* and Catherine Holly of *Suddenly Last Summer,* among others—through whom Williams explores the tensions between a romanticized view of spiritual love and the more earthly passions of the flesh. Blanche's desire for "magic," Alma's resistance to the facts of John Buchanan's anatomical chart, Marguerite's high-flown literary pretensions, and the madness of Catherine that blocks out the violent results of blunt sexuality are different means to romanticize or obscure the brutal facts of sexuality, but these extraordinary women are also seeking a transcendence that is probably unattainable.

Williams also sought this transcendence, but in *Something Cloudy* he is prepared to come down to earth. For Kolin, the play negotiates with *Menagerie* "on the level of the gut and the gonads . . ." (Kolin 46), a notion that might be extended to suggest that these two plays function as complementary, presenting a complete portrait of Williams—the guts, the gonads, and the heart. They do so not only in that the older play features Williams's view of himself as a young writer and *Something Cloudy* has him exploring this young writer from the perspective of a life lived but because the plays in tandem demonstrate two significant sides of Williams's essential nature so fully. One is an eternal romantic longing for a gentler, more compassionate world, a world in which, as he so passionately writes in *Camino Real*, it is possible for the violets to break through the rocks. The other in *Something Cloudy* is, despite his youth, already something of the world-weary cynic, a man of flesh—corrupt, self-absorbed, and fully human. Although the August of 1940 is short on compassion, the August of 1980 is filled with it and recognizes his sins and failings, longing to do the impossible—to remake the past.

Something Cloudy represents an essential change in its author's views. If in his earlier works Williams memorably underscores the desire he and his characters feel for a more romanticized life as they escape into faded memories of a kinder world, the Williams of *Something Cloudy* recognizes with no lack of melancholy that such romanticism cannot survive, as Kip and Clare cannot survive—and, perhaps, as August's lofty artistic ambitions cannot survive in the commercialized theatrical marketplace of the Fiddlers. Tied together with the brutalizing aspects of sexuality, Williams's self-portrait depicts a damaged but surviving spirit with little choice but to participate in a corrupting world.

Aside from exploring homosexuality, Williams's autobiographical bent also leads to his struggles as an artist. August's ruminations on theatre and the artist's life seem, at first, a decidedly secondary concern, but the contradictory combination of pride and insecurity Williams had in his accomplishments as a playwright emerge fully here as well as his resistance to pressures to compromise his work. The pitfalls of the artistic life are dealt with in both *Notebook* and *Something Cloudy*. August vacillates about making changes in his play for his producers, the Fiddlers, but is interrupted by Clare who, he notes, appears as a conscience. The temptation to satisfy the Fiddlers' demands are great—August needs their financial support—and he flirts with giving in to his own exigencies of desperation. American society's devaluation of the artist concerned Williams in his last years (if not earlier); in *Notebook*, he similarly depicts the struggles of older (Arkadina, Trigorin) and younger (Constantine, Nina) artists weighing somewhat different, but equally constricting exigencies. August recognizes the venality of the Fiddlers, but he cannot fully escape them—he is, for better or worse, depending for survival on their commodification of his art. Caroline Wales recognizes this exigency—she knows how to play the Fiddlers but seems better able to communicate with August, a fellow artist. The Fiddlers, who essentially see August as nothing more than a commodity, allow Williams to vent his spleen at the condescension and greed of those who cannot make art but can only compromise it and sell it.

Clare and Kip serve as purer spirits able to recognize the value of art in their desire for transcendence—they cannot make art, but they do not want to sell it or see it compromised; they require it to lift them out of reality. Williams's art sustained his life on many levels, but it finally proved not to be enough. Clare seems to be speaking for Williams when she sadly notes, "We all live on half of something—some on less" (Williams 52). However, Williams cannot leave it at that—at one point, listening to music emanating from August's silver Victrola, he has Kip exclaim on the power of art: "Music like this makes even tonight's sky clearer than it is" (Williams 63). Art, like dreams, can be clarifying but only to those able to recognize its true worth. August—seeing the future—pointedly tells Clare that as an artist he will make many mistakes, "but they'll be my own mistakes, I'll never concede to manipulation by—," and a prescient Clare agrees, "Don't—don't ever. In the end you'll take pride in having never" (Williams 8). Combining the young playwright's artistic searchings and the older writer's honest assessment of his career-long achievements is also effectively established by Williams to underscore the autobiographical connections. Tellingly, August, clearly speaking for his author, says that "Artists always continue a theme with variations. If lucky, several themes with numerous variations" (Williams 11). *Something Cloudy* is, of course, a variation on the recurring autobiographical theme of Williams's dramatic accomplishment that began with *The Glass Menagerie*.

August also speaks of the difficulties of maintaining autonomy as an artist in a thoroughly commercialized theatre. The play provides an interlude in which he finds himself in an argument with the flamboyant Tallulah Bankhead, a character representing the tumult and frustrations of Williams's theatrical adventures. He spurns the theatre's (and Bankhead's) excess, its commercialism, and its inherent falseness (as represented by Bankhead's notoriously camp performance of Blanche DuBois in *A Streetcar Named Desire* at New York's City Center in February 1956). However, he is also drawn to it and, despite his anger at Bankhead for what he regards as a gross caricature of his most famous character, he speaks of loving her and what she represents. In the scene, as their anger subsides, Bankhead admits her love for August, leaving him to reflect on the play's guiding conceit, "Life is all—it's just one time. It finally seems to all occur at one time" (Williams 59). This Pirandellian reflection on time leads to the most intriguing thematic chord in *Something Cloudy*.

The splintering and freezing of time—a rare commodity, as August ruefully laments: "Time, time, we all want more of that than there is of it to be had" (Williams 62), is a variation on a recurring Williams theme, for example as seen in Big Mama's rueful realization of the rapid passage of time as a grandfather clock chimes in the distance in *Cat on a Hot Tin Roof*. The play's fractured time is enhanced by the dreamlike environment Williams creates, as made clear by his description of the setting which has a spectral quality of a time and place from a past remembered through the mists of forty intervening years. The blurring of time underscores the significance of dreams and illusions in the play as, for example, when Clare talks of escaping into her dreams and speaks of them as "the truest things in the world . . ." (Williams 29).

The unique conflation of time and the sketchy, fractured environment of *Something Cloudy* permit a breathtaking, instantaneous movement from past to present—a thorough, simply accomplished compression of the concepts of time and location that permits not only an exploration of a range of themes with economy and directness but allows past and present to co-exist simultaneously.

Williams's skill at establishing a concurrent past and present for the play is displayed within this setting with an impressive conciseness. As August puts a record on his Victrola, he and Clare instantly establish the folding together of two times and their ability, within the play's conceit, to simultaneously be part of both:

> CLARE: You have a strange voice.
> AUGUST: Are you sure you hear it?
> [*We hear the record, Ravel's* Pavane pour une infante défunte.]
> CLARE: It isn't as clear as it was, that summer.
> AUGUST: Forty years ago, Clare. (Williams 11)

Reminding August that she is in 1940, Clare underscores this by adding a light touch of irony: "Let's drop the metaphysics, play it straight, play it not like summer long past but as it was then." (Williams 13) Williams wipes away the rose-colored glow of memory, de-emphasizing his trademark lyrical language that even the characters themselves acknowledge, as when Clare points out that they are speaking strangely.

The play's double exposure (as its first director, Eve Adamson, described it) of time extends into the characters themselves—August is at once seen as man/artist, young/old, and understanding/uncomprehending, while other characters represent heterosexual/homosexual, strong/weak, aesthetic/prosaic, and compassionate/brutal. It is also through August that Williams most effectively accomplishes the feat of exploding time, as the character himself realizes. That none of the others exist anymore—be it the fictional Clare or the "real" characters including Kip, Tallulah Bankhead, etc.—contributes to the audience's recognition of this as a memory play much like *The Glass Menagerie* but extending beyond its structure via August's full presence in both 1940 and 1980. Tom Wingfield occasionally speaks directly to the audience from some unspecified present, reflecting on the past but is imbued with little of the rueful omniscience or sense of the seeming simultaneous flow of time that allows August to fully realize his past and present personas.

Something Cloudy is no less lyrical than earlier works like *Menagerie,* but the greater realism and frankness of the themes, action, and characters of *Something Cloudy* at times purposely diffused and overshadowed the lyrical elements. On one hand, Williams seems to be eschewing lyricism in language (except with Kip and Clare, two ethereal beings of memory, and, occasionally, August, a writer given to poetic inflections), and, on the other, the skewing of time and memory in *Something Cloudy*—the overlapping of moments from August's/Williams's early and late life. Past and present lap back and forth as the sea laps on the shore near August's Cape Cod shack.

On the most obvious level, the *Something Cloudy* of the play's title refers to a cataract on one of August's eyes. This ocular metaphor—another layer of double exposure—allows August to see himself both as he *was* (cloudy) and as he *is* (clear). An older, wiser, more compassionate August observes his more callow youthful self, a being at times clouded by impetuousness, selfishness, and sexual appetite, along with the uncertainties of an as-yet unrealized creative future. Abrupt shifts in perspective via the double exposure of time permit Williams to focus on two key notions also implied by the title, something his characters refer to as life's "exigencies of desperation" (the cloudy) and "negotiation of terms" (the clear), the meanings of which become evident throughout the course of the play.

Beyond, or because of, the double exposures of the play, Williams is able to reveal his impassioned need to confront his memories (both comforting and painful) and to identify the junctures when choices made placed him on the road to his present—in this case, circa 1980—and the inevitable shadows of loves and losses gone by. Although they are gone—or belong exclusively to 1940—fading reflections are still present in 1980. Conflicting critical views find that Williams either attempts a self-serving, self-justification or is too harsh in his self-portrait. Neither is true—Williams aims to show himself, warts and all. His clear-eyed self-judgment suggests Williams was attempting what Eugene O'Neill accomplished in his most elegiac works, *Long Day's Journey into Night* and *A Moon for the Misbegotten*—to pay a debt to and to forgive his dead and, at the same time, to find some measure of forgiveness for himself. Perhaps only in the drama can the past be revisited so fully and autobiography explored as critically.

Tracking Williams's dramatic journey from its beginnings to *Something Cloudy* reveals an evolution of his use of the drama as confessional autobiography that culminates in this final work. The stage in his assured dramaturgical hand is transformed into a mode for exploring and exposing life's transitional events as well as those individuals who touched him. With particular emphasis on the challenge of his Homeric artistic ambitions, his turbulent reckoning with his sexual orientation and the complexities inherent in the connections between spiritual love and baser sexual pursuits, and the fleeting mysteries of time, Williams, for whom the stage was always autobiography, completes his story.

Works Cited

Clum, John. "*Something Cloudy, Something Clear:* Homophobic Discourse in Tennessee Williams." *The South Atlantic Quarterly* 81 (1989): 161–179.

Feingold, Michael. "The Playwright as Stinker." *Village Voice* 16–22 September 1981: 89.

Hughes, Catharine. "Specters." *America* 10 October 1981: 202.

Kolin, Philip C. "*Something Cloudy, Something Clear:* Tennessee Williams's Postmodern Memory Play," *Journal of Dramatic Theory and Criticism*, Vol. XII, No. 2, Spring 1998, pp. 35–55.

Mann, Bruce J. "Memories and Muses. *Vieux Carré* and *Something Cloudy, Something Clear*," in *Tennessee Williams. A Casebook* edited by Robert F. Gross. New York/London: Routledge, 2001, pp. 139–152.

Novick, Julius. "Review: *Something Cloudy, Something Clear*." *Back Stage* 26 October 2001: 43.

Rader, Dotson. "The Art of Theatre V: Tennessee Williams," originally published in *The Paris Review*, 81 (Fall 1981), pp. 145–185, reprinted in *Conversations with Tennessee Williams* edited by Albert J. Devlin. Jackson, MS: UP of Mississippi, 1986.

Williams, Tennessee. *Something Cloudy, Something Clear*. New York: New Directions, 1995.

Thomas Keith

A HOUSE NOT MEANT TO STAND —
TENNESSEE'S HAUNTED LAST LAUGH[1]

A House Not Meant to Stand: A Gothic Comedy (1982) is a landmark play in the Williams canon for several reasons. *House* was the last of Williams's new plays professionally produced during his lifetime; it is his only full-length play written in real time; it is one of only six full-length comedies out of all of Williams's eighty-plus plays; and, like some other late Williams plays, *House* reveals the rigors and fears Williams faced—physical, mental, and emotional—during the last ten years of his life and career. While Williams often used drama to deal with his youth and his past, it was through this dark comedy that he was best able to convey his experiences of old age. Various drafts and draft titles of *House* show something of the evolution of Williams's thinking as he developed this haunting final comedy.

From November 8th through the 23rd, 1980, Chicago's Goodman Theatre presented an evening of three one-act plays by Tennessee Williams, *A Perfect Analysis Given by a Parrot*, *The Frosted Glass Coffin*, and *Some Problems for the Moose Lodge*, under the collective title *Tennessee Laughs* (Goodman 1980). Produced by Gregory Mosher (the Goodman Theatre's Artistic Director from 1978 through 1985), the combination was instigated by local director Gary Tucker, who had befriended Williams and was especially attracted to the newest short play, *Some Problems for the Moose Lodge*, which had never been performed. With Tucker directing, the evening was generally well received and shortly after opening night, Williams flew home to Key West (Jaeck). Playwright Richard Nelson approached Gregory Mosher suggesting that *Moose Lodge* would make a successful full-length play and urged him to pass along the idea to Williams (Mosher). Mosher contacted Williams who enthusiastically began rewrites. Working with the same characters, Williams expanded *Moose Lodge* and, by the following year, several re-writes and several titles later, *A House Not Meant to Stand* premiered in the Goodman's Studio Theatre. The production ran from April 2 through May 23, 1981, but Williams was dissatisfied and told Gregory Mosher that the intimacy of the Studio Theatre was too confining for the play's comic characters and that the set looked far too stable for a house on the verge of collapse (Goodman 1981; Mosher). Both felt that the play needed further structuring and tightening and so Williams went back to work rewriting *House*. With a new director at the helm, Belgian-born Andre Ernott, the third incarnation of *House* opened on the Goodman's large main stage space on April 16, 1982—closing out its limited run on May 23, 1982, just nine months and two days before Williams's death on February 25, 1983 (Goodman 1982).[2]

A House Not Meant to Stand is the story of Cornelius and Bella McCorkle of Pascagoola [*sic*], Mississippi, a late-middle-aged couple who return home one midnight from the Memphis funeral of their older son, Chips. The McCorkles's daughter, Joanie, has recently been admitted to an insane asylum, and their younger son, Charlie, out of work again, is upstairs having sex with his pregnant, born-again Christian girlfriend as the McCorkles enter. Bella is in mourning for Chips, but it is clear that she has long been in an emotional fog; when she can manage to focus on anything, it is her desire for all three of her children to return home to her and be together as the loving family they once were. It is her haze that shields Bella from the constant verbal abuse of her defeated and insensitive husband who is trying to get his hands on Bella's family inheritance, a large amount of cash she has hidden somewhere in their home—the exact location of which she has, in fact, forgotten. As the play progresses, Cornelius's attempts to find the money are interrupted by a series of eccentric characters whose visits to the McCorkle residence increase the chaos in a house already filled with turmoil. Cornelius is finally defeated by the ghost of their older son who appears to Bella and tells *her* the location of the money. Bella slips deeper in her private world until "spirits," representing her three offspring as young children, appear to her, and as they reenact the blessing before a meal, Bella dies.

The initial short play, *Some Problems for the Moose Lodge,* contains the same basic elements and characters as *House,* save for Cornelius's quest for his wife's inheritance, the dilapidation of the house, and the presence of any ghosts (Williams *Moose*). In fact, without Cornelius's quest for money, it is virtually without a plot and is one of Williams's lighter one-acts—a rather gentle sketch of a dysfunctional family. The set description could be any one of dozens of Williams plays set within a shabbily furnished living room. In *Moose Lodge* Cornelius has two monologues and several smart remarks about his wife's weight and her eating habits, which, while drawing a parallel with the sedentary life and shallow desires of Cornelius, are a set-up for Bella's relationship with food, about which jokes and cheap shots are revisited throughout the short play. Cornelius is also more vituperative in *Moose Lodge* in his condemnation of their dead son, Chips, who, according to Cornelius, "looked pretty as a girl laid out in his casket" (Williams *Moose* 21). Instead of being obsessed with recent plastic-surgery, neighbor Jessie Sykes is preoccupied with and quite descriptive about her painful hemorrhoid condition. The one-act ends with Bella preparing food, well after midnight, for her grown children (who are, of course, not present) as Jessie watches her with bewilderment.

Williams's notes, drafts, and revisions on *House* during 1981 and 1982 record his search for a core theme. A master of play titles, Williams's prospective titles for *House* are clues to how his thinking evolved. The title *Some Problems for the Moose Lodge* was plainly chosen for comic effect; the Moose Lodge itself is not essential to the action of the play but rather an offstage location referred to a few times.

In the next titled draft, *The Dancie Money*, Williams clearly shifted his focus by introducing Cornelius's interest in Bella's inheritance, and it is that which drives the action through to the middle of the second act (Williams *Dancie*). At the end of *The Dancie Money*, the voices of Bella's ghostly children are *heard*—supplied by dramatic sound effects, however spooky, rather than characters in the play. The title *The Dancie Money* speaks for itself—the play gained a plot with Bella's family inheritance and Cornelius's attempts to uncover it. As with *Moose Lodge*, the set of *The Dancie Money* is not described as anything out of the ordinary.

In one fragment tentatively titled *Our Lady of Pascagoola*, Williams's describes Bella in a fashion not included in the final version (Williams Unfinished III):

> "Bella should be presented as a grotesque but heart-breaking *Pieta*. She all but sense-lessly broods over the play as an abstraction of human love and compassion—and tragedy . . .
> Whenever she appears the play is suspended as all turn to regard her as if she were indeed an unearthly apparition. Despite the great accretion of flesh, there is a quality of grace and loveliness about her . . ."

As Williams developed the character of Bella, her deep sense of loss, obsession with the past, and physical deterioration became the theme of the play. Perhaps Hannah from *Night of the Iguana* is the Williams character that most closely corresponds to Bella's role of compassionate mother and comforter. However, no matter how emotional Williams's rendering of Bella, making her character overweight allows an actress to more readily exploit the comic potential of her lines. When deciding on a southern city in which *House* would take place, Williams must have appreciated the onomanapoetic humor in the name Pascagoola [Pascagoula] and his idiosyncratic way of spelling it—in his stage directions for one draft he even adds, in parenthesis, "not far from Yazoo City," which may have been another possible location for the play (Williams *House* I). *Our Lady of Pascagoola* is a title which embodies both Williams's vision of Bella's boundless compassion as well as the comic potential of the McCorkle family and their self-destruction. *The Legendary Bequest of [a] Moonshine Dancer, Laundry Hung on the Moon*, and *For Tatters of a Mortal Dress* are other titles considered by Williams which spring from Bella's character and signal an attempt to make Bella's concerns the theme of the play (Williams Unfinished I). Other prospective titles, *Being Addressed by a Fool, A House Not Meant to Last Longer Than the Owner*, and *What Odds Are Offered by the Greek in Vegas?* reflect a concentration on Cornelius's self-doubts, mortality, and ambitions, financial and political (Williams Unfinished I). Still other draft titles, *The Disposition of the Remains, Terrible Details (A Gothic Comedy)* and *Putting Them Away* experiment with the sad lives of the McCorkle children as the play's focus; the first two relating directly to Cornelius's indifference and Bella's agony regarding the death of Chips, and the latter a double entendre referring to Chips's interment and Joanie's confinement to a mental ward (Williams Unfinished II, IV, V). Williams settled on *A House Not Meant to Stand* for the second Goodman production and did not change the title again. As a title, *A House Not Meant to Stand* beautifully encompasses Bella's obsession with the past, Cornelius's obsession with himself, and the McCorkle children's frustrated lives by placing them all within the metaphor of the deteriorating house, which symbolizes the deterioration of their family and, in turn, represents the breakdown of America.

In the initial stage directions of *House* Williams writes that he will not try to describe the dilapidation of the house without the contribution of a "highly gifted" designer and then proceeds to describe the set in spatial terms (Williams *House* III). It is unfortunate that Williams did not go into greater detail about the condition of the set or include descriptions from earlier drafts of the play (Williams Unfinished I). Without understanding the state of the house, the rest of the play cannot be fully appreciated. In the stage directions Williams referred to the play as a "Southern Gothic spook sonata," which suggests the poetic dimension of *House* but is not quite a "genre" in and of itself as Williams states. In one draft fragment Williams goes to great lengths to describe the extreme decay and disarray of the McCorkles' house and indicates that there is nothing naturalistic about the set—in one instance he predicts that the audience will be "appalled" by the extravagance of the set's decomposition and that the rise of the curtain should produce in the audience a "shock of disbelief" (Williams Unfinished I). Williams further explains that the setting for the play represents "a far excursion from any kind of theatre" he had attempted previously. Throughout his plays Williams defined locations with expressionistic suggestions of natural settings, such as the dominating skyline in *Fugitive Kind,* the bed and large scrim in *Cat on a Hot Tin Roof,* and the screens and black stage in *The Milk Train Doesn't Stop Here Anymore* (Williams *Fugitive; Theatre III; Theatre V*). In *A House Not Meant to Stand* Williams is asking for something that could be called hyper-realistic. The McCorkle house is dilapidated far beyond what its middle-class inhabitants could be expected to live in; hence Williams's subtitle of "Gothic" to describe the comedy comes into play. Once the abnormal nature of the environment is established, the action of the McCorkles arriving home adds a mad quality to the characters' most commonplace behavior. Even Cornelius's self-pitying complaints about having to live in such a terrible house become understatement, while the other characters absurdly appear to be oblivious to the condition of the house. There is one area of the stage which stands out amid the mess, and that is a dining room covered by a transparent scrim where Bella spends much of her time and where her ghostly children appear to her.

As the play begins, the McCorkles enter a most unnaturalistic set: water dripping everywhere, great portions of walls and ceiling rotted away or hanging precariously, failing electricity and chaotic disarray from the furniture to the stairs and doorways. Cornelius addresses his first lines to the audience instead of to his wife; however, they eventually engage in relatively naturalistic dialogue. Cornelius's speeches to the audience are always indicated by stage directions and appear intermittently during the first act. Bella has only one short line that is directed to the audience. Jessie Sykes has even more lines directed to the audience than does Cornelius. None of the other characters show any awareness of the audience, and none of Williams's drafts prior to the final version use the conceit of talking to the audience (Williams *Moose, Dancie, House* I, *House* II). It is not clear-cut whether Williams decided on a pattern for the use of this device as he did with Tom's narration of *The Glass Menagerie* or if he merely used it as the notion struck him, though the latter is more likely the case since the device is dropped entirely in the second act except for one speech from Jessie. A possible contrast Williams was undertaking, if the anomaly of Bella's one line to the audience is excluded, is that Cornelius and Jessie address the audience directly and are the more animated, comic, and aggressive spouses of Bella and Emerson, who are both accused of suffering from dementia—the former nearly paralyzed by the present, the latter confused by it. In fact, there is no indication in Emerson's dialogue or stage directions that he is anything but eccentric. Bella has moments of clarity that make it questionable to pin that label on her. She seems to spend the entire play in a haze that varies in aspect from something like dementia to a kind of pathetic rapture. Distinguishing Cornelius and Jessie from their spouses in this way further reenforces their indelicate, greedy natures; both are tormented by the lack of money and show little or no love for their families.

Ghosts, in one form or another, are a recurring element in five of Williams's later plays. *Clothes for a Summer Hotel*, in which the characters move back and forth through time and sanity, is subtitled "A Ghost Play"; the Writer who narrates *Vieux Carré* enlists his personal ghosts to act out the play; *Something Cloudy, Something Clear* takes place in two dimensions, the summer of 1940 and the summer of 1980, both places visited by apparitions directly out of Williams's life; and conjuring the spirits of the famous is one of the essential comic ingredients of *Will Mr. Merriwether Return from Memphis?* (Williams *Theatre VIII, Something, Merriwether*). Though the ghosts in *House* are quite visible to the audience during their short scenes, they can hardly be considered literal—two of the McCorkles' adult children are still alive during the play and the spirits that come to Bella are young children. Whether or not the last scene of the play succeeds depends upon how the other stylistic elements are handled. If the set is made sufficiently unreal in its decay, if Cornelius and especially Bella move in their separate orbits, if the abrupt transitions are navigated by the comic characters of Jessie, Emerson, Charlie, Stacey, and Cornelius, then the other worldly appearance of the specters in Bella's dining room, as Jessie and Dr. Crane continue quarreling over the discovered money, would seem a reasonable sequence in an unreasonable world. If those elements are not achieved, then it is easy to see how the appearance of Bella's ghostly children could come off as a sentimental and unsuccessful device. Aside from the homage to Strindberg, Williams's description of *House* as his own

"Southern Gothic spook sonata" would most sensibly refer to the haunted lives of all the living characters in the McCorkles' haunted house and not merely to the two short scenes in which spirits appear near the end of the play. The "ghosts" in *House* do not belong to the total world of the play, only Bella's world—they are parts of Bella's broken heart reassembling itself, finding her a way to ultimately let go of her sorrow.

The choice to make the action continuous from the beginning to the end of the play, what is referred to earlier as "real time," is particularly out of character for Williams. In all of his other produced full-length works, there is some passage of time, however brief, between scenes and acts, and so it is reasonable to conclude that this structural device for *House* was a choice. While the extreme condition of the house belies the comparatively normal dialogue, the style of dialogue belies the pace indicated by action presented in real time. It would have been easier for Williams to justify certain transitions in the play had he chosen to break up the action into scenes—Jessie's sudden appearances, the first entrance of Charlie's girlfriend Stacey, Bella's time away from the house and her truck accident, the arrival of the police, or had Williams even increased the decay of the set by degrees or perhaps brought Charlie and Cornelius back toward the end of the play. But confining the action of the play to the two hours between midnight and two A.M. forces those transitions to be made in front of the audience, which helps to remove the "normalcy" of a drawing room comedy and heighten the humor. A good example of this is the whole sequence of events from the middle of Act I through the earlier part of Act II, beginning with a talk between Charlie and Cornelius about Bella's condition and ending when police drag the two men away. Williams might well have achieved something tighter and well made, in the traditional sense, had he broken up the events into short scenes, with their transitions and expository gaps in time. As written, however, the action is often messy, the transitions abrupt and awkward, and hence the comedy charges forward at a pace that complements the primary themes of the play: the chaos and inevitable decay of society, and obsession with a gentle past that could not survive.

As *House* evolved and those themes solidified, Williams must have understood, whether he made a conscious choice or not, how a comedy could integrate his strong feelings and fears about old age into something an audience could absorb. Had he pursued a dramatic story instead it might have been far too unrelenting, especially Bella's character. That same instinct for finding the humor in his most intimate pain may have sprung from the natural inclinations for self-protection and self-deprecation, long known as personality traits of the playwright. During the last decade of writing, Williams attempted, by degrees, to unmask the autobiographical nature of his characters that were previously extended into the realm of dramatic fiction. His pattern was fairly consistent: Clare and Felice from *The Two-Character Play* and *Out Cry* are, while still placed within a dramatic conceit, overt representations of a youthful Williams and his sister Rose (disguised with less fictional cover than Laura and Tom from the *Glass Menagerie*) (Williams *Theatre V*). He dealt more directly with his sex life in *Small Craft Warnings* wherein openly gay Quentin's dialogue often telegraphs passages from Williams's nonfiction *Memoirs* that appeared a few years later (Williams *Theatre V* 260–261, *Memoirs* 208–211). In *Vieux Carré*, amidst the other distant memories of his first month in New Orleans in 1939, Williams candidly transferred his first sexual experience to a dialogue (*Theatre VIII* 22–25). Williams went even further in *Something Cloudy, Something Clear* as he grappled with his love life in Provincetown during the summer of 1940—the main character of August, a writer, is distinguishable from the young Tennessee in name only and other characters, Kip, Hazel, Frank Merlo and Tallulah Bankhead, are not even given the theatrical guise of a new name (Williams *Something*). Those are all primarily dramatic works which deal in memory and reconstruction of the past. When Williams delved into his *contemporary* life as fodder for his later plays, the treatment tended to be comic. In the case of *Kirche, Küche* [*sic*] *und Kinder* the result bordered on the ridiculous with a batty character named Miss Rose spouting gentle absurdities—some of which surely came straight from Rose Williams during one of her many visits with her brother in New York City or the sanitarium where she lived (Williams *Kirche*). The Countess in *This Is (An Entertainment),* a domineering matron with grand pretensions, is Williams's sometimes pithy, sometimes unkind tribute to his long-time friend Maria St. Just (Williams *This Is*). The elderly spinsters of *Will Mr. Merriwether Return from Memphis?* are mischievous, sexually aware, and full of humor that puts them at far remove from, say, the starving spinsters Miss Carrie and Mary Maude in *Vieux Carré* (Williams *Merriwether; Theatre VIII*).

Cornelius pontificates from his armchair (when he can get to it), never lacking for an unkind word, complaint, or egocentric ambition, and is as impotent as he is loud. Bella wanders the decomposing house as if she is beginning to fade into it or into the past she longs for, becoming a spirit herself. Into this haunted world enter several outsiders, all but one arriving to make a contribution to the chaos. The one exception is the McCorkles' younger son Charlie. Williams seems to have needed Charlie for certain interactions and exposition but failed to flesh him out as a complete person. Charlie is the straight man in a play that doesn't need one. Charlie is also one of the McCorkle children and as such would have benefited from having as complete a story line as his off-stage siblings.

The rest of the visitors, however, survive well enough as comic relief, and most of them seem to have stepped out of other plays, paying a call on the McCorkles to keep *their* play alive. Jessie Sykes, a traditional comic female in the Tennessee Williams vein, could easily make an appearance in *A Lovely Sunday for Creve Coeur* or *Tiger Tail* and seem right at home. Jessie is a sort of female Cornelius, only with a bit more get-up-and-go. Greedy, self-possessed, and insensitive, Jessie must have been a pleasure for Williams to write because her comic speeches are better constructed than Cornelius's and turn up far too often for the minor role she serves in the play. Jessie's husband, Emerson Sykes, is a benign version of Cornelius and shares his Moose Lodge brother's monetary desires. While Cornelius threatens to have Bella committed for mental breakdown but can take no action, Emerson is at the mercy of his wife who, due to her high energy and lack of conscience, succeeds in having him put away. Jessie and Emerson Sykes play out two extremes of old age; Emerson the feeblest kind of simpleton, is incapable of survival while Jessie is the most aggressive survivor in the play.

Six-foot-four-inch police officer Pee Wee Jackson is a sexual sight gag who went to school with Charlie and takes Cornelius and Charlie away in the squad car after their fight. Jessie's delight that Pee Wee's knock at the McCorkle door could be that of a "sex-fiend" she believes to be on the loose is a terrific build-up for Pee Wee's entrance. Described as powerful and handsome, Pee Wee is the one character in *House* who parallels the homoerotic sexuality present in other late Williams comedies and in which Williams seemed to delight—the ominous "Man" in *Kirche, Küche und Kinder* and the parade of scantily-clad servants in *This Is (An Entertainment)*. Pee Wee also gives Jessie a handsome young man to lose control over. She exhibits the very sexual obsession she attributes to her husband and uses as the excuse to have him committed. Emerson does have a sexual obsession and it is revealed when he meets Charlie's very pregnant-looking fiancée, Stacey, as she comes downstairs in her rain-soaked teeshirt. Stacey efficiently puts Emerson in his place only to turn up later as the most cartoonish character of the group. During the time Williams began writing *House,* Ronald Reagan was elected president and the conservative movement, later misnamed "The Moral Majority," was becoming visible in America. Williams's choice to make Stacey what he calls "a born again Christian" must have been his not so subtle comment on current events. Stacey is one of the funniest characters in the play and her "holy-roller" fit, which comes out of nowhere, is riotous. The appellation of born-again Christian, however, is really a misnomer since what Stacey acts out as she speaks in tongues and rolls on the floor is really a parody of a Pentecostal. Stacey, however, is not merely a comic device. While Charlie is attentive to and protective of his mother, Stacey is the outsider most sensitive to the cruelty in the McCorkle house. She is kind to Bella and, in seeming contradiction to her religion, she is extremely sympathetic to the late Chips, going so far as to describe homosexuals she has known in a positive light which is an irritation to Cornelius and a comfort to Bella.

Tennessee Williams infused nearly all his work with the names, places, and personages of his life, frequently those of his early life in Mississippi, Tennessee, and Missouri. Williams's mother and sister, Edwina Dakin Williams and Rose Isabel Williams, represented by personality traits, speech, manner, or psychology, appear in one form or another in most of Williams's plays and many of the short stories. Williams's father, Cornelius Coffin Williams, on the other hand, was less fertile material, perhaps too distant and painful a figure in Williams's life, and his presence in Williams's works is more elusive. Certainly he became the famous father who worked for the phone company and "fell in love with long distance," appearing only as a portrait above the mantle in *The Glass Menagerie,* and to some extent, though arguably only in a general sense, added to the character of Big Daddy in *Cat on a Hot Tin Roof.* But the patriarch of the Williams family did not get the memorable and loving treatment accorded to his wife and daughter. If Williams's father is rarely reflected in Williams's plays, his younger brother, Dakin, is excluded entirely, that is, until one considers the main character of *A House Not Meant To Stand*, Cornelius McCorkle—an unmistakable composite of Williams's father, brother, and Tennessee himself. Blustering, temperamental, abusive, ludicrous, and sentimental by turns, the character of Cornelius exhibits none of the sexuality, cunning, or energy of Stanley, Brick, Val, Shannon, Chance, Chicken, or Quentin, the dignity of Big Daddy, or the innocence and playfulness of Mangiacavallo or Kilroy—in the gallery of Williams's leading male characters, Cornelius is a cranky buffoon, rather without precedent.

In addition to assuming the same first name of Williams's father, Cornelius assumes his namesake's role as the aggressive and contemptuous father who counters what he sees as the overprotection and smothering of his children by his wife. Everything about the character Cornelius McCorkle reflects Cornelius Williams's character through a soft light. Where Mr. Williams, from all accounts, was more remote and hence more salient and wounding in his personal attacks on his children, Mr. McCorkle rains a continual assault of less vicious but more sustained insults down on his spouse and offspring. When Mr. Williams deigned to speak to his son Tom, he often referred to him as "Miss Nancy" (Leverich 53); when Cornelius responds to a description of his dead gay son as "the handsomest boy at Pascagoola High" by correcting it with "the prettiest girl at Pascagoola High" one gets the impression that he never had the nerve to say it to his son's face, and thus his cruelty comes over as black humor. That his son's homosexuality is a subject Cornelius loves to ridicule, is a telling connection to the real Cornelius, and it must have been satisfying for Tennessee to finally put that scorn on stage in such way as to garner laughs and a few groans instead of gasps or pity for the object of contempt—with *House* it became Cornelius who was to be pitied, not the gay sons, neither the fictional one who moved away and died, nor the real one who moved away and made a success of his life. While Mr. Williams drank his way through his failure as a businessman, life with his frigid wife, and his profound disappointment in Rose and Tom, Mr. McCorkle revels in his failures—his failed runs for political office and his dysfunctional children—bragging to anyone who will listen about his contempt for his older son's homosexuality, his daughter's madness and promiscuity, and his younger son's laziness and failure.

The absent father of *The Glass Menagerie* works as a brilliant off-stage antagonist, and yet it is quite possible that the true nature of his father's behavior was too painful for Tennessee Williams to have even considered writing it into a character in that play. Nearly forty years later in *House,* it seems Williams still felt more comfortable drawing his father as a comic menace rather than the intensely painful figure he was in life. It is also likely that by 1980 Williams had come to better terms with his father (who died in 1957) as demonstrated by the beautifully written 1960 essay "The Man in the Overstuffed Chair" and would not have been immediately inclined to draw the abusive father of his childhood but rather a man he understood himself to be more like than he had ever realized in his youth: "I almost feel as if I

Peg Murray as Bella and Scott Jaeck as Charlie in the Goodman Theatre's mainstage production of *A House Not Meant to Stand*, Chicago, 1982. Photo by Lisa Ebright. Used by
permission of The Goodman Theatre, all rights reserved.

am sitting in the overstuffed chair where he sat, exiled from those I should love
and those that ought to love me" (Williams *Collected* xv). (There is even a stage direction in *House* which indicates that "Em[erson] supports [Cornelius] feebly to
an overstuffed chair" [Williams *House* III 55].)

This is where the aging Tennessee Williams enters the character. Cornelius is as
fascinated as he is tormented by what he perceives to be his failing health and the
battery of medications he takes. Williams's own hypochondria often clouded the
true nature of his physical debilitation in his later years, and when Cornelius's
character details his prescription drugs for his son Charlie, their uses, their ingredients, and even how to spell them, it must have been from Williams's recent experience. Because Williams's real and perceived physical problems and the loss of
his youthful looks troubled him, it would be only natural that he turn those feelings into laughable elements in Cornelius's narcissistic character. By 1980 when
Some Problems for the Moose Lodge was produced, Williams was tired. He had been
certain with every play he'd written for the previous twenty years that it would be
his last. Having been haunted by his mortality since he was boy and, having lived
to the age of 69, must have felt more worry than ever that his fears would come
true at any moment. Cornelius rails against corrupt politicians, rapacious and

controlling corporate interests and their brain-washing advertisements, the population explosion, and the moral decline of society—all in a very general way,
which was how Williams usually handled such matters—yet, he cannot help but
also tell stories about dementia, incontinence, and death, all concerns that had become immediate for Williams. It is not incidental that with each draft of *House,*
Cornelius's weight increased until he bore the paunch that Williams did at that
time (Williams *Dancie, House* I, II & III). While the core of Cornelius's ambi-
tiousness, greed and insensitivity are unquestionably created from elements of
Williams's father, Williams himself is also in evidence in Cornelius's paranoia, hypochondria, and coarse humor which all, in the end, create contradictions in the
character that help to make him a better match for the intensity of Bella.
Cornelius's ambitions and failures must have resonated directly with Williams's
own feelings of neglect and perhaps with the part he played in what he saw as his
own professional promise unfulfilled. Acknowledging all that in a comic character, drawn from his father, gave Williams a chance to have a laugh at some of his
deepest pain.

Bella bears a strong affinity to the first and foremost Tennessee Williams southern belle and mother figure, Amanda Wingfield from *The Glass Menagerie,* in one
very important aspect: they are both women who are obsessed with the past and
unable to function in the present without relying on their memories of times and
people long gone. However, that is where the similarity ends. If anything, Bella
could, ironically, be dubbed the "anti-Amanda" or for that matter, even the ultimate counterpoint to the typical Tennessee Williams southern belle. Bella,
created over thirty-five years later, shares none of Amanda's temperament, her ag-
gression, flirtatiousness, or self-absorption. Bella's children are precious to her,
and her love for them is unconditional. Amanda's children are precious to her,
and she places all her own failed dreams and hopes on their shoulders, relentlessly
pushing them away from her. Not only is Amanda proud of the beauty she pos-
sessed in her youth—as an aging woman she wears her sexuality like a corsage—
Bella could not be less concerned with her appearance. Bella overeats and seems
to have little or no awareness of the weight that endangers her health and about
which her husband continually scolds her. Amanda's eccentricities are vivid, over-
bearing, and often charming, though she is never privy when the joke is on her.
Amanda is the kind of eccentric character that audiences wait on to hear the next
droll thing they will say. Bella's eccentricities are low-key; the steadiness with
which she moves through her personal fog is almost unnerving, and she has the
ability to break free of it on occasions of complete clarity and dash off a stinging
line to whomever she pleases, then just as quickly she recedes into her more comfortable state of mild confusion. Bella seems to understand that her life has disin-
tegrated, and her resolve to reclaim her children is, as it turns out, more realistic
than Amanda's different goal. In the face of difficult odds, Amanda fights with
the world at hand, her children, and even with her absent husband to give her
children the life she feels that she and they have been deprived of. She plots; she
plans; she is cunning, and when her most ambitious scheme ends in failure and

the departure of her son, she rises like a phoenix, ready it do it all over again. Bella, on the other hand, turns first toward the unlivable house, and then more and more inward; she finds the money with the assistance of her older son's ghost. Then Bella creates her own closure in the fantastic production of spirits that stand in for her three children as she remembers them in childhood, which gives her the moment from the past she has sought so desperately and, having succeeded, she dies. There couldn't be a much more dramatic contrast between two Williams characters who rise from the same source—with Bella, it's as if a Williams southern belle had left the Episcopalian rectory and joined a Buddhist monastery. Williams had long since distanced himself emotionally from his mother by the time she died in 1980, but as he developed the character of Bella, the death of Edwina/Amanda could not have been far from his mind. And there is no doubt that for Williams, Amanda was the ultimate dramatic portrait of his mother, despite her life-long protests to the contrary. Perhaps Bella is in part a tribute to the gentleness that Edwina did possess but rarely exhibited and at the same time a portrait of the longing for better times that both he and his mother experienced.

It is fitting that Williams's last contribution to the professional theater was this curious and jarring comedy with its components of old age, mortality, money, insanity, homosexuality, religion, and ghosts. *A House Not Meant to Stand* is haunted not only by visions of ambition, decay, and loss but by the long shadow of Tennessee Williams.

Notes

1. Quotations from the work of Tennessee Williams used by arrangement with The University of the South. Copyright © 2002 by The University of the South. Excerpt by Tennessee Williams from *The Glass Menagerie,* copyright © 1945 by The University of the South, © renewed 1973 by The University of the South. Reprinted by permission of New Directions Publishing Corp. Excerpt by Tennessee Williams from *The Collected Stories of Tennessee Williams,* copyright © 1980 by The University of the South. Reprinted by permission of New Directions Publishing Corp. All rights whatsoever in these plays are strictly reserved and application for performance, etc., must be made before rehearsal to Casarotto Ramsay & Associates Ltd., National House, 60–66 Wardour Street, London W1V 4ND. No performance may be given unless a licence has been obtained.
2. Williams wrote at least four distinct drafts of *House* as well as dozens of rewrites of various scenes; fragments and revisions are still surfacing and likely will be for some time to come (Williams *Dancie; House* I–II; *Unfinished* I–V). Unless otherwise indicated, the version referred to in this chapter is the "final version" of the play as it was performed at the Goodman in the spring of 1982 (Williams *House* III). Further research will have to be done to incorporate any small changes, cuts, or revisions Williams may have made in 1982, either at the Goodman or when the same production was mounted briefly for a Miami theater festival in June of that year (Clarke and Alva).

Works Cited

Clarke, Gerald, and Marilyn Alva. "Sweating It out in Miami." *Time Magazine,* June 28, 1982: p. 69.
Goodman Theatre Studio, theater program for *Tennessee Laughs,* Chicago, November 8–23, 1980.
Goodman Theatre Studio, theater program for *A House Not Meant to Stand,* Limited Engagement, Chicago, April 2–23, 1981.
Goodman Theatre, theater program for *A House Not Meant to Stand,* Chicago, April, 1982.
Jaeck, Scott, interview with Thomas Keith, Chicago, Illinois, August 22, 2001.
Leverich, Lyle. *Tom: The Unknown Tennessee Williams.* New York: Crown Publishers, 1995.
Mosher, Gregory, interview with the author, New York City: May 31, 2001.
Williams, Tennessee. *Collected Stories.* New York: New Directions Publishing, 1985.
——. *The Dancie Money: A Gothic Comedy,* unpublished manuscript. Chicago: Goodman Theatre Archive (typescript, 76 pp.) "January 1981"
——. *The Disposition of the Remains.* Unfinished, typed fragment with title. Harvard Theater Collection, no date. (Williams, Unfinished V)
——. *Fugitive Kind.* New York: New Directions Publishing, 2001.
——. *A House Not Meant to Stand: A Gothic Comedy.* Unpublished manuscript. New York: Columbia University Library (typescript with revisions, in three scenes, 100 pp.) "April, 1981 (Post-Goodman Studio Version)" (Williams, *House* I)
——. *A House Not Meant to Stand: A Gothic Comedy.* Unpublished manuscript. New York: Columbia University Library (typescript with revisions, in two scenes, 100 pp.) "April, 1981 (Post-Goodman Studio Version) Revised February 1982" [Lyle Leverich copy] (Williams, *House* II)
——. *A House Not Meant to Stand: A Gothic Comedy.* Unpublished manuscript. Chicago, New York: Goodman Theater Collection, New Directions Files (typescript with revisions, in two acts, 102 pp.) "April 27, 1982." (Williams, *House* III)
——. *Kirche, Küche und Kinder.* Unpublished manuscript. New York: New Directions Archive.
——. *Memoirs.* New York: Doubleday & Co., 1975.
——. *Not About Nightingales.* New York: New Directions Publishing, 1998.
——. *The Notebook of Trigorin.* New York: New Directions Publishing, 1997.
——. *Putting Them Away.* Unfinished (IV), typed fragment with title. Harvard Theater Collection. (Williams, Unfinished IV).
——. *Some Problems for the Moose Lodge.* Chicago: Goodman Theatre Archives (typescript, 33 pp.) "revised 11/10/80."
——. *Something Cloudy, Something Clear.* New York: New Directions Publishing, 1995.
——. *Spring Storm.* New York: New Directions Publishing, 1999.
——. *The Theatre of Tennessee Williams Vol. I, Vol. III, Vol. V and Vol. VIII.* New York: New Directions Publishing, 1971, 1971, 1976 and 1992.
——. *This Is (An Entertainment).* Unpublished manuscript. New York: New Directions Archive.
——. Unfinished, title page, typed, undated, with the following titles:
The Legendary Bequest of Moonshine Dancer
A House Not Meant to Stand
Laundry Hung on the Moon

(then handwritten):
What Odds Are Offered by the Greek in Vegas?
For Tatters of a Mortal Dress
The Legendary Bequest of a Moonlight Dancer
Scenery of
on the next page a draft begins with the title:
Being Addressed by a Fool
Columbia University Library. (Williams, Unfinshed I)
———. Unfinished, typed page with revisions, undated, one page:
Revised ~~Play~~ (then handwritten): *Terrible Details* (A Gothic Comedy) Harvard Theater
Collection. (Williams, Unfinished II).
———. Unfinished, typed page of notes with annotations, undated, no page number: *"Our
Lady of Pascagoola"* (possible title). Harvard Theater Collection. (Williams, Unfinished
III).
———. *Will Mr. Merriwether Return from Memphis.* Unpublished manuscript. New York:
New Directions Archive.

NOTES ON CONTRIBUTORS

PHILIP C. KOLIN, Professor of English at the University of Southern Mississippi and Founding Co-editor of *Studies in American Drama, 1945–Present,* has published widely on Williams. Among his books are *American Playwrights Since 1945* (1989), *Confronting Tennessee Williams's* A Streetcar Named Desire: *Essays in Critical Pluralism* (1993), *Tennessee Williams: A Guide to Research and Performance* (1998), and *Williams:* A Streetcar Named Desire (in the Cambridge UP Plays in Production Series, 2000). Kolin is currently editing the *Tennessee Williams Encyclopedia* and has also edited special issues of the following journals on Williams—*Mississippi Quarterly, Southern Quarterly,* and *Studies in American Drama, 1945–Present.* His essays on Williams have appeared in *Missouri Review, Theatre History Studies, Tennessee Williams Literary Journal, The Tennessee Williams Annual Review, Journal of Dramatic Theory and Criticism, Theatre Survey, American Drama,* and *The Magical Muse: The Theatre of Tennessee Williams.* Kolin is also the Theatre Reviews Editor for the *Tennessee Williams Annual Review* and the General Editor for the Routledge Shakespeare Criticism Series.

ROBERT BRAY, Professor of English at Middle Tennessee State University, is the Founding Editor of the *Tennessee Williams Annual Review* and the founding director of the Tennessee Williams Scholars' Conference, held each March in New Orleans. His most recent work includes articles in *The Historic New Orleans Quarterly* as well as the introductions to New Directions editions of *The Glass Menagerie* and *Vieux Carré.*

UNA CHAUDHURI is Professor of English and Drama at New York University. She is the author of *No Man's Stage: A Semiotic Study of Jean Genet's Plays,* and *Staging Place: The Geography of Modern Drama,* and the editor of *Rachel's Brain and Other Storms,* a book of scripts by performance artist Rachel Rosenthal. She was also the guest editor of the special issue of *Yale Theater* on "Theater and Ecology." Her co-edited volume *Land/Scape/Theater* will be published in 2002.

GEORGE CRANDELL is Head of the Department of English at Auburn University. He has published articles in American humor and modern drama as well as *Tennessee Williams: A Descriptive Bibliography* and *The Critical Response to Tennessee Williams.* He is currently working on a descriptive bibliography of Arthur Miller.

JAMES FISHER, Professor of Theatre at Wabash College, is the author of five books, including *The Theater of Tony Kushner: Living Past Hope* (2001), numerous essays and reviews on all aspects of theatre and drama, and a recent article in *Text and Presentation* on Williams's *The Notebook of Trigorin*. He has also written on *The Roman Spring of Mrs. Stone*, *Camino Real*, and homosexuality in Williams. Fisher was named Indiana Theatre Person of the Year in 1997.

VERNA FOSTER teaches modern drama, Shakespeare, and dramatic theory at Loyola University of Chicago. She has published numerous essays on Renaissance and modern drama, especially tragicomedy, on which topic she has completed a book-length study. Her most recent publications include an essay on *A Streetcar Named Desire* as tragicomedy in *American Drama*.

ROBERT F. GROSS is Director of Theatre and Professor of English and Comparative Literature at Hobart and William Smith Colleges. He is the editor of *Tennessee Williams: A Casebook* and *Christopher Hampton: A Casebook*, as well as the author of *S.N. Behrman: A Research and Production Sourcebook*.

ALLEAN HALE, Adjunct Professor of Theatre, University of Illinois, has edited four Williams plays for *New Directions*, including *Not About Nightingales, Fugitive Kind*, and *Stairs to the Roof*, and has published numerous articles, and consulted on three TV documentaries on the playwright.

NORMA JENCKES, Associate Professor in the Department of English and Comparative Literature at the University of Cincinnati, is editor of *American Drama* and Director of Helen Weinberger Centre for Study of Drama and Playwriting. She has published widely on George Bernard Shaw, British and Irish drama, and American playwrights.

THOMAS KEITH, originally from Cleveland, Ohio, is an editor at New Directions Publishing. He edited *Robert Burns: Selected Poems & Songs* (Caledonia Road Publishing, 2001) and has written a variety of critical articles for *The Barns Chronicle, Studies in Scottish Literature*, and *Robert Burns in America*. Along with Peggy Fox, he is the co-editor of *The Selected Letters of Tennessee Williams and James Laughlin* to be published by W.W. Norton in 2003, and is a contributor to the *Tennessee Williams Encyclopedia*.

FELICIA HARDISON LONDRÉ is Curators' Professor of Theatre at the University of Missouri-Kansas City, Honorary Co-Founder and Dramaturg of the Heart of America Shakespeare Festival, and secretary of the board of the College of Fellows of the American Theatre. The first of her ten books was *Tennessee Williams: Life, Work, and Criticism* (1989) as well as Williams essays in *American Playwrights since 1945* (1989), *The Cambridge Companion to Tennessee Williams* (1997), *The Tennessee Williams Literary Journal* (Fall 1999), and *Encyclopedia of American Literature of the Sea and Great Lakes* (2001).

MICHAEL PALLER teaches theatre history at the State University of New York at Purchase. He has published on Tennessee Williams in *The Tennessee Williams Annual Review, The Tennessee Williams Literary Journal*, and in the anthology *Magical Muse: The Theatre of Tennessee Williams* and *The Tennessee Williams Encyclopedia* (Greenwood Press). He was the dramaturg for the Russian premiere production of *Small Craft Warnings* at Moscow's Sovermenik Theatre directed by Richard Corley in 1997. He has written widely on theatre and books for *The Washington Post*, the *Cleveland Plain Dealer*, *The Village Voice*, and other publications.

GENE D. PHILLIPS, S.J., teaches literature and film history at Loyola University of Chicago. He is the author of *The Films of Tennessee Williams*, and has contributed essays on the plays and films of Tennessee Williams to *Confronting Tennessee Williams's* A Streetcar Named Desire, *The Encyclopedia of Stage Plays into Film*, *Video Versions: Film Adaptations of Plays on Video*, and *The Tennessee Williams Encyclopedia*.

TERRI SMITH RUCKEL teaches writing at Louisiana State University. She contributed "A 'Giggling, silly bith, voluptuary': Tennessee Williams's *Memoirs* as Apologia Pro Vita Sua" to *Tennessee Williams: The Non-Dramatic Work*, in the Fall 1999 special issue of *The Southern Quarterly*. She is currently working on entries for *The Tennessee Williams Encyclopedia* and is completing a project that studies intersections of gender, race, and "Southern sexuality" in contemporary Southern women's writings. She is a frequent reviewer for *World Literature Today*.

ANNETTE J. SADDIK is an Associate Professor of English at Eastern Michigan University, where she teaches courses in twentieth-century drama. Her recent publications on Williams include a book on the later work, *The Politics of Reputation: The Critical Reception of Tennessee Williams' Later Plays* (1999) and an article on *Suddenly Last Summer* and "Desire and the Black Masseur" in *Modern Drama* (1998). She is currently preparing several entries for *The Tennessee Williams Encyclopedia*.